TEACH YOURSELF BOOKS

PSYCHOLOGY TODAY

This book is a symposium: a collection of coordinated contributions by individual authors, each of whom is a specialist in his particular field and a member of the Department of Psychology at Nottingham University. Coordinator, editor and part contributor to this symposium is Bill Gillham, a lecturer in psychology at Nottingham University.

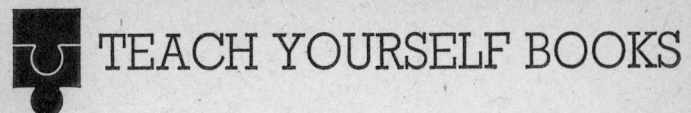
TEACH YOURSELF BOOKS

PSYCHOLOGY TODAY

Contributing editor

W. E. C. Gillham

ST PAUL'S HOUSE   WARWICK LANE   LONDON EC4P 4AH

First printed 1975

Copyright © 1975
W. E. C. Gillham, Ch. *1, 10, 13*; D. J. Wood, Ch. *2, 7*;
P. R. W. Barnes, Ch. *3*; G. M. Stephenson, Ch. *6*;
D. J. Smail, Ch. *14*; C. I. Howarth, Ch. *16*
The English Universities Press Ltd, Ch. *4, 5, 8, 9, 11, 12, 15*

All rights reserved. No part of this publication may be reproduced or transmitted in any form or by any means, electronic or mechanical, including photocopy, recording, or any information storage and retrieval system, without permission in writing from the publisher.

ISBN 0 340 19498 7

*Printed and bound in Great Britain
for The English Universities Press Ltd by
Hazell Watson & Viney Ltd, Aylesbury, Bucks*

Contents

	Preface	vii
1	Introduction W. E. C. Gillham	1
2	Developmental Psychology D. J. Wood	9
3	The Psychology of Personality P. R. W. Barnes	23
4	Experimental Psychology G. Underwood	42
5	Physiological Psychology R. G. Stevens	58
6	Social Psychology G. M. Stephenson	81
7	Psycholinguistics and the Psychology of Communication D. J. Wood	100
8	Mathematical Psychology R. B. Henry	116
9	Animal Behaviour T. R. Cox	133
10	Psychopathology W. E. C. Gillham	149
11	Behavioural Pharmacology T. R. Cox	170
12	Parapsychology A. Gauld	190
13	Educational Psychology W. E. C. Gillham	203
14	Clinical Psychology D. J. Smail	217

15	Occupational Psychology	G. C. Simpson	232
16	The Uses of Psychology	C. I. Howarth	256
	Index		277

Preface

This book is a joint enterprise, having been written by members of a large and diverse university department of psychology. Each chapter has an individual author, a specialist in the content area it covers. The attempt has been, in every case, to present a comprehensive summary in language no more technical than the subject-matter necessarily requires; this means, inevitably, that some chapters are more difficult than others—for example, the chapter on mathematical psychology—but have been included to make the book as comprehensive as possible. Chapter headings are more or less conventional and, accordingly, debatable; such an organisation into traditional content areas does, however, in the editor's opinion constitute an advantage in an introductory text. The reader can sample first those chapters which have the most immediate value or appeal, and then go on to read others which are more difficult or more technical. Each chapter can be used as a basis for further study and the books recommended for further reading have been selected to enable the reader to pursue those topics which interest him most. The advanced student can go on to a study of the detailed individual references.

In what we hope will be recognised as a 'multi-level' text, the intention has been to present our material in such a way that it is accessible to the intelligent layman, co-professionals, the student in secondary or higher education whose course includes a psychology component, as well as the beginning honours student in psychology. Implicit in such an intention is the belief that psychology has nothing to gain, and a great deal to lose, in taking the form of an esoteric, exclusive science and profession.

W.E.C.G.

Acknowledgements

The main acknowledgement must be to my wife, Judith, who, during the writing and editing of the book, read and advised from the standpoint of the 'typical' non-specialist reader; all chapters have had some modification following her scrutiny—in terms of style as well as clarity of expression. Such infelicities and obscurities as remain are, of course, the responsibility of the individual authors concerned.

Additional thanks are due to Margaret Grainger who typed, with uniform accuracy, chapter manuscripts of varying form and legibility.

Acknowledgements are gratefully given to the following authors and publishers for permission to reproduce, or derive from, copyright tables and diagrams:

J. S. Bruner and Harvard University Press for Fig. 2.1 from *Toward a Theory of Instruction*; Ulric Neisser and Scientific American Inc. for Fig. 4.2 from 'Visual search', *Scientific American*, *219* (6), p. 97 (bottom) (copyright © 1964 Scientific American Inc. All rights reserved); G. Sperling and the Human Factors Society for Fig. 4.4 from 'A model for visual memory tasks', *Human Factors*, *5*, 19–31; E. S. Gollin and Southern Universities Press for Fig. 5.12 from 'Developmental studies of visual recognition of incomplete objects',

Perceptual Motor Skills, *11*, 289–98 (Fig. 1 on p. 290); T. Millon, H. I. Diesenhaus and John Wiley & Co. Inc. for Table 10.1 from *Research Methods in Psychopathology*; M. Rutter, J. Tizard, K. Whitmore and the Longman Group Ltd for Table 10.2 from *Education, Health and Behaviour*; the Controller of Her Majesty's Stationery Office for Table 10.3 from *Criminal Statistics for England and Wales 1972*; G. B. Todd and A. N. Fairbairn for Table 13.1; and K. F. H. Murrell and Chapman & Hall Ltd for Fig. 15.6 from *Ergonomics: Man in his working environment*.

W.E.C.G.

'The professional psychologist writes no prescriptions. He has no secret remedies. The good that he can do he can only do with the full and free co-operation of an educated and critical laity.'

C. A. Mace

I

Introduction

W. E. C. Gillham

Seventy years ago one of the innovators of modern psychology described it as having a long past but only a short history. That is still true: some form of study of human behaviour and human experience is as old as recorded history and one can reasonably assume that such preoccupations were pervasive even in pre-historical times. Modern psychology, what Ryle (1949) has called 'a partly fortuitous federation of inquiries and techniques', was, to use O'Neil's phrase, 'a city founded in the seventh and eighth decades of the nineteenth century on a very old site' (O'Neil, 1968).

As a more or less defined discipline psychology is barely a hundred years old; it is largely a phenomenon of the twentieth century—having its most vigorous growth in the last forty years or so—and has been characterised during the past decade by a broadening of its base as a science and, perhaps most significantly, by a radical extension of its practical applications.

Eighty years ago William James, brother of the novelist Henry James, and perhaps the best stylist that psychology has produced, defined the new discipline as 'the Science of Mental Life', that is of 'feelings, desires, cognitions, reasonings, decisions and the like'. Quite clearly such a 'mentalistic' view of the content of psychological study necessarily involved introspective report—individuals reporting on their conscious experience—

as the *major* technique for obtaining scientific evidence. Not that James saw psychology only as the study of what Ryle has called 'mind-stuff'; he was concerned to point out that 'no mental modification ever occurs which is not accompanied or followed by a bodily change'. Nor did James presume that his attempts to delineate the subject area were definitive and in this respect observed that 'we gain much more by a broad than a narrow conception of our subject. At a certain stage in the development of every science a degree of vagueness is what best consists with fertility.'

James' predictions were to prove correct, for during the first two decades of the twentieth century, diametrically opposed approaches to human behaviour were to emerge in Europe and North America. In Europe the 'depth' psychologists, of whom Freud was the most brilliant and the most powerful figure, proposed explanations of human psychological development in 'intrapsychic' terms of hypothetical constructs such as the 'id' or 'unconscious' and unobservable forces of 'psychic energy', whilst in the United States, under the leadership of J. B. Watson, 'behaviourism' emerged as the methodology which was to dominate academic psychology for the next half-century. Watson was reacting, not to the Freudians, but to that conception of psychological study represented by the work of James and others. '"States of consciousness"', he wrote, 'like the so-called phenomena of spiritualism, are not objectively verifiable and for that reason can never become data for science.' Behaviourism, he proclaimed, was a 'fresh, clean start in psychology'. His definition of psychology as 'that division of natural science which takes human behaviour—the doings and sayings, both learned and unlearned, of people as its subject matter' can be compared with the definition by William James quoted above.

The influence of Watson's work on psychology as an academic science has been very extensive and remarkably enduring. Thus his description of the aims and methods of behaviouristic psychology as constituting 'attempts to formulate, through systematic observation and experimentation, the generalisations, laws and principles which underlie man's behaviour' are mirrored in a recent and excellent introductory text in the behaviourist tradition (Wright *et al.*, 1970) where psychology is defined as 'the application to human behaviour . . . of the observational and experimental methods of science'.

Although broadly influential, Watson's most distinctive contribution, which has now acquired pejorative connotations, has come to be known as stimulus-response (S-R) psychology. He was unequivocal in his assertion that it was necessary to conceptualise human behaviour in such terms; thus he wrote, 'we may say that the goal of psychological study is the *ascertaining of such data and laws that, given the stimulus, psychology can predict what the response will be; or, on the other hand, given the response, it can specify the nature of the effective stimulus*' (italics in the original).

In this sort of formulation, and in the name of science, subjective human experience was reduced to the status of an 'intervening variable' and 'inner man' became a cypher. In consequence, because of its pursuit of the status of a natural science, psychological investigation became, at once, excessively empirical and technical and, in theoretical and practical terms, relatively trivial. This 'trivialising' was the inevitable result of the attempt to develop laws of behaviour exclusively in S-R terms since many important behaviours were not amenable to such a reduction, either because the 'stimulus' or the 'response' could not be adequately determined, or because the role of the 'intervening variable' was so complex that 'responses' could not be defined in stimulus terms whatever formula was allocated. It is now more readily appreciated that an individual in a physically standard stimulus setting experiences it more or less uniquely—and responds accordingly; to an important extent the physical properties of the external world are *optional* for him, i.e. some stimuli are not effective, but also the organisation and value (i.e. the meaning) given to the stimuli selected are, to some degree, personal and individual. An appreciation of these factors, and an attempt to grapple with them, has been the force behind the considerable current interest in cognitive psychology (see, for example, Neisser, 1967).

To define psychology, as we might now do with general acceptance, as the scientific study of human behaviour and human *experience* is the broadening of the subject referred to in the opening paragraphs; it also means that the *science* of psychology is not just that of another natural science. As Laing (1967) says, 'Natural science knows nothing of the relation between behaviour and experience ... But this relation is the copula of our science—if science means *a form of knowledge adequate to its subject*. The relation between experience and behaviour is the stone that the builders will reject at their peril. Without it the whole structure of our theory and practice must collapse.'

If psychology has now come of age it is because it has achieved a more adequate 'form of knowledge'; as Howarth observes in the final chapter of this book, 'Old controversies about whether psychology should be concerned with "mental life" as revealed by introspection or with "behaviour" as revealed to an outside observer, are now happily of little interest since so many studies have shown the usefulness of both introspection and the observation of behaviour, particularly in checking conclusions based on the other.' And if 'behaviourism' has warranted criticism, its corrective influence on the development of psychology must also be taken into account. Psychology developed out of philosophical speculations as to the nature of man when these came to be influenced by advances in the biological sciences. From this union psychology retained a philosophical, speculative character and a dualistic, mind/body approach to behaviour and 'mental life' which presented insoluble conceptual and methodological problems; these are brilliantly expounded by Gilbert Ryle in his classic of philosophical psychology *The Concept of Mind* (1949).

The quality of explanation or *theory* is one index of the status of an academic discipline; but no matter how elegant or sophisticated a theory may be, the touchstone of its validity is its ability to account for a wide variety of evidence and its capacity for generating hypotheses—results that should follow if the theory is correct. By this means a theory can be tested—and confirmed, disproved or modified. A respect for evidence and the willingness to test out one's theoretical position are the hallmark of the scientist. Theories that are not capable of being challenged are probably not to be considered as 'scientific'. As the distinguished French psychologist, Paul Fraisse, has said: 'This very necessary discipline does not lead to the sort of extravagant theories which satisfy those minds more concerned with the aesthetic appeal of a thesis than its truth.'* (Vurpillot, 1972.)

An insistence on the discipline of 'accountability' (or, when experimental procedures are feasible, of 'testability') in scientific psychology does not mean that only 'behavioural' data are acceptable; it does mean that different kinds of data, obtained perhaps in different ways but relating to a common area, should fit together in terms of some common explanation; a theory that can account for a variety of data is a 'strong' one. Thus, assumptions about how people feel and think need to be related to overt signs of these subjective experiences in some meaningful fashion, particularly if these thoughts and feelings are supposed to 'cause' people to act in certain ways; so, for example, a system of psychotherapy which claimed to treat psychological disorder but produced no change in the accepted behavioural manifestations of that disorder should be considered of questionable validity.

The concern with evidence is more than a methodological preoccupation: it highlights the central concern of science which is *truth* and therefore, by implication, the controversion of prejudice. Whilst scientific evidence can be used to support prejudice it can, of course, then be challenged in scientific terms. Prejudice which rests on unverifiable theories is immune from such appraisal.

The extension of knowledge within an academic discipline necessarily involves *research*. For some research psychologists

* Present writer's translation.

this has the exclusive connotation of experimental investigation, in common with other, largely experimental, natural sciences; thus, in the present book, Underwood (Chapter 4) writes of psychology being 'firmly within the grasp of experimental science'. But, in fact, much of human behaviour is incapable of being subjected to the controlled variation of conditions that constitutes the experimental method. This does not mean that such behaviour is inaccessible to scientific investigation; what it does mean is that the research psychologist selects techniques which are appropriate to what is being investigated. For example, the way in which people bring up their children—an area of behaviour of great theoretical and practical importance—has been studied by our colleagues, John and Elizabeth Newson (Newson and Newson, 1963; 1968), by means of sensitive and detailed interviewing techniques; the direct and systematic *observation* of behaviour in a natural setting (e.g. of how children interact in play situations) is another approach which is 'non-experimental' but not 'unscientific'.

It may be a matter of some surprise to the reader that in describing the evolution of scientific psychology there has been only passing reference to the work of Freud. This is largely because scientific psychology represents a different tradition, despite extensive borrowing from what Ryle has called 'psychology's one man of genius'; the influence of some of his ideas is recorded in the chapters of this book dealing with psychopathology and the growth of personality. Freud, however, placed himself in a position of relative isolation when, with the arrogance of genius, he propounded a theory of human psychology which sought to explain everything but was largely unassailable from the point of view of critical appraisal; instead of a theory which was accountable in consistent behavioural terms, behaviour was interpreted, and, where necessary, reinterpreted, to fit the theoretical system. It can easily be seen why this was unacceptable to psychologists, who sought to be scientists whether this role was conceived in broad or narrow terms or not.

Yet Freud's influence on man's conception of himself has been very great—as, indeed, has the influence of psychology as a whole. But if psychological ideas have been pervasive, until recently professional psychologists working on applied problems in society were a comparative rarity. In part this has been due to uncertainty about exactly what sorts of roles the psychologist should take up. Should he be like a doctor with apparently mysterious practices and restricted, exclusive skills? It seems likely that, for the psychologist to be effective, such a role would be undesirable and that his understanding is only going to be implemented if he shares it with others; as C. A. Mace once commented, 'the chances are that only a layman will be on the spot when psychology needs to be applied'. Such a novel role for an 'expert' constitutes a challenge to competence. When skills and understanding are treated as the exclusive property of a profession, it is easy to camouflage limitations which can only be inimical to growth. A distinguished British scientist once said that he never felt quite satisfied with a theorem until he felt he could explain it to the next man he met in the street; the future vigour of psychology is likely to depend on its ability to do just that.

References

James, W. (1890), *Principles of Psychology* (2 vols). London: Macmillan.

Laing, R. D. (1967), *The Politics of Experience* and *The Bird of Paradise*. Harmondsworth: Penguin Books.

Mace, M. (ed.) (1973), *Selected Papers by C. A. Mace*. London: Methuen.

Neisser, U. (1967), *Cognitive Psychology*. New York: Appleton-Century-Crofts.

Newson, J., & Newson, E. (1963), *Infant Care in an Urban Community*. London: George Allen & Unwin.

Newson, J., & Newson, E. (1968), *Four Years Old in an Urban Community*. London: George Allen & Unwin.

O'Neil, W. M. (1968), *The Beginnings of Modern Psychology*. Harmondsworth: Penguin Books.

Ryle, G. (1949), *The Concept of Mind*. London: Hutchinson.
Vurpillot, E. (1972), *Le Monde Visuel du Jeune Enfant*. Paris: Presses Universitaires de France.
Watson, J. B. (1919), *Psychology from the Standpoint of a Behaviorist*. Philadelphia: J. B. Lippincott.
Wright, D. S., Taylor, A., et al. (1970), *Introducing Psychology: An Experimental Approach*. Harmondsworth: Penguin Books.

Recommended further reading

O'Neil, W. M. (1968), *The Beginnings of Modern Psychology*. Harmondsworth: Penguin Books.
Ryle, G. (1949), *The Concept of Mind*. London: Hutchinson.
Wright, D. S., Taylor, A., et al. (1970), *Introducing Psychology: An Experimental Approach*. Harmondsworth: Penguin Books.

2

Developmental Psychology

D. J. Wood

From 'the infant mewling and puking in the nurse's arms' man progresses through his seven 'parts' to return at last to 'second childishness and mere oblivion'. In its widest frame of reference, developmental psychology could be seen as embracing all the seven ages of man, and to be the study of such changes and transitions and of the factors which affect all aspects of the growth and development of an individual or a species. The study of muscular growth, the investigation of moral development, the changes in the capacity for thought—all such variations with time and age are potentially part of its area of study.

This chapter, however, like the major part of the work in the field, focuses on intellectual or cognitive development—the study of such capacities as thinking, remembering, perceiving and problem-solving. Furthermore, it only travels about as far as Shakespeare's fourth age of man, its main concern being the origins and growth to maturity of intellectual abilities.

The normal neonate (or newborn) enters the world equipped with all the raw material of the intellect. Current research indicates that all his sensory capacities are functioning at birth. He can co-ordinate both eyes—albeit for only short periods—to focus light onto his retinas (no mean feat when one realises that this demands the co-ordination of twelve different eye muscles). He responds differentially to changing visual patterns (Fantz,

1961; Fantz, Ordy and Udelf, 1962), indicating that his visual system is functioning with a fair degree of resolution and selectivity. He also responds differentially to sound patterns (Eisenburg, 1965), showing a similar degree of development in the auditory system. On the action or 'effector' side he can soon move all parts of his body, producing, potentially at least, all the movements necessary for holding a tool, playing a piano or even painting a reproduction Rembrandt. When, a few weeks into life, he begins to babble, he similarly produces much of the raw material of language. Whilst there is some debate as to whether every child really does produce all possible sounds in the babbling stage—it seems unlikely—he does eventually produce a wider range of sound patterns than is required for his own language and, under different conditions, sufficient to enable him to produce any other language. What he lacks initially, of course, is both the *intention* to do any of these things and the *skill* to do them. Whilst he can *spontaneously* produce the spectrum of movements, he does not and cannot produce them as *deliberate actions* to fit the demands of specific occasions or needs: he does not integrate them in the service of any plan of action.

Looked at from this one perspective, then, the early stages of intellectual development can be characterised as the ever-growing achievement of *control* by the individual over his own body and, in consequence, control of his environment and other individuals. He learns or discovers how to bring the spontaneously produced raw material of action under voluntary control and gradually discovers various environmental signs and contingencies which signal when specific types of actions should take place. So, for example, the baby must gain control over his arms, eyes and general posture, so that when he catches sight of an attractive object he can move his arm in a suitable path to intercept the object and adjust his hand and fingers to take possession of it at the appropriate moment.

In fact, there has been a great deal of disagreement in the last few years as to just how much such apparently simple control over actions has to be learned by the infant through experience, and how much is innate. Piaget, a Swiss psychologist and epistemologist, to whose work we shall be returning, has suggested that the child must discover or 'co-ordinate' the various aspects underlying any experience—'schemas' as he calls them (see, for example, Piaget and Inhelder, 1969). The sight, sound, feel and taste of any object are initially, he argues, quite separate in experience and the infant must discover their interrelationships. This explains why, for example, it is usually about four months before the infant will reach readily and in a variety of everyday contexts for a desired object. Before this time he may stare at it, move his mouth in anticipation, grasp his clothing and so on, but he will not—and apparently cannot—reach out skilfully to grasp it. Another major piece of evidence cited by Piaget for his general theoretical position is the infant's failure to search for hidden objects. If a baby of about four months is shown an object, like a rattle for example, which is dropped or otherwise hidden from sight, it is extremely unlikely that he will look around for it or indicate in any way that he appreciates its continued existence. The absence of search is, for Piaget, symptomatic of the fact that the baby has no concept of an object, no 'object permanence'. He only 'thinks' that things exist when he himself is in direct contact with them. Another implication of this argument—one which is pursued later—is that the infant has no memory for objects; no images and no symbols with which to represent a thing in its absence. This memory, argues Piaget, can only come into existence when the child has co-ordinated the various 'schemas' or aspects of experience. However, a number of recent experimental studies have cast some doubt on Piaget's views on object permanence; it does not seem to be the case that the neonate must learn or discover the relationships between various parts of an experience. His movements in the presence of an attractive object are far from random or unsystematic even in the first weeks of life. Rather, they reveal an 'appreciation' in behaviour of certain characteristics or properties of the object seen. Large objects are met with different movements from small ones; and the baby's hands tend to take a suitable grasping posture to fit the shape of the object seen (Bruner and Koslowski, 1972; Bower, 1972). In one particularly striking experiment, babies were supplied with small pairs of 'distorting' spectacles. These contained prism lenses which shift or refract incoming light rays so that objects appear to the wearer to be in a different place to their true location. T. G. R. Bower, who did this experiment (Bower, Broughton and Moore, 1970), claims that the infants not only moved their arms towards an (imaginary) object thus seen but also displayed clear signs of distress when they failed to contact it (since, of course, it was not where they 'expected' it to be).

If one accepts Bower's interpretation, then it follows that not only are 'seen' and 'felt' positions already co-ordinated very early in life but also that the sight of an object arouses an expectancy of its palpability or touchability which, when violated, produces distress. This one example illustrates an issue which continually crops up in psychological enquiry. Bower's work implies that the relationships between all the senses or modalities are *inborn* or, at least, soon *acquired*. For Piaget, they must be *discovered*. For many years, prevailing opinion in psychology has tended to favour the latter position—'empiricism' or 'environmentalism' as it is often called. Its basic argument is that all phenomena can be traced back to experiences of one form or another. The other position—'nativism'—argues that many of our capacities are inborn and are not determined by experience in any fundamental sense. Although few, if any, psychologists really propound one extreme position or the other, they continue to disagree about the relative importance of the two factors: nature and nurture. There has been a definite swing towards nativism in the last decade or so and it now seems reasonably clear that there does exist some genetic prestructuring of behaviour. The conclusion is particularly well illustrated by some of the work in psycholinguistics (Chapter 7).

It may well be, then, that the infant's world is integrated and structured at birth so that sight, sound, touch and smell are co-ordinated. But even the most casual observation will testify that the infant still lacks *skill* in operating his bodily systems. The first few years of life are marked by the achievement of ever-increasing control by the child, first over the relatively gross movements of the limbs, vocal cords and so on and gradually over finer aspects of precise movements.

But we have yet to establish the importance and significance of the study of such seemingly trivial accomplishments in a consideration of intellectual abilities. How does simple *action* tie in with thought?

One of the most compelling statements to emerge from current psychological enquiry is Piaget's assertion that 'thought is internalised action'. He argues that the structure of mental activity in thinking derives from the constraints and strictures acting upon prior physical actions. This is an extremely difficult concept to grasp fully. Hopefully, the following discussion will help to enrich and clarify the statement, though a true understanding will demand much more thought and study.

Although there is some controversy surrounding the infant's ability to think about or remember objects in their absence, it is clear from a variety of studies that the capacity to remember the nature and structure of events increases with age over the first years of life. As we have already seen, the infant is reluctant if not totally incapable of searching for a dropped object until around six months or so, when he will eagerly peer after a dropped toy. Indeed, he will doubtless make quite a game of dropping things and then 'retrieving' them with his eyes. As he discovers the structure of everyday events—like the behaviour of objects under the influence of gravity—he begins to *anticipate* the increasingly remote consequences (in time and space) of his actions. This growth and development are revealed to the observer by such things as the anticipatory movements of his head, hands and eyes. The friendly adult disappears from sight only to reappear shortly thereafter with an explosive 'peekaboo'; the six- or seven-month-old will soon learn where and when to look for such reappearances. Great games can be played with him by first building up and then violating this expectancy, whether by 'missing a turn' or by popping up somewhere else. Knowledge of event structures breeds anticipation, and friendly violation of that anticipation breeds, in its turn, humour and laughter.

So the child starts to reveal an increasing knowledge about the structure of recurrent events. He becomes correspondingly more *selective* as to where, when and to what he will attend. Whereas in the early days of life any loud noise or bright light will arouse and hold his attention, with age he becomes more selective and idiosyncratic.

So, increasing anticipation is indicative of the child's growing memory for event structures; knowledge both of the various consequences of his own actions and of those of other agencies. This developing memory leads, gradually, to an increasing degree of deliberateness and autonomy in his actions. Anticipation of consequences leads to the possibility of an evaluation of actions *before* they take place. Thus, thoughts—anticipations of action consequences—start to take the place of full-blown actions.

Piaget argues that there are, in fact, four stages in intellectual development; four stages during which the infant's initial dependence upon the immediate situation, when his 'sensory-motor' intellect is bounded by what he can immediately perceive and do, gives way to a capacity to think about things in terms of abstract propositions; to use systems of symbols and operations as in mathematics and logic.

The first, sensory-motor stage, is characterised by the child's apparent lack of *representation* and during this stage, as we have already seen, he is supposedly learning the relationships between different facets of everyday experience. Then, usually during the second year of life, he begins to show clear and increasing signs of memory for absent objects and events. He will imitate the actions of people who are not present, for example, thus indicating that he has some mental 'currency' with which to represent them. This second stage is labelled 'pre-operational'. Although the child now has the capacity to represent things, he only displays 'static imagery'. He cannot yet operate upon or 'transform' these representations in his head; he can perform no mental operations. An example of the type of study used to substantiate this view should illustrate the distinction.

The pre-operational period usually lasts until around age seven or eight. An average five-year-old will, on request, draw simple objects—even if they are not present in his view. He will probably be able to draw two squares, for example. However, if he is asked not only to draw them but to draw what they look like when one is placed on the other and pushed so that it overlaps the bottom one, he will almost surely fail. A seven-year-old, on the other hand, will probably succeed. This, argues Piaget, shows that the younger child cannot transform the images of the two squares 'in his head'. He has 'static' but not 'kinetic' or transformational representations (Piaget and Inhelder, 1969).

This apparent lack of any ability for mental operations is also held responsible for the pre-operational child's inability to solve a variety of problems which, on first sight, look quite trivial. For example, suppose the pre-operational child is shown two identical beakers, each filled with liquid to the same level, and he is asked which, if any, contains more to drink. Usually he will quite happily say that they contain the same amount. If, however, one is poured without spillage and in full view of the child into another, differently shaped container, then the child will almost certainly change his judgements. He will say that they now contain different quantities—usually selecting that with the highest liquid level as the one containing most to drink. Thus, even though he can see the pouring taking place and will agree that they were the same to start with, he cannot 'see' that they 'must' be still the same. Pour them back into the original containers and he will once again agree that they are equivalent.

Piaget points out that to appreciate the 'conservation' of the liquid's volume the child must see that the loss or gain in one dimension—height, breadth or width— is compensated for by changes in the others. He must, to use Piaget's terminology, be able to 'co-ordinate' the three. But, since he cannot perform mental operations, cannot transform the equation in his head, so to speak, he is incapable of appreciating this logic and continues to change judgement on the basis of what he can see happening in the most dominant dimension—height.

This intriguing phenomenon and a number in a similar vein have stimulated a great deal of research (see, for example, Elkind and Flavell, 1969). The child's apparent 'illogicality' in such situations has proved remarkably stable. Piaget's interpretation is not, however, without competitors, as the following example illustrates.

Paradoxically enough, if the child is shown the liquid being transferred but can only see it disappearing behind a screen and cannot see what happens to it on the other side, he will maintain his initial judgement that the quantities are the same. Only when the screen is removed and the child can see what the new height is will he be likely to change judgement. J. S. Bruner suggests that this result is symptomatic of the 'pre-empting' quality of perceptual information for a child of this age. His changes in judgement are not due to an *incapacity* for mental operations but to the short-circuiting of such thoughts by the sight of the liquid levels. Thus, for Bruner, the child fails because he makes an inappropriate selection of information in such situations and not because he is incapable of certain types of mental operations (Bruner, 1968, 1971; Bruner, Olver and Greenfield, 1966). Indeed, Bruner's general position is that the 'repertoire' of intellectual activities of the infant and child is fundamentally the same as that of the adult. What differentiates infantile from mature thought is not a different set of mental operations or mental structures but different degrees of *skill* in extracting the necessary information from events and in recognising what is most appropriate in order to solve problems—failures of attention, representation and coding rather than a lack of logical abilities.

To return to the proposed four stages: Piaget argues that by age eight or so the child, now adept in the transformation of certain types of mental representations, enters the 'concrete operational' stage. The concrete operationalist will not make errors in conservation tasks; he is quite capable of intellectual operations such as the co-ordination of several dimensions. Still, however, he is limited in his logical capacities, for he can only perform such operations upon the representations of real or 'concrete' events—like the dimensions of a volume of liquid. He cannot as yet afford similar treatment to abstract, formal material. Any problem which is expressed in terms of hypotheticals like x's and y's, any of which contains abstract propositions, will not be solved. It must be rendered concrete and refer to real things before solution can be guaranteed. By the teens, according to Piaget, the child may enter the stage of full intellectual maturity—the stage of 'formal operational' thought. Now he can think about and operate upon abstractions; he can argue in terms of abstract postulates and suppositions and construct hypothetical possibilities which may never exist in reality. He can start to understand the logician, the philosopher and the moralist.

Piaget's proposed stages have been used as the basis of this chapter not because they offer the only theory of development or because his ideas are necessarily the most acceptable. Rather, they have been adopted because Piaget was the first contemporary theorist to present a full and coherent view of intellectual development. His wealth of ideas and range of observations have provided the framework for the majority of recent research in developmental psychology. However, there are a number of issues and questions which fall somewhat outside or beyond Piaget's formulation. By discussing these we may also gain greater insight into other possible views of intellectual development.

A question of central importance concerns the role of adults in the intellectual development of the child. Just as different cultures possess different languages, so too they have their own methods of rearing and educating their children in their particular values and skills. They face different types of problems and need correspondingly different technologies—both mental and mechanical—to solve them. Although there is a good deal of evidence for certain universal patterns in human development no matter where it occurs, an adequate theoretical perspective must acknowledge and explain the many important differences. In short, it must specify how the adults in a culture communicate the complex ideas and complicated skills needed by their children. Obviously, the child will not reproduce in isolation the whole mental and physical achievements of man in general or his culture in particular. Somehow he is assisted and shaped in his development so as to rediscover and reinvent in a short time enough of these achievements to permit his survival and guarantee his position as a useful member of his society.

A second related question concerns the nature of technological and intellectual changes which occur from generation to generation. The evolution of man takes place not only in terms of physical mutation but also in terms of mental development. New skills, intellectual revolutions, scientific discoveries and so on all fundamentally affect and eventually change the intellectual abilities of later generations; a cumulative, dynamic, evolutionary process. The intellect is, in a sense, 'supra-generational', in that each generation launches itself from the intellectual shoulders of the ones preceding it.

It would be both presumptive and misleading to imply that developmental psychology has greatly clarified these questions. However, a number of interesting first steps have been taken.

For some years, J. S. Bruner has been concentrating on two major lines of study which reflect on these issues. He and his colleagues have performed a variety of investigations which are designed to illustrate and substantiate the view that the infant, from birth, is an intelligent and active problem-solver whose intellectual abilities are, in a fundamental way, similar to those of the mature adult. Bruner postulates three modes of representation for knowledge: in action (*enactive*), in images (*iconic*) and in various *symbolic* media (see Bruner, Olver and Greenfield, *op. cit.*). In this respect, his views resemble those of Piaget, who employs a similar set of distinctions. However, unlike Piaget,

Bruner argues that the child always has the capacity to utilise any type of representation and is limited only by his relative lack of expertise and skill. Whereas Piaget says that intellectual development is paced by maturational stages, Bruner argues that it is only the nature and degree of experience with a given type of task which determines what level of sophistication the individual will develop.

Another major difference between the two theoretical approaches, and Bruner's second line of study, is the attempt to characterise the part played by adults in the instruction of the child and, through this, to gain insights into the relationships between culture and cognitive growth (Bruner, 1966; 1971). Bruner argues that any concept or idea, no matter how formal or involved, can be communicated to a child if it is presented and developed in a way that the child can initially comprehend and assimilate. Thus, whereas Piaget places the onus on stages of development, saying that these dictate the levels of intellectual achievement, for Bruner it is determined jointly by the present skills and aptitudes of the child and by the way in which the task is presented to him by his culture.

In one study which illustrates this argument, the aim of the experimenters (or teachers as they really become in this type of investigation) was to show that eight-year-olds could understand formal equations like the quadratic function $(x+1)^2 = x^2 + 2x + 1$. What they did was to present the children with blocks which they named an 'x square', 'x' strips and '1' strips. Fig. 2.1 illustrates how the blocks can be arranged so as to exemplify the quadratic function, for an '$(x+1)$ square' is made up of an 'x' square, two 'x' strips and a '1' strip. Given periods of play with the blocks in classroom instruction sessions, the four children involved eventually grasped the nature of the quadratic function—they could in fact 'see' the principles involved. Indeed, Bruner and his co-worker in the study, Kenney, report (Bruner, 1966) that some children taught by this method could be guided to generalise the lesson to weights on a beam balance where the same quadratic rule holds. Thus, the children ac-

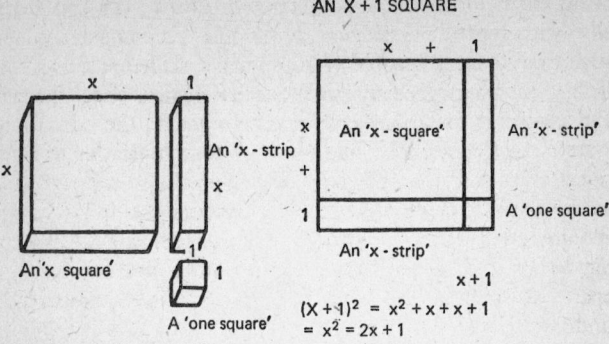

Fig. 2.1 Visual representation of a quadratic function (after Bruner, 1966).

quired some abstract rule and not simply a set of naming rules applicable only to the sets of blocks.

The significance of such studies, beyond the general theoretical implications, rests in their obvious educational implications. Where a complex, abstract task can be expressed in a way which is *perceptually* accessible to a child, then it can be used to provide a good initial basis upon which an expert can start to instruct him in the more formal characteristics of the task. Having played with the 'perceptual' material and discovered the relationships between various perceived configurations and the actions which must be performed to produce them, the child achieves a basis of knowledge from which, according to Bruner, he can abstract more formal rules or principles.

At a more general theoretical level Bruner has attempted to follow through such ideas by trying to establish relationships between different patterns of education and general cognitive abilities. In some 'traditional' cultures the child is gradually and informally 'inducted' into his role in society: there are no formal institutions of learning, no 'school' within which the act of 'learning' is set apart from the general cultural milieu. The child in such a culture almost literally follows in the footsteps of his elders, picking up and doing whatever he can and gradually, with sporadic assistance, developing his competence until such time as he is capable of occupying a skilled role as a fully fledged member of society. In Western societies, where the tasks and problems to be faced continually change, the educational system must concentrate not upon the communication of traditional skills but upon the development of those more abstract abilities which underlie the capacity to change skills and rapidly acquire new ones. So, in technological societies, the act of learning has been removed from on-going work situations and set apart. Learning is seen as an end, an act in itself, not as some undifferentiated part of everyday social life.

Bruner traces the effects of such varying educational practices upon general cognitive abilities such as problem-solving. The Western child, educated to see his actions as separate, accountable and self-determined, can deliberately transfer actions from one situation to another; thus operations used to solve one problem can be used to solve other, novel, problems that arise. This is not the case in some traditional societies. In these instances, although an individual may be in possession of all the necessary component skills to solve a problem, he will not do so because he does not have a problem-solving 'attitude'. He has grown up without anyone systematically commenting upon his actions as though they were separate, *optional* entities. In consequence, they remain an undifferentiated part of a specific skill and inseparable from it, rather as a name 'belongs' to a specific class of objects. So, for example, the women of certain Indian tribes can weave intricate blanket patterns but may well be unable to 'see' that similar, and much simpler, operations are involved in making strings of beads and other articles of that kind.

The fascination—and real importance—of developmental psychology is that it explains man's diversity, as in the preceding instances, as well as his common character; for these, and related reasons, its great importance as an area of study is increasingly being recognised.

References

Bower, T. G. R. (1972), 'Object perception in infants'. *Perception*, *1*, 1, 15–30.

Bower, T. G. R., Broughton, J. M., & Moore, M. K. (1970), 'The co-ordination of vision and touch in infancy'. *Perception and Psychophysics*, 9.

Bruner, J. S. (1966), *Toward a Theory of Instruction*. New York: Norton.

Bruner, J. S. (1971), *The Relevance of Education*. New York: Norton.

Bruner, J. S., Olver, R. R., & Greenfield, P.M., *et al.* (1966), *Studies in Cognitive Growth*. New York: John Wiley.

Bruner, J. S., & Koslowski, B. (1972), 'Visually preadapted constituents of manipulatory action'. *Perception*, *1*, 1, 3–14.

Eisenburg, R. B. (1965), 'Auditory behaviour in the human neonate: a preliminary report'. *Jour. of Speech and Hearing Research*, 7, 245–69.

Elkind, D., & Flavell, J. H. (eds) (1969), *Studies in Cognitive Development: Essays in Honor of Jean Piaget*. New York: Oxford Univ. New York: Holt, Rinehart & Winston.

Fantz, R. L. (1961), 'The origin of form perception'. *Scientific American*, 204, 66–77.

Fantz, R. L., Ordy, J. M., & Udelf, M. S. (1962), 'Maturation of pattern vision in infants during the first six months'. *Journ. of Comparative and Physiological Psychology*, 55, 907–17.

Piaget, J., & Inhelder, B. (1969), *The Psychology of the Child*. London: Routledge & Kegan Paul.

Recommended further reading

Bruner, J. S. (1966), *Toward a Theory of Instruction*. New York: Norton.

Bruner, J. S., Olver, R. R., & Greenfield, P.M., *et al.* (1966), *Studies in Cognitive Growth*. New York: John Wiley.

Elkind, D., & Flavell, J. H. (eds) (1969), *Studies in Cognitive Development: Essays in Honor of Jean Piaget*. New York: Oxford Univ. Press.

Piaget, J., & Inhelder, B. (1969), *The Psychology of the Child*. London: Routledge & Kegan Paul.

3
The Psychology of Personality

P. R. W. Barnes

People who are studying psychology for the first time often assume that the subject is mainly concerned with an understanding of an individual's personality—what it is that makes him who he is. The other chapters in this book hopefully will counterbalance this assumption, but it remains the case that the study of personality, its structure, assessment and origins, is a central feature of the psychologist's task. In so far as psychology is about people, and a person's personality is central to how he will behave and respond, both in real-life situations and in the often artificial settings in which psychologists carry out their work, the significance of the study of personality pervades all aspects of the subject.

To try to define personality with any precision could well take up the remaining space available for this chapter. Definitions abound; Gordon Allport (1937) summed up the situation rather neatly when he wrote 'everyone, it seems, knows what personality is, but no one can precisely describe it'. It is perhaps sufficient to make clear from the outset that we are not merely using the word in the everyday sense of 'having a lot of personality' by being outgoing in social situations. Whilst it is true that our culture may value and reinforce certain types of personality rather than others, the psychologist's interest is in every aspect of personality.

The aim of this chapter is to introduce the reader to some aspects of the study of personality and the issues that they raise; particularly useful for further reading are Allport (1961); Hall and Lindzey (1957); Lazarus and Opton (1967); Mischel (1971); and Vernon (1964).

If we start out with some sort of common-sense definition in mind of what is meant by personality we are faced at once with the question of how to categorise or classify it. Hippocrates, an ancient Greek physician, described four categories or types of temperament: choleric (irritable), melancholic (depressed), sanguine (optimistic) and phlegmatic (calm). An individual's temperament was determined by the predominance of one of four body humours—yellow bile, black bile, blood and phlegm—and was therefore constitutionally determined.

Since then psychologists have employed other type labels; Sheldon, as we shall see, has explored the relationship between types of body build and types of personality, and Jung distinguished between extraverts and introverts.

Although there is a certain tidiness about being able to pigeonhole people in this way, some critics of this approach have argued that the individual's personality is too complex for it to be assigned wholeheartedly to any one category. However, not all typologies are categorical, and some of the most important ones are in the form of dimensions; people are not wholly extravert or wholly introvert but can be placed somewhere on a line between the two extremes. The use of type descriptions, then, is an attempt to sum up something basic to an individual's personality in just a few words. Some typologies are based upon clinical experience—the originator's conception of the fundamental personality patterns following from observations of his fellow men—and others have a firmer 'scientific' footing, being derived from the statistical analysis of a large amount of information from a large number of people.

An alternative way of viewing personality is to talk in terms of traits rather than types. A trait is 'any distinguishable relatively enduring way in which one individual varies from another' (Guilford, 1959). So that when, in everyday language, we talk about someone as being aggressive or friendly or honest we are attributing him with certain personality traits. Such judgements are usually based on our observations of how that person behaves and reacts in a variety of situations, and there is an implicit assumption that to describe someone as honest, for example, enables us to predict how he will behave in certain situations in the future. Whether such assumptions are wholly justifiable is open to doubt. A classic study (Hartshorne and May, 1928-9) of the character exhibited by children engaged in a variety of activities in several different situations indicated that a habit such as honesty might be evident in one situation (e.g. when given the opportunity to steal money) but not in another (e.g. cheating in a game). Although there was some overlap, it was argued that this was insufficient to justify the notion of general traits. This does not mean that character or personality is merely a collection of specific habits, but that many of the trait dimensions we use are too general and vague for us to place people on them with any degree of accuracy.

Part of the problem may be the actual choice of trait dimensions. The English language provides a large number of adjectives which could be used as trait labels; Allport and Odbert (1936) found as many as 18 000 in the dictionary. Because many of these words are synonymous this list can be reduced to about 170 traits, and since many of these are closely related—an individual who shows evidence of trait A also being likely to show evidence of trait B—the list can be reduced still further.

Here one encounters a major area of dispute amongst psychologists interested in personality (Holt, 1962). We acknowledge that every individual on this planet is unique; at the moment of conception each human being receives his own peculiar genetic endowment, and his experience of life from that point on serves to mould him into a person whom it would be impossible to replicate. Even identical twins who share the same genetic endowment can never have the same experiences, however zealously their parents strive to bring them up the same. But however unique the individual may be in terms of the character traits he exhibits, if we are to be able to describe his personality in such a way that he can be compared with other people, then it is necessary to categorise his standing on those traits which are judged to be most important—in other words, we need to be able to generalise.

A leading proponent of the *idiographic* approach—that concerned with the individual—was Gordon Allport (1961). He argued that it was more important to understand 'man in particular' rather than 'man in general'; psychology, in its attempt to copy the procedures of the natural sciences, had tended to concentrate on the latter. By contrast, he advocated a more intensive and extensive study of the single case, seeing how the individual's character traits relate to one another and how he behaves and reacts. This is similar in many respects to the task of the biographer in trying to understand and explain the complex structure of an individual's life, his relationships with other people and why he took a particular decision at a particular point in time.

But, retort the 'tough-minded' psychologists, what is the point of concentrating upon the individual in depth? Even if one did come to such an understanding of 'man in particular' one would still have to generalise it to other people or else it would be of little scientific value. This search for broad and preferably universal laws characterises the *nomothetic* approach. H. J. Eysenck, a prominent spokesman of this viewpoint, argues that 'to the scientist the unique individual is simply the point of intersection of a number of quantitative variables' (Eysenck, 1952). But if one accepts this approach it is necessary to decide which are the most important quantitative variables—which traits are sufficiently common and all-embracing to act as the main dimensions of human personality differences. One way to a solution to this question is provided by a complex statistical technique called factor analysis (Child, 1970). As already noted, there is a varying degree of correspondence or correlation between traits, and factor analysis is used to identify those with the highest degree of correspondence and to distinguish them from other clusters which are similarly highly internally correlated. The data on which these calculations are based are usually the results of a large battery of tests together with ratings and observations of behaviour.

Factor analysis has been likened to a sausage machine—what comes out is dependent upon what goes in and what happens in the intervening process. There is more than one way of conducting a factor analysis, and different interpretations have emerged. Eysenck found three bipolar dimensions of personality which were *orthogonal*, that is they were completely independent of one another. These dimensions were extraversion–introversion (in effect a measure of sociability), neuroticism–stability (emotionality) and psychoticism–non-psychoticism (the tendency towards an abnormal mental state). If these three dimensions are seen as occupying three-dimensional space, then it is possible to place an individual at a particular point in that space depending on where he stands on each of the three factors.

R. B. Cattell (1965), on the other hand, has produced a larger number of factors; the exact number has varied, but sixteen are most frequently quoted. He labels these dimensions with neologisms (new words) to reduce the likelihood of their being confused with descriptive labels in use in everyday speech; thus the outgoing, warm-hearted individual is described as *affectothymic* by contrast with the reserved and critical *sizothymic*. Because of the larger number of factors, the individual's personality is represented by a profile, showing the relationship of his scores on the sixteen factors. Although Cattell argues that it is necessary to consider all these factors in relation to one another, he does concede that, for simplicity, they can be reduced to four second-order factors, one of which—exvia–invia—is similar to Eysenck's extraversion–introversion dimension.

The difference between Eysenck and Cattell is that, although they agree about the need for a scientific, nomothetic approach to the study of personality, Cattell believes in description at the level of the trait whereas Eysenck concentrates on the type level as being more relevant to his theory of personality structure.

The theory of personality put forward by Sigmund Freud is in sharp contrast with the type and trait approaches already described (Hall, 1954). Whereas the latter concentrated upon the conscious and stable manifestations of personality, Freud pointed to the importance of unconscious forces which were in a continuous state of flux. As with much of the rest of psycho-analytic theory, Freud's ideas on personality derived, in the main, from his experiences with neurotic patients. Freud likened personality to an iceberg; the bulk of it is submerged and hidden from view. As such it is only accessible via a roundabout route, in particular through symbolic representation. He divided the structure of the personality into three distinct but interacting parts. The most basic is the *id*, which is the source of the driving force behind the individual. The id discharges tension in accordance with the pleasure principle, and its impulses are largely sexual or aggressive in form. These impulses have to be controlled by the *ego*, which is the tip of the iceberg and is in contact with the reality of the external world. The ego is governed by the reality principle, the aim of which is to postpone the discharge of energy until the appropriate object appears in the environment. In the course of normal development the individual's ego is formed out of the pleasure-seeking id under parental guidance. The third part of the personality is the *super-ego*, which represents the ideal rather than the real and strives for perfection as distinct from pleasure or reality. In terms of Freudian theory the super-ego is the conscience, and it involves the internalisation of parental control in the form of self-control.

Freud claimed that these three parts are not fixed and immutable but are in continual conflict. In the well-adjusted individual the ego is in control of both the id and the super-ego and is 'maintaining commerce with the external world in the interest of the total personality and its far-flung needs' (Hall, 1954). Disharmony and maladjustment appear when the ego surrenders too much of its power to the id, to the super-ego or to the external world. The extent to which the ego is differentiated from the id and the form that it comes to take depend upon individual human experience (see below).

The approaches described so far (with the exception of Allport) have tended to apply some sort of a common external structure to the individual's personality, be it the Freudian trio or the factor analytically derived trait dimensions. By contrast, other approaches—and ones which seem to be attracting increasing interest—see the individual as playing a more active role in dictating the shaping and presentation of his own personality. George Kelly (1955; and see also Bannister and Fransella, 1971) has formulated a personal construct theory in which the individual is seen as creating his own personality dimensions. In his day-to-day life man is, as it were, a scientist, formulating hypotheses about himself in relation to the world about him and testing them in terms of his experiences at the hands of other people; he attempts to anticipate and control the events in his life. His personality is less fixed, and may well change in response to events in the world as he adopts a new role appropriate to a particular situation.

This range of theories of the nature and structure of personality is reflected in the variety of ways by which psychologists have attempted to assess the individual's personality. The aim of this sort of assessment, as Sundberg and Tyler (1962) have put it, is 'the systematic collection, organisation and interpretation of information about a person and his situations'. The frame of reference within which this information is collected, organised and interpreted will depend upon the theoretical inclination of the psychologist, and, to some extent, on the purposes for which the information is required. The latter may be to assist in the diagnosis of a particular clinical condition, or to indicate one form of treatment or therapy rather than another; it may be for educational or vocational guidance purposes, or for personnel selection; or it may be for the further investigation of personality itself—its structure and growth, and its relation to other variables such as how the individual was brought up during the formative years of childhood.

A large number of techniques have been developed with a view to satisfying some of these needs, but there is space here to outline only a few. For further general information on personality assessment the reader is referred to Anastasi (1961) and Vernon (1964), and for more detailed information about particular tests to Buros (1972). The selection of a test or technique for use in a given situation will depend on a number of factors, the most important being the proven validity and reliability of the measuring instrument. By validity is meant the extent to which the test measures what it claims to measure; just because the content of a test appears, on the surface, to be measuring some aspect of the personality is no guarantee that that is what is actually being measured. In the end, as Vernon (1964) puts it, 'a test measures itself, and its further validity rests entirely on its established relations to other behaviours. It is the network of its relations to other variables and to real-life situations that gives its meaning.' The reliability of a test is the accuracy with which it measures what it claims to measure. One measure of reliability is the degree of agreement between the test scores for the same individual made at two separate points in time; poor agreement indicates low reliability, and the test is as much use as an elastic tape-measure. On the other hand, it may be that what is being measured is itself not stable, and that the change in situation from one occasion to the next is a real one and not an artefact of a poorly constructed test. There are several ways of determining the reliability and validity of a personality test and these are explained in most books on psychological testing, e.g. Anastasi (1961).

Perhaps the best-known personality tests are those labelled 'projective'. Frank (1939) summarised the purpose of these techniques as being to answer 'the problem of how we can reveal the way an individual personality organises experience in order to disclose or at least gain insight into the individual's *private world* of meanings, significances, patterns, and feelings'. Such an approach has its roots in psychoanalytic ideas of the nature of personality. A variety of techniques have been used to gain insight into this private world (Anastasi, 1961; Lindzey, 1961): associations of words or shapes; construction of stories; completion of sentences or stories; choosing or ordering material such as photographs, pictures or words; and expression through play, drawing and painting.

An examination of one of these tests, the Rorschach technique, will clarify some of the principles involved. Hermann Rorschach, a Swiss psychiatrist, described a technique for the investigation of personality using ten cards, on each of which was printed an ink blot symmetrical about a vertical axis. The subject is shown the cards one at a time and is asked to report what he sees and what the blot makes him think of. His responses are scored using a complicated system which notes where on the card the subject reports seeing whatever it is he sees, the qualities of the blot that determine the concept reported—form, movement, colour or shading—the subject-matter of the concept, the popularity of the response in terms of the frequency with which it is reported by others, and the accuracy with which the reported concept fits the blot area used (Klopfer and Davidson, 1962).

From an analysis of these responses the experienced Rorschach interpreter claims to be able to describe certain important facets of the individual's personality, including his intellectual status, the originality of his thinking, the breadth of his interests, his general emotional tone, his responsiveness to people, his control of emotional impulses, his self-confidence and his sexual adjustment. These claims are hotly contested (e.g. Eysenck, 1957a), and, indeed, studies have shown that widely different interpretations and judgements can be made by different experts confronted with the same set of responses.

A contrasting approach to assessment has evolved from the trait and type theories of personality. These are the personality inventories or questionnaires in which the subject is required to say whether a particular description of behaviour or feelings does or does not apply to him—'Do you like to mix socially with people?', 'Are you inclined to be moody?' and so on. These and similar questions are presented on a printed sheet and the subject typically selects one of a small number of alternative answers (yes/no; often/sometimes/never). Depending on his response he makes a score as laid down in the manual of instructions, and the scores from individual questions are combined to produce an overall score for a particular trait. Because the test has been tried out on a large number of people (the standardisation sample) during the stage of its initial construction, it is possible to say how one person's score compares with the scores of a representative population—how extreme it is on any particular trait. These inventories are straightforward to administer and score and, unlike most projective techniques, they are designed to be used with a group of people at one sitting. As a result they are frequently used in industrial personnel selection and in education; in this respect Cattell's Sixteen Personality Factors Questionnaire and Eysenck's Maudsley Personality Inventory are popular choices.

In some respects the information sought in these questionnaires is similar to that which one might try to elicit in an interview. Presenting the questions in this fashion apparently makes the process more objective because such things as the interviewer's tone of voice and his response, whether favourable or unfavourable, to the answers given cannot influence what is said. On the other hand, the inflexibility of the questionnaire necessarily limits the range of information obtained and might prevent significant avenues of an individual's personality from being explored. However, the personality questionnaire is far more than this. The questions or statements that are included are not chosen haphazardly but are selected from a much larger number of similar questions in accordance with their statistical relationship to one another (as determined by factor analysis) and their ability to predict how people will behave in other situations. To some extent the name given to the personality trait is irrelevant so long as it is an effective predictor. Indeed, many personality tests were developed for the expressed purpose of weeding out people who would otherwise prove to be unsuitable in a particular situation, e.g. working under stress. One way in which the validity of these tests is established is by comparing the scores of people who have been differentially classified according to some other criterion. For example, if a group of people who have been judged to be neurotic by a psychiatrist answer certain questions in a way which is noticeably different from people not so classified, then those questions are valuable discriminators of neurotic people.

These questionnaires and inventories are open to criticism both at a technical level and in more general terms. One common criticism is that they are open to faking by the person who wishes to put over a particular impression of himself. Whyte (1956), for example, has written an amusing guide on how to cheat at personality tests and what types of personality it is advisable to portray in certain situations. In a more serious vein, Vernon (1964) accounts for the comparatively poor agreement between test scores and the external criteria of the traits they are supposed to measure in terms of an understandable tendency to give socially desirable responses, together with other attitudes which are an artefact of the assessment situation and have little to do with the individual's basic personality.

It follows from Kelly's approach to personality that any attempt to assess personality must begin and end with an understanding of how the individual construes his own interpersonal environment. There is little point in placing him somewhere on a trait dimension if that particular dimension has no meaning for him—if it isn't part of his construct system. Instead, the individual is placed on equal terms with the psychologist in determining the basis upon which his constructs are to be explored. Kelly's technique for investigating personal constructs is the Repertory Grid, a set of bipolar dimensions on which the individual arranges the significant features of his life. Various techniques have been developed for constructing such grids. One requires the subject to think of three people who are important to him—his wife, his mother and his father, for example—and to say in what ways one of them differs from the other two. It might be that his wife and his mother are gentle and his father harsh—the gentleness-harshness dimension is thus established as one which is significant to that person and one on which other aspects of his experience and feelings may usefully be evaluated. Often people will volunteer twenty or so such constructs, and these can usually be reduced in number by statistical techniques which indicate whether some constructs are so closely related as to be considered the same for practical purposes.

Using the terminology introduced earlier, this is basically an idiographic technique to guide the psychologist's understanding of the person and the person's understanding of himself. Because the form the grid takes is not under the psychologist's control it is impossible to have norms for comparison, although attempts have been made along these lines, such as a test of schizophrenic thought disorder (Bannister and Fransella, 1966) which measures the looseness or tightness of an individual's construct system—the extent to which the various constructs relate to one another in a consistent way.

Kelly's approach brings us closer to the sort of technique that we tend to use in everyday life, which, in its more formal state, takes the form of a face-to-face interview (Hetherington, 1970). The interview has often been criticised as too subjective and open to bias in the form of the preconceptions of the interviewer and his susceptibility to undue influence by first impressions of dress, accent, manner and so on. Also, too much reliance is placed upon the skill and intuition of the person conducting the interview to make it a generally acceptable and reliable device. Although it is difficult to say with any precision what distinguishes the good interviewer from the poor one, Allport (1961) has suggested that the ability to judge others is dependent on maturity and experience of life, intelligence, similarity with the person being judged, and a level of cognitive complexity similar to or greater than that of the person being judged. Despite its limitations the interview continues to be extensively used in situations requiring some form of personality assessment, and more often than not it is accepted and relied upon by both interviewer and interviewee alike. In this respect it is perhaps significant that, after an extensive review of a wide range of techniques of personality assessment, Vernon (1964) concluded that neither clinically oriented or psychometrically oriented psychologists have 'succeeded in providing acceptable or practicable methods of diagnosis which are consistently more accurate than the unsophisticated methods that we ordinarily use in understanding people in daily life'. The broad issue is further explored in Chapter 14 (Clinical Psychology).

Whatever their theoretical stance on the nature of personality, one question has been of paramount interest to psychologists, namely the origins of our developed personality—how we become the person we are. A broad distinction can be made here between those who have stressed the biological determinants of personality patterns and those who have investigated the experiences the individual has had, particularly in childhood.

Freud claimed that every child passed through certain phases of development, and that personality characteristics could be shown to stem from the experiences received at each stage (Hall, 1954). The stages were linked to the three main erogenous zones: the mouth, anus and genitals; these are the parts of the young child's body which are subject to the greatest degree of excitation, and the extent to which the urge to suck, defecate and masturbate is allowed or frustrated is reflected in certain identifiable personality types. Frustration of oral gratification by too abrupt weaning may result in oral aggressiveness in the form of biting; the infant is seen as trying to hold on to things so as to prevent a recurrence of the traumatic weaning experience. Subsequently, this aggressiveness may show itself in other guises—sarcasm and a cynical regard for other people—or the individual may experience anxiety over these aggressive feelings and react by saying only kind things about other people. A further possibility is that the oral aggression becomes projected onto others, and the individual sees himself as the butt of their aggression. Similarly, obsessional habits and narcissism are associated with fixations at the anal and phallic stages respectively, although in these instances as well the relationship is not straightforward and intervening mechanisms might well produce a result opposite to the one anticipated.

Freud's theory was based on the recollections of his patients, and the accuracy of such retrospective evidence, particularly when it refers to childhood events, is highly questionable. Memory is selective, and the power of suggestion is such that Freud's questions may have triggered off certain recollections rather than others. Attempts to verify the theory (Kline, 1972) have produced ambiguous results. Rather than rely on this dubious retrospective evidence, the longitudinal study provides an alternative way of investigating the link between childhood experiences and adult personality. By following the same sample of people from early childhood through to adulthood, collecting information by means of interviews, observations and standardised tests, it becomes possible to relate childhood experiences and patterns of child-rearing to the developed adult character. So far few such studies have come to fruition, though the National Child Development Study (Davie *et al.*, 1972) and a study in Nottingham (Newson and Newson, 1963, 1968) have been in progress for some years.

It remains questionable how conclusive such studies can be in pointing to the precursors of particular personality patterns. Yarrow *et al.* (1968), for example, tried to replicate some of the findings from a much-quoted American study by Sears *et al.* (1957), but by and large they failed to find the same relationships between parental characteristics and child characteristics. This may be attributable to an overemphasis on the view of the child as a 'tabula rasa' onto which the personality is inscribed by the action of his parents and other environmental influences. More recently, the emphasis has been on the two-way nature of adult/child relationships (Schaffer, 1974). Even the youngest child has an individuality of his own which makes certain types of parental treatment appropriate and other types inappropriate. It is perhaps too soon to attribute to the infant a personality in the sense that it has been described here, but an analysis of the reciprocal relationships that he strikes up with his parents may well prove worthwhile in the long term.

An important attempt to link personality to biologically determined characteristics of the individual has been made by William Sheldon (1940, 1942). In his view there is a biological structure which plays a major role in determining observable physique and in moulding an individual's behaviour and temperament. Refining ideas traceable to the ancient Greeks, he devised a technique for measuring human physique along three basic dimensions: *endomorphy*, characterised by a roundish appearance weak in bony and muscular development; *mesomorphy*, an athletic physique with large bones and muscles; and *ectomorphy*, a long slender appearance, lacking in muscular development. Each dimension is viewed as a seven-point scale, and the individual somatotype—the pattern of these three primary components of physique—is expressed by three figures. Thus an individual rated 7-1-1 is extremely high in endomorphy and very low in mesomorphy and ectomorphy. As a guide to identifying somatotypes Sheldon produced atlases of men and women, illustrating the possible combinations of the three types. Having established a stable way of assessing physique he went on to identify three types of temperament: the *viscerotonic*, sociable, relaxed and comfort-loving; the *somatotonic*, energetic, assertive, courageous; and the *cerebrotonic*, tense, restrained and preferring solitude. In his early investigations Sheldon claimed a very high degree of association between these categories of temperament and body type (the relationship being in the order given above), but subsequent studies have shown a more moderate correspondence. A comparison of delinquent and non-delinquent boys, for example, showed that the physiques of the former tendered toward mesomorphy at least twice as often as those of the latter.

This example, and the other evidence of a relationship between physique and temperament, raises questions about the nature of the link: do they both emanate from the same constitutional source, or are there factors which mediate between the two, or, even, are both the product of similar environmental influences? The child with the athletic, mesomorphic build is more likely to be successful in physical conflicts with his peers and to be 'rewarded' for such behaviour; might not this make him more likely to come into conflict with the law? Alternatively, a particular type of home environment might encourage physical strength and an athletic physique, and at the same time expose the child to influences which might lead to delinquent behaviour. Sheldon himself seems to favour the idea of selective experience, the physique making certain styles of behaviour more appropriate than others, but whatever the mediating mechanism may be, the association between physique and personality remains as an interesting challenge to psychologists.

A further example of a biologically based theory of personality development is that proposed by Eysenck (1957b, 1965). There are individual differences (which are largely inherited) in the structure of the brain and the central nervous system, and in particular in the excitatory and inhibitory mechanisms which affect the transmission of nerve impulses and, thereby, learning (see Chapter 5 (Physiological Psychology)). Taking a lead from early workers such as Jung and Pavlov, Eysenck has postulated a link between extraverted and introverted patterns of behaviour and neurological function. The extravert has weak excitatory and strong inhibitory potentials, whereas the introvert has strong excitatory and weak inhibitory potentials. This affects the way in which the personality is acquired. Introverts learn (can be conditioned) more readily, and so come to absorb the rules of society; they become oversocialised and tend to prefer thought to action. Extraverts, on the other hand, are only poorly socialised and are predisposed towards action rather than thought. Eysenck's theory is well articulated and much of it is open to experimental verification (Eysenck, 1970). It raises the further possibility that, in so far as the workings of the nervous system can be controlled through stimulant and depressant drugs, the basis of personality can be controlled.

This brief review of the various ways in which psychology has conceptualised 'personality' may well leave the reader asking himself: 'But which one is right?' The answer is that they are all valid to some extent; they all account for some of the variation—within people and between them—that we meet in everyday life. In psychology, as in other forms of knowledge, it is clear that different theories represent different ways of looking at the same class or kind of phenomena. Some theories are more suitable for some aspects than for others—rather in the way that different lenses and filters on a camera are suitable for different scenes and different conditions. Theories are ways of looking at the world, psychological theories are ways of looking at human behaviour. Of one thing we can be quite sure: that any attempt to explain or understand human personality will only account for part of its richness and diversity and, at best, will account for it only very inadequately.

References

Allport, G. W., & Odbert, H. S. (1936), 'Trait-names: a psycholexical study'. *Psychol. Monogr.*, 47, No. 211.

Allport, G. W. (1937), *Personality: A Psychological Interpretation*. New York: Holt, Rinehart & Winston.

Allport, G. W. (1961), *Pattern and Growth in Personality*. London: Holt, Rinehart & Winston.

Anastasi, A. (1961), *Psychological Testing*. New York: Macmillan.

Bannister, D., & Fransella, F. (1966), 'A grid test of schizophrenic thought disorder'. *Brit. J. Soc. Clin. Psychol*, 5, 95-102.

Bannister, D., & Fransella, F. (1971), *Inquiring Man*. Harmondsworth: Penguin Books.

Buros, O. K. (1972), *The Seventh Mental Measurements Yearbook*. New Jersey: Gryphon.

Cattell, R. B. (1965), *The Scientific Analysis of Personality*. Harmondsworth: Penguin Books.

Child, D. (1970), *The Essentials of Factor Analysis*. London: Holt, Rinehart & Winston.

Davie, R., Butler, N., & Goldstein, H. (1972), *From Birth to Seven*. London: Longman.

Eysenck, H. J. (1952), *The Scientific Study of Personality*. London: Routledge & Kegan Paul.

Eysenck, H. J. (1957a), *Sense and Nonsense in Psychology*. Harmondsworth: Penguin Books.

Eysenck, H. J. (1957b), *The Dynamics of Anxiety and Hysteria*. London: Routledge & Kegan Paul.

Eysenck, H. J. (1965), *Fact and Fiction in Psychology*. Harmondsworth: Penguin Books.

Eysenck, H. J. (1970), *Readings in Extraversion–Introversion*. Vols 1–3. London: Staple Press.

Frank, L. K. (1939), 'Projective methods for the study of personality'. *J. Psychol.*, 8, 389–413.

Guilford, J. P. (1959), *Personality*. New York: McGraw-Hill.

Hall, C. S. (1954), *A Primer of Freudian Psychology*. New York: Mentor Books.

Hartshorne, H., & May, M. A. (1928), *Studies in Deceit*. New York: Macmillan.

Hartshorne, H. & May, M. A. (1929), *Studies in Service and Self-control*. New York: Macmillan.

Hetherington, R. R. (1970), 'The Clinical Interview'. In Mittler, P. (ed.), *The Psychological Assessment of Mental and Physical Handicap*. London: Methuen.

Holt, R. R. (1962), 'Individuality and generalization in the psychology of personality'. *J. Personality*, 30, 377–404. Reprinted in Lazarus, R. S., & Opton, E. M. (eds)—see below.

Kelly, G. A. (1955), *The Psychology of Personal Constructs*. Vols 1 & 2. New York: Norton.

Kline, P. (1972), *Fact and Fantasy in Freudian Theory*. London: Methuen.

Klopfer, B., & Davidson, H. H., *The Rorschach Technique*. New York: Harcourt, Brace & World.

Lindzey, G. (1961), *Projective Techniques and Cross-cultural Research*. New York: Appleton-Century-Crofts.

Newson, J., & Newson, E. (1963), *Infant Care in an Urban Community*. London: George Allen & Unwin. (Harmondsworth: Penguin 1965.)

Newson, J., & Newson, E. (1968), *Four Years Old in an Urban Community*. London: George Allen & Unwin. (Harmondsworth: Penguin 1970.)

Schaffer, H. R. (1974), 'Early social behaviour and the study of reciprocity'. *Bull. Br. Psychol. Soc.*, 27, 209–16.

Sheldon, W. H., Stevens, S. S., & Tucker, W. B. (1940), *The Varieties of Human Physique*. New York: Harper.

Sheldon, W. H. & Stevens, S. S. (1942), *The Varieties of Temperament*. New York: Harper.

Sears, R. R., MacCoby, E. E., & Levin, H. (1957), *Patterns of Child Bearing*. New York: Harper & Row.

Sundberg, N. D. & Tyler, L. E. (1962), *Clinical Psychology*. New York: Appleton-Century-Crofts.

Vernon, P. E. (1964), *Personality Assessment*. London: Methuen.

Whyte, W. H. (1956), *The Organization Man*. New York: Simon & Schuster.

Yarrow, M. R., Campbell, J. D., & Burton, R. V. (1968), *Child Rearing: an Enquiry into Research and Methods*. San Francisco: Jossey Bass.

Recommended further reading

Allport, G. W. (1961), *Pattern and Growth in Personality*. London: Holt, Rinehart & Winston.

Hall, C. S., & Lindzey, G. (1957), *Theories of Personality*. New York: John Wiley.

Lazarus, R. S., & Opton, E. N. (eds) (1967), *Personality*. Harmondsworth: Penguin Books.

Mischel, W. (1971), *Introduction to Personality*. New York: Holt, Rinehart & Winston.

Vernon, P. E. (1964), *Personality Assessment*. London: Methuen.

4
Experimental Psychology

G. Underwood

Experimental method in psychology

Psychology may be described as the study of behaviour, and experimental psychologists hold the belief that the most accurate method of studying behaviour, and the method which yields the greatest understanding of behaviour, involves the techniques of scientific investigation. In general, this means defining a range of stimuli which the human being or animal will receive, describing the effects of these stimuli upon behaviour which can be observed, and inferring the nature of the processes in the nervous system through which a certain stimulus has a certain behavioural effect. In simpler terms, experimental psychologists attempt to explain *why* certain patterns of behaviour are produced using a particular method of enquiry.

Experiment is a fundamental method of investigation in science, and the aims of experiments are to understand and predict the events of nature. Some of the uses of the knowledge of understanding and predicting behaviour have been to control behaviour, but this does not necessarily have authoritarian overtones. By designing traffic signs which allow car driving behaviour to be more efficient we are, in a sense, controlling that behaviour. Control may come through prediction of an event under certain circumstances, but understanding of the cause–effect relationship is not necessary for control. For instance, it has been observed that if a cup of coffee is drunk between finding a telephone number in the directory and dialling that number, then the number is dialled incorrectly. We may then construct hypotheses as to *why* misdialling takes place, but observation of these events is all that is necessary to control the outcome: if we wish to dial correctly, then we must not drink coffee between finding the number and dialling. We have, in this simple example, a competitor to the experimental method, and this is the method of enquiry of *naturalistic observation*. Naturalistic observation describes the regularity and predictability of behaviour, but gives no evidence as to why behaviour of one variety rather than another is produced. In the previous example the antecedent condition of coffee-drinking might be the cause of misdialling, but the 'naturalist' would never know for certain, nor would he know for certain why coffee-drinking should affect the behaviour of using a telephone dial. Any number of hypotheses might be produced about cause–effect relationship, but they could only be tested and distinguished between by using the experimental method. Previous experience might indicate that misdialling has little to do with the coffee itself, but is due to the time taken to drink the coffee between finding the number and dialling—this interval could be critical by allowing forgetting of the number. Another hypothesis might consider the effects of caffeine upon the motor task of dialling or upon remembering the number. These hypotheses are not differentiated between by the observation that an antecedent condition of coffee-drinking leads to misdialling.

As an alternative to the naturalistic observation approach, the experimental approach would attempt to determine the specific cause of the misdialling behaviour by a process of observing the effects of isolated conditions. Effects of caffeine upon any number of component tasks might be determined, and similarly the effects of drinking coffee upon remembering telephone numbers or any number of interpolated tasks. The basic method is to control the factors which may influence the event in question, to hold all these factors constant except one and to vary this factor to determine whether or not it influences the event. So, to investigate the specific effects of caffeine, we might try two tests at finding and dialling a number. One test would have the person being tested drink coffee as an interpolated task, and the other test would have a person drink water or some other liquid between finding the number in the directory and dialling it. If the person misdials in the 'coffee' *treatment* (or *condition*) but not in the 'water' treatment, then on the basis of this and other tests using different telephone numbers (to ensure that the effect is not specific to that telephone number) and people (to ensure that the effect is general throughout the sample of the population being tested) we might conclude that the cause of the misdialling effect was in some direct way related to the coffee, and not simply due to the time taken to drink the coffee—provided that we have ensured that the people being tested were made to drink the water as slowly as did the coffee-drinkers. This is what is meant by holding all other factors constant. If we had allowed thirty seconds to drink the water and three minutes to drink the coffee, then two factors would have been varied—substance and duration—and the difference in results might be due to either of the treatments. This is the basic principle behind the experimental method in psychology—one group of people (known as 'subjects') is given one treatment and another group of subjects (or group*s* in more complicated experimental designs) is given another treatment which differs from the first in only one factor. All other factors are held constant, and so any variation in the effect over the treatment groups is in some way due to the treatments. Factors which are varied or held constant may be referred to as *independent variables*, whereas the behaviour resulting from the treatments may be referred to as the *dependent variable*.

The independent variables in psychological research are stimulus events, and the dependent variables are behavioural or response events. That is, we vary the stimuli presented to subjects and observe the effects of these stimuli upon subjects' responses. Stimuli take the form of physical energy—visual, auditory, tactile, etc.—and in the simplest situations may be words spoken to the subject or presented visually on paper. In the example used above there are two stimulus sources present—the telephone number and the coffee. Responses are changes in behaviour, and may be a vocal output, or the pressing of a lever, or dilation of the pupil of the eye, or, of course, the absence of these or other activities where previously they were present. In the example above, the response is the dialling behaviour, and the feature of interest is whether the number dialled corresponds to the number found in the directory.

The range of behaviour now studied by experimental psychologists is immense, and here we come to a somewhat confusing distinction. Although the *experimental method* in psychology may be applied to the study of any behavioural phenomenon, the full extent of which is indicated by the remaining chapters of this book, there exist a particular breed of workers who have come to be known as *experimental psychologists*. In a broad sense the term could refer to a psychologist interested in any aspect of behaviour, but whereas the social psychologist, for example, could use a method of naturalistic observation, the experimental psychologist could by definition only use the experimental method. Experimental psychologists have interested themselves specifically in such behavioural phenomena as perception, memory, learning, skilled behaviour, problem-solving and decision-making. The common factor between these phenomena is that they are all exhibited in the normal behaviour of the adult individual. The remainder of this chapter will deal with the problems of describing and understanding some of these phenomena, and the attempts which experimental psychologists have made to deal with these problems.

The scope of human psychology

Perception
Consider the psychological processes that are operating as you read a sentence from a piece of paper, any sentence. As you

read the letters the conversion from visual symbols to meaningful
words and phrases is performed rapidly and without your having
to be aware of the conversion, unless the language is unfamiliar.
When the European comes across Arabic or Chinese text for the
first time, the symbols do not associate themselves into words or
phrases but remain as meaningless visual stimuli. To describe
the situation in a slightly different way, the Arabic symbols are
seen but they are not perceived. Perception therefore may be
described as 'effort after meaning', in which some organisation
or interpretation is imposed upon the signals arriving at the
sense organs. Perception depends upon sensation, but there is
not a one-to-one correspondence between, say, the pattern of
receptor cells fired on the retina and the pattern which is perceived. This may be established with the use of two examples.
First, two different sensations can give rise to the same perception. A series of handwritten 'A's, written by different people
and having different styles, were found to be easily recognisable
by subjects tested by Neisser and Weene (1960). These characters had different stimulus properties but resulted in the same
perception: they all had the quality of 'A'ness. Second, two
identical sensations can give rise to different perceptions, and
this is demonstrated by the example provided by Selfridge
(1955). Fig. 4.1 is easily read and understood, but the identical
stimuli 'Ħ' are read by most people as an 'H' in one context and

THE CAT

Fig. 4.1   From Selfridge (1955).

an 'A' in the other context. It appears that perception is dependent upon the stimuli presented, but not totally determined
by them. These two examples serve to indicate the problems of
pattern recognition—the problem of how stimuli are converted
into meaningful events.

Psychologists have devised two general theories to explain how we recognise patterns, or categorise the stimuli presented, and they are the template-matching and the feature-analysis theories. The template-matching theory considers that a figure which is presented is recognised by comparing it with a model which is stored in memory. Thus, each time we see the letter 'A' and recognise it, we do so by comparing it with a specific model of an 'A'. By having a series of models we are able to recognise each of the letters of the alphabet. However, pattern recognition cannot be as simple as this, for we are able to recognise a great many sizes of 'A's, and if the 'A' is tilted on presentation it is still recognised without too much difficulty. To get round these objections the template-matching theory could postulate a great many templates—templates for all sizes and orientations of letters—but this seems inefficient in comparison with an addition to the basic theory of pre-processing for size and orientation. So, the strong version of the theory says that each stimulus is re-orientated and resized where necessary before matching against the stored model, or template. However, the theory still cannot handle the phenomenon of recognition of handwritten symbols —there are an infinite number of ways of writing 'A', each of which is recognisable. Template theory would have to postulate an infinite number of templates for us to be able to recognise each of these variations, and this is clearly not the case in view of the finite capacity of the human brain. Again, the theory could argue that pre-processing eliminates irrelevant features from the handwritten 'A', and only the basic shape is matched. Template theorists could hedge like this indefinitely, so in the meantime we shall look at the alternative theory.

The feature-analysing model of pattern recognition suggests that characters are recognised by first testing them for various specific features. For the purposes of the present discussion it is not necessary to know exactly what these features are, but they may be such qualities as the presence of a vertical line in the character, or parallel lines, incomplete circles or oblique angles. In this way it is easy to describe an 'A' as having the qualities of an acute angle with point uppermost and a horizontal line at the midpoint of the character. Two analysers could be involved here, one for 'acuteness, upwards' and one for 'horizontal line, halfway'. Using such features the whole alphabet and dozens more characters could be uniquely described, and therefore analysed efficiently, with far fewer templates than would be necessary to perform the same function. Note that this model analyses characters independently of their size and, with knowledge of the degree of rotation, independently of rotation.

As an empirical test between these two models of pattern recognition, consider an experiment reported by Neisser (1964). Subjects were presented with lists of letters, as in Fig. 4.2. The task, with each list, was to search for the letter 'Z' and press a response key as soon as this target letter was found. The time between presentation of the list and the pressing of the response key was recorded, and this was the dependent variable. The independent variable was the shape of the letters in the list to be searched. If you try this task for yourself you will find that searching for the 'Z' is much easier with list (a) than with list (b), and this was the result found by Neisser using a large number of subjects and a large number of lists with target letters in many positions over the different lists. The interesting point here is that, whereas the template-matching theory predicts no difference between search times for the 'Z' in each list, the feature-analysis theory predicts the obtained result. How? Template-matching theory argues that when reading lists of letters each letter is compared with a model of the target 'Z', and this comparison process continues until a match is found. If each letter is compared with the template, then the shape of the letters should make no difference to the time taken for the comparison. Feature-analysis theory suggests that the critical features of the 'Z' (e.g. horizontal parallels, oblique line) are used in the search, and that it is these features which are looked for when scanning the list. So, with a list composed of letters dissimilar in shape to the 'Z', the comparison process is simple—the only letter possessing any of the critical features is the

(a)	(b)
ODUGQR	IVMXEW
QCDUGO	EWVMIX
CQOGRD	EXWMVI
QUGCDR	IXEMWV
URDGQO	VXWEMI
GRUQDO	MXVEWI
DUZGRO	XVWMEI
UCGROD	MWXVIE
DQRCGU	VIMEXW
QDOCGU	EXVWIM
CGUROQ	VWMIEX
OCDURQ	VMWIEX
UOCGQD	XVWMEI
RGQCOU	WXVEMI
GRUDQO	XMEWIV
GODUCQ	MXIVEW
QCURDO	VEWMIX
DUCOQG	EMVXWI
CGRDQU	IVWMEX
UDRCOQ	IEVMWX
GQCORU	WVZMXE
GOQUCD	XEMIWV
GDQUOC	WXIMEV
URDCGO	EMWIVX
GODRQC	IVEMXW

Fig. 4.2 Is it easier to find the 'Z' in list (a) or list (b)? (From Neisser, 1964.)

target letter itself. With the list containing 'E's, 'X's, and 'V's, however, critical features abound, and the search is slower because a particular combination of critical features must be searched.

Here we have an experiment which tests between two theories of pattern recognition, comes out in favour of one theory and against the other theory. Whereas naturalistic observation may have come to the same conclusion eventually, by manipulating the stimuli presented to the subjects and by taking objective measures, we have established which theory best describes behaviour, in an efficient and conclusive manner.

Other perceptual phenomena investigated by experimental psychologists include the operation of the constancies—a plate lying on a table is not 'seen' as an elliptical object but as a circular object. Why? The pattern of stimulation on the retina is that of an ellipse, as could be proved by taking a photograph, but that is not how we perceive the plate. A plate remains circular, regardless of its orientation, and this is the phenomenon of shape constancy. Similar phenomena operate on the perception of size (people in the distance are not 'seen' as midgets, which is what their retinal size would indicate) and colour (a white plate in red light is 'seen' as a white plate, again going against the information given by the retina). The perception of movement (real and apparent) and depth are issues which are also of interest to experimental psychologists.

Memory

Given that information (e.g. a telephone number, a sentence from a book or a drawing) has been perceived, an intervening process which could lead to an incorrect response is that of storage in memory. An efficiently perceived item of information may be forgotten during the interval between presentation time and retrieval time, making recall impossible. This is a phenomenon common to us all. We are constantly forgetting addresses, telephone numbers, where we have placed objects, or that we should have called at the shops on the way home. We forget so much that we often surprise ourselves by remembering even the most trivial details of events long past, the appearance of rooms not visited for many years, or a small inconsequential event on a distant holiday. The phenomena of remembering and forgetting are so important to our behaviour that experimental psychologists have devoted a great deal of effort to their study, and some of the specific points that they have been investigating include: how information is entered into and stored in memory; how many kinds of memory we have; what the mechanisms are by which forgetting takes place; how we organise the information in memory; and how we retrieve the information which is stored.

As an illustration of some of the difficulties of investigating an intangible area such as memory, and some of the ingenious ways which experimental psychologists have found to get round these difficulties, consider an experiment reported by Sperling (1960).

One of the earliest experiments in psychology, performed by Erdmann and Dodge in 1898, investigated the apprehension of information during reading: how many letters can be seen and remembered with a very brief exposure of the type gained by an eye fixation whilst reading at normal speed. Erdmann and Dodge found that four or five unrelated letters could be reported with an exposure duration of a tenth of a second. The processes involved here must include perception of the letters, storage in memory for the period between presentation and response, retrieval from memory and output (response) of the information retrieved from memory. However, things are not quite as simple, as Sperling (1960) has shown. In his experiment subjects were shown three rows of unrelated letters with four letters in each row, of the type shown in Fig. 4.3. This display of twelve letters was shown for one-twentieth of a second.

```
S N T R
P K F A
D L J M
```

Fig. 4.3 A display of the type used by Sperling (1960).

Immediately after this display the subject heard a tone, and this tone indicated which of the three rows of letters the subject was to report. A high tone cued the top row, a medium tone the centre row and a low tone the bottom row. The important point here is that the tone is heard *after* the letters have been removed from sight, and until the tone is heard the subject is not sure which row will have to be reported. From Erdmann and Dodge's experiment we might have expected that subjects would have four or five letters available, and as these letters would be distributed over three rows then only $\frac{4}{3}$ or $\frac{5}{3}$ letters, on average, would be reported from any one row. However, subjects were able to report about three letters of the four required on each test trial (i.e. about 75 per cent recall on average). They could recall about three letters from any of the three rows, and since they did not know which row would be cued for recall this must mean that they could have recalled about 75 per cent of any row. Hence the subjects must have had 75 per cent of the total display available for recall after the presentation had finished; that is, about nine of the twelve letters were in some form of memory after the display had been terminated. Whereas the early experiment had suggested that the 'span of apprehension' is four or five letters, the Sperling experiment shows clearly

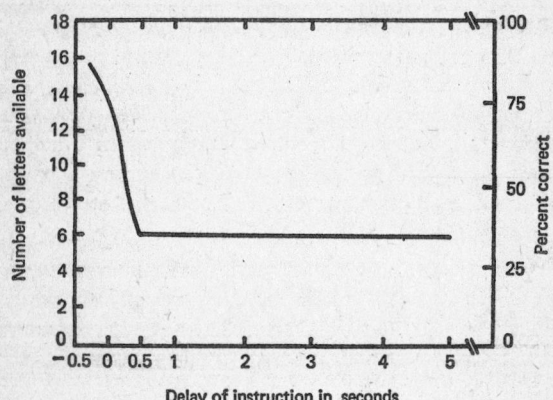

Fig. 4.4 The effect of delaying the cue-tone upon recall. (From Sperling, 1963.)

that this is not the case. However, an explanation of this discrepancy is provided by recall data when the tone cueing the row is delayed. With an 'immediate' cue we infer that about nine letters are available, but if the cue is delayed for just one second then only 4·3 letters are available—a similar figure to that reported by Erdmann and Dodge. What is happening in this one-second interval? Sperling has concluded that his experiment provides evidence for a visual memory system which decays extremely rapidly, within one second in fact, and this decay function can be seen in Fig. 4.4. This diagram shows the result of an experiment reported by Sperling in 1963, and which is essentially similar to the 1960 experiment, except that the onset of the cue-tone was an independent variable which was varied systematically and the number of letters in the display was eighteen instead of twelve. The number of letters reported (from which the number of letters available is inferred) drops sharply from about 75 per cent of the number presented to about 30 per cent as the tone is delayed from 0 seconds to $\frac{1}{2}$ second. Thereafter it makes little difference to the number of letters reported how long the cue is delayed.

From this experiment several points emerge. The observation of Erdmann and Dodge that with a brief exposure we are able to recall four or five letters from a large display is quite emphatically not the whole story. Secondly, the existence of a special type of memory is indicated—a memory system which can hold a large amount of information for a very short period of time. Experimental psychologists are now developing theories to explain how information is transferred from this very short term memory system into other longer term memory systems, and at what point in the process of transfer meaning is extracted from the displays held in these systems. This brings us to the third point, for although we have considered Sperling's experiments under a heading of 'Memory' they might just as validly have been included in the section headed 'Perception'. The experiments deal with the presentation and report of visual information, a task performed effortlessly many times a day—we look at something and read it out, or respond to it in some other way. The psychological description of the processes involved is not quite as straightforward as this, however. One of the problems is for us to say at what point the items have been perceived. It is quite likely that the subject makes no attempt to transfer the items from the visual memory system until he hears the tone cueing a particular row. If the letters are perceived or recognised after the tone has been heard, then the processes of perception and storage in memory are not compartmentalised in a distinct and orderly manner but continuously interact, and a 'pre-perceptual' memory may well be in operation here. This does not make for easy writing of textbooks on the subject of how we process information and respond to it, and the reader should be aware that the headings 'Perception', 'Memory' (and, for that matter, 'Skills', 'Learning', 'Decision-making' and 'Problem-solving') are a convenience. They do not, or should not, imply a neat ordering of the behaviour which they might describe.

The two experiments described in some detail so far, those by Neisser (1964) and Sperling (1960), serve to indicate the type of enquiry favoured by experimental psychologists. They are representative of investigations into those areas of human behaviour which we might describe as 'perception' and 'memory', but the same principles of enquiry are employed by all experimental psychologists, and so the following two sections will contain only an outline of the problems under discussion in the areas of 'Learning and skilled behaviour', and 'Decision-making and Problem-solving'.

Learning and skilled behaviour

If we are to adapt to our environment, then we must be able to acquire knowledge of that environment, and specifically of the consequences of our actions in the environment. We must be able to recognise the occurrence of desirable outcomes to our behaviour and to organise our behaviour around attempts to obtain these. To psychologists this involves the description of the processes by which associations between events are built; the description of the effects of 'reinforcement' (and, more problematically, why partial reinforcement—the reinforcement of only a proportion of the total number of correct responses—should be so effective); the description of the effects of punishment upon behaviour (and why punishment can act as 'reinforcement' under certain circumstances); and under which conditions the learning of one task can aid performance on another task. Problems facing psychologists working in the related area of skilled performance include the description of the limits of performance which we may expect from human operators in, for instance, vigilance tasks (too few stimuli presented for efficient performance) and overloaded tasks (too many stimuli competing for the subject's attention for efficient performance). We are also interested in the description of the changes which may occur within the human operator between non-skilled and skilled performances on any task. This will involve an understanding of how the operator organises the task perceptually and comes to appreciate the predictability of the task—how one stimulus is invariably associated with another stimulus, and how one response necessarily leads to another response in the same task. Differences in the strategies of acquiring information from displays indicate an appreciation of this predictability, and with practice the unskilled performance may come to be a skilled performance through the simultaneous processing of information which had been processed sequentially when the task was attempted initially.

Problem-solving and decision-making

To understand the processes which are used when we solve a problem it is necessary to understand how the problem is perceived, what strategies are used during the process and what are the limitations imposed upon problem-solving by such psychological factors as memory. For example, try solving the following problem for yourself: 'If the puzzle you solved before you solved this one was harder than the puzzle you solved after you solved the puzzle you solved before you solved this one, was the puzzle you solved before you solved this one harder than this one?'* (Restle, 1969). How do you organise or classify the problem? What strategies do you use to solve it? Do you attempt

---

* The solution is that only two puzzles are referred to in the question, and 'this one' is harder than 'the puzzle you solved before you solved this one'.

to visualise a set of puzzles of differing difficulty, for instance? What are the effects of 'mental set' (or expectation) in the problem-solving situation? In other words, what assumptions do you make about the problem, and what advantages and disadvantages do these assumptions have? By using problem-solving as an experimental task, psychologists have been able to study the processes involved in thinking, a topic which has not been respectable scientifically until the last few decades. Closely associated with the area of problem-solving is that of decision-making, which may be viewed as the problem of how we select between available courses of action. What are the factors which influence that selection, and how do we assess values and costs when deciding? One of the problems here is to describe how psychological value (utility) varies with individuals, and how 'utility' is used when making the decision. For example, the prospect of winning £1 will not have the same value for all individuals, and even with two individuals to whom £1 has similar value we cannot be sure that they would both make the same decision in a situation where they were sure of winning £0·10 *or* had one chance in ten of winning £1. Decision-making rarely follows a logical course. Given that we would choose eggs rather than sausages, and would choose sausages rather than fish, this does not mean that we would choose eggs rather than fish, as transitivity would dictate.

Psychology is now firmly within the grasp of experimental science. By the application of the techniques of scientific investigation during the last hundred years we have come to understand a great deal about how and why people behave as they do, the limitations imposed upon their behaviour by psychological processes and the facilities available to them when responding to the environment.

References

Erdmann, B., & Dodge, R. (1898), *Psychologische Untersuchungen über das Lesen*. Halle: M. Niemeyer.

Neisser, U. (1964), 'Visual search'. *Scientific American*, 219 (6), 94–102.

Neisser, U., & Weene, P. (1960), 'A note on human recognition of hand-printed characters'. *Information and Control*, 3, 191–6.

Restle, F. (1969), 'Mathematical models and thought: A search for stages'. In Voss, J. F. (ed.), *Approaches to Thought*. Columbus, Ohio: C. E. Merrill.

Selfridge, O. G. (1955), 'Pattern recognition and modern computers'. *Proceedings of the Western Joint Computer Conference*. Los Angeles.

Sperling, G. (1960), 'The information available in brief visual presentations'. *Psychological Monographs*, 74, (No. 11).

Sperling, G. (1963), 'A model for visual memory tasks'. *Human Factors*, 5, 19–31.

Recommended further reading

Dodwell, P. C. (1972), *New Horizons in Psychology 2*. Harmondsworth: Penguin Books.

Gregory, R. L. (1966), *Eye and Brain*. London: Weidenfeld & Nicolson.

Lindsay, P. H., & Norman, D. A. (1972), *Human Information Processing*. London: Academic Press.

Neisser, U. (1967), *Cognitive Psychology*. New York: Appleton-Century-Crofts.

Underwood, B. J. (1966), *Experimental Psychology*. New York: Appleton-Century-Crofts.

Wright, D. S., et al. (1970), *Introducing Psychology*. Harmondsworth: Penguin Books.

5
Physiological Psychology
R. G. Stevens

Over the last hundred years or so there has developed a multi-disciplinary approach to the study of behaviour. This has been termed physiological psychology and its subject-matter is the relationship between brain and behaviour. The reason why psychologists have been interested in brain function is that such knowledge will extend their understanding of psychological processes. Although at present it is not possible to explain such complex behaviour as social interaction, for example, in terms of brain function, other psychological processes like memory, attention and motivation have been profitably studied by physiological psychologists.

Physiological psychology has borrowed techniques from psychology, physiology, anatomy, biochemistry and pharmacology. Because of some of its parent sciences, the premise on which it is based is that psychological processes are the product of a mechanism, the brain. For most contemporary psychologists this proposition would be readily accepted, but for a few, psychological processes, which are the basis of mind, must be beyond physical explanation. Descartes, the seventeenth-century scientist and philosopher, was the first to treat the brain as a mechanism which controls behaviour, and no rational contemporary scientist would deny this. The argument of those who consider that mind is not a function of the brain must therefore go like this:

Behaviour which is dependent upon sensations and responses is conceivably the product of exceedingly complex brain processes. But there can be no feasible mechanism which would produce consciousness, cognition, empathy, etc.—the foundations of mind.

However, the brain is enormously complex and we are only at the very beginning of understanding it. It is therefore more advantageous for the development of psychology if we initially suppose that mind can be explained by the functioning of the brain. Moreover, if we ever completely understand how the brain works the problem will be resolved.

Because of the diversity of areas studied by physiological psychologists, this chapter can only provide a brief overview of the subject. Therefore, three topics have been selected, which will demonstrate some of the processes underlying important aspects of behaviour and in which there is considerable current interest. These topics are hunger, vision and memory. But before discussing these subjects a brief review of some neuroanatomy and the events underlying neurotransmission is required.

The mammalian nervous system is structurally divided into two parts: a peripheral portion, consisting of the nerves which lead from the spinal cord to the various parts of the body, and a central portion, which is functionally subdivided into a major portion called the central nervous system (CNS) and a secondary part called the autonomic nervous system (ANS). The CNS is also physically divided into the brain and the spinal cord, and it is responsible for the processes involved in sensing, thinking, remembering and acting in a voluntary manner. Information is transmitted to and from the brain and spinal cord by the peripheral nervous system, which consists of bundles of nerve fibres, commonly called nerves. Control of various involuntary processes like heart beat, digestion and excretion are performed by the ANS. Although from its name, autonomic, it would be expected that the ANS is autonomous or independent of the CNS in function, in reality the two systems closely interact at several levels. For example, there are few of us who have not suffered from digestive disorders in situations of stress, such as before examinations or the undertaking of tasks which we are unsure we shall be able to perform adequately. In these ex-

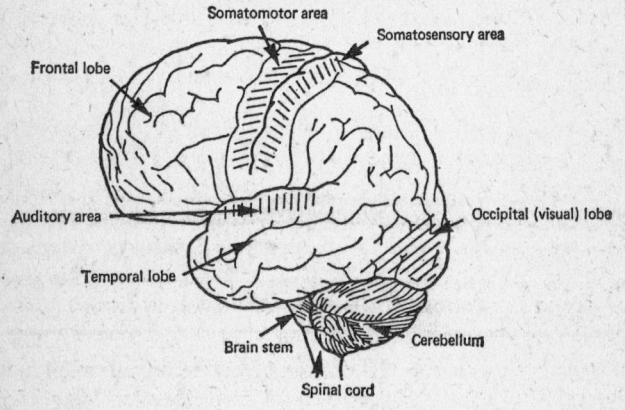

Fig. 5.1 A side view of the left cerebral hemisphere. Note the convoluted appearance of the surface of the hemisphere.

amples, functions of the CNS like expectations are affecting ANS functioning. Alternatively, if we see a distressing event such as a car accident, our perception of the situation (a CNS function) is affected by our emotional responses which are intricately linked to the ANS.

A human brain weighs 1300 to 1500 grammes. Its most conspicuous surface feature is the pinkish-grey wrinkled cerebral cortex, which is responsible for processing visual, auditory and tactile information and for producing voluntary movements and speech. The pinkish-grey colour of the cerebrum comes from the presence in it of *neurons*, the information-processing cells of nervous tissue. There are estimated to be 10 000 million neurons in the cerebral cortex and these neurons, like all others in the nervous system, have three basic features. There is the cell body which contains a nucleus and which is sometimes shaped like a pyramid, a star, a sphere or a pear. Twig-like projections run in all directions away from the cell body and frequently one of these is much longer than the others; this is the *axon*. The other twig-like projections are *dendrites*. Many cerebral cortex neurons project their axons into the middle of the brain and then down the spinal cord. These axons are usually covered by *myelin*, a fatty sheath, which gives the middle of the brain a yellowish-white appearance.

Neurons are cells which are specialised (a) to transmit information as nerve impulses, (b) to pass this information to other neurons and (c) to receive information from other neurons. These processes are interlinked, but for the sake of clarity they will be discussed separately and in the above order. A nerve action potential or impulse is set up at the point where the axon joins the cell body (see Fig. 5.2). Action potentials are all-or-nothing events, since once set up they travel down the axon away from the cell body at a constant amplitude and velocity. The action potentials are the means by which information is transmitted between various points in the nervous system. Most of our understanding of the events underlying the action potential comes from the studies of the biophysicists Hodgkins and Huxley (1939). They showed, by inserting very fine glass tubes into the fluid-filled interior of axons, that there is a voltage between the inside and the outside of axons which is maintained at a level of about -70 millivolts (the resting potential). An energy-consuming biochemical process, which has been given the apt name of the sodium-potassium pump, maintains this voltage. This pump concentrates sodium ions* in the fluid outside the cell and potassium ions inside the cell. A nerve impulse

---

* Ions exist in solutions and are electrically charged particles.

when recorded from an axon consists of a complete reversal of the voltage across the cell membrane, which briefly makes the inside of the axon 30 mV positive with respect to the outside. The impulse occurs when the sodium-potassium pump briefly stops working; sodium ions which were concentrated outside

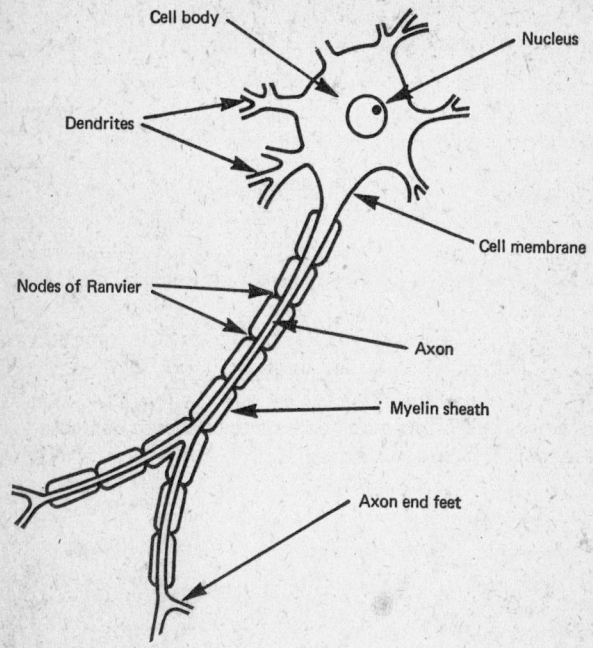

Fig. 5.2 A diagrammatic representation of a typical neuron showing the three divisions, dendritic, cell body and axonal.

the cell by the pump rush into the cell, which then makes the cell more electrically positive on the inside. Lagging briefly behind the influx of sodium ions into the axon is an efflux of positive potassium ions from the cell, making the inside negative again.

Physiological Psychology 63

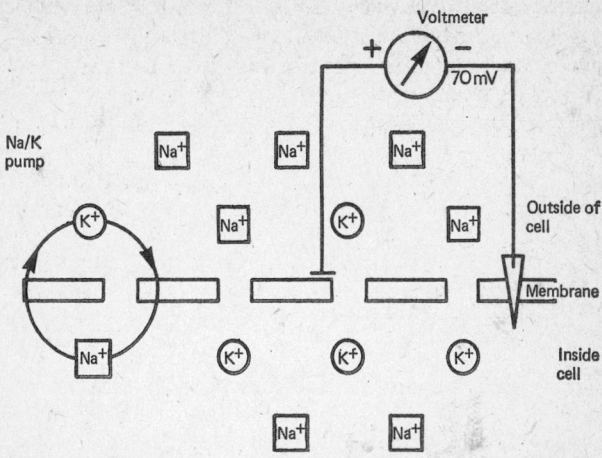

Fig. 5.3 A section across a nerve cell membrane. There are more positively charged sodium ions outside the cell than inside and fewer potassium ions outside the cell than inside. The sodium-potassium pump returns the potassium ions (K^+), which escape from inside the cell, and at the same time removes sodium ions (Na^+) from inside the cell.

The permeability of the axon membrane to sodium ions is dependent on the voltage across it. This is the reason why neurons can be stimulated electrically. If the voltage across the axon membrane is reduced from 70 mV to about 60 mV, sodium ions will start entering the cell, making the inside even less negative and thus initiating the nerve impulse. This effect also accounts for the nerve impulse travelling down the axon. The ion currents spreading ahead from the region of the impulse cause a decrease in the voltage across the membrane, thereby initiating a further local breakdown in the sodium-potassium pump.

When a nerve impulse reaches the end of the axon it has to influence the activity of other neurons. The axon ends in several tiny fibrils which appear to contact the dendrites or cell bodies of other neurons. However, at the junction, called the *synapse*, between neurons there is, in fact, a minute liquid-filled gap.

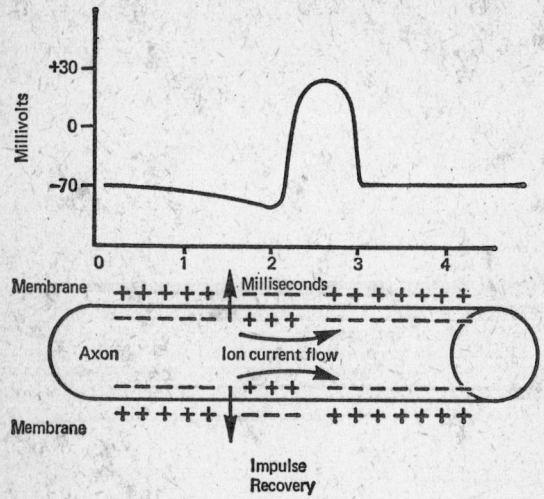

Fig. 5.4 The nerve action potential consists of an initial flow of sodium ions (Na^+) into the cell which produces the positive-going spike. This is followed by an escape of potassium ions (K^+) from the cell which again makes the inside of the cell negative. Local currents set up by the movement of these ions depolarise the cell membrane in the region in front of the nerve action potential, so triggering a similar response there.

The nerve impulse causes the release into this gap of chemical transmitter substances. These cause a change in the permeability of the membrane of the so-called post-synaptic neuron. There are two types of transmitter substance, one which reduces the voltage across the membrane (excitatory) and the other which increases it (inhibitory).

An impulse will be initiated in the post-synaptic neuron, provided that the excitatory transmitter can reduce the resting potential across the cell membrane from 70 mV to 60 mV where the axon joins the cell body. Since a nerve cell can receive both excitatory and inhibitory transmitter substances (but not from the same neuron), it can act as a decision-making switch. An

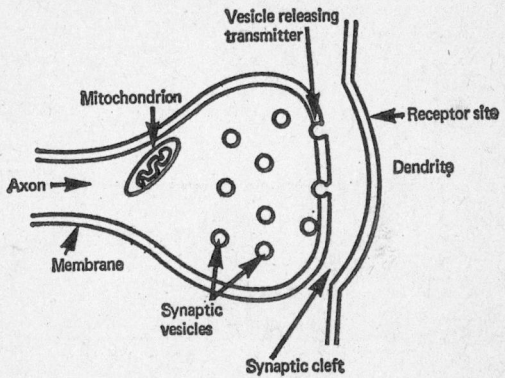

Fig. 5.5 A synaptic bouton which terminates the axon end feet. The synaptic vesicles contain neurotransmitter substances; when a nerve action potential reaches the synaptic bouton, some of the vesicles release their contents into the gap between the nerve cells. The transmitter substances, on reaching the receptor site of the post-synaptic cell, cause a change in voltage across the cell membrane.

impulse is only initiated when the addition of excitatory and inhibitory effects produces a sufficient change in voltage across the cell membrane.

In summary, neurons transmit information between various parts of the nervous system. They can also produce and control muscle movements and the secretions from glands. But further, neurons also act as logical switches, deciding whether as well as where information will be transmitted.

Vision

The nervous system can only process information in the form of nerve impulses, but as environmental information is in the form of light, sound, heat, pressure and so on, specialised sensory receptors have been evolved. These receptors are adapted to detect only one type of information, but in addition to detecting

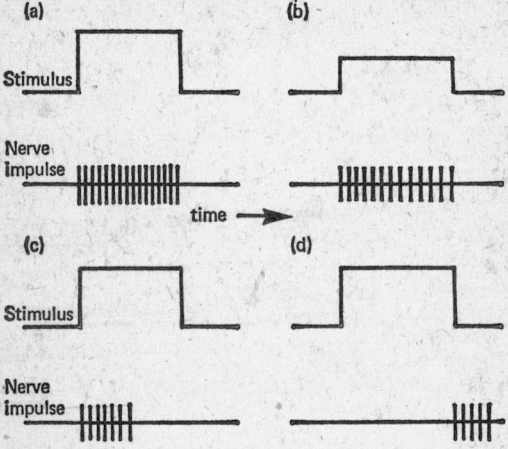

Fig. 5.6 Examples of ways by which neurons can code various types of information. (a) and (b) The strength of the stimulus is coded by the frequency of firing in the neuron. Note in both cases the duration of the stimulus is also coded. (c) A neuron which only fires at the onset of a stimulus, and (d) a neuron which fires at the termination of a stimulus.

the presence or absence of stimuli they also code such characteristics as intensity and duration in the form of nerve impulses. Because nerve impulses cannot vary in amplitude, the information is coded by which nerves are firing and the frequency of firing.

Since the environment is constantly bombarding our receptors with stimuli, how is it that we do not live in a world of buzzing confusion, responding to now this and then that new stimulus? The answer lies in the complex neural networks in our brain which impose order on the information coming from our sensory receptors. A crucial aspect of these networks is that they detect features and patterns from the receptor information.

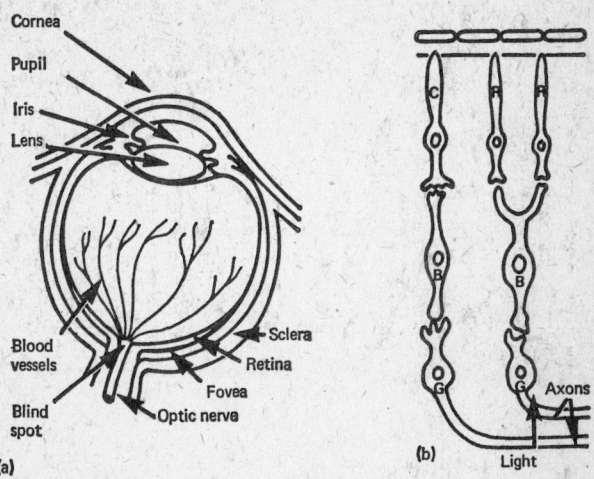

Fig. 5.7 (a) A cross-section through an eye showing the principal parts. (b) Light reaching the receptor cells in the eye (the rods (R) and cones (C)) first passes through two layers of nerve cells, blood vessels and the axons which form the optic nerve. The bipolar cells (B) are activated by the receptors and in turn stimulate the ganglion cells (G), which conduct directly to the brain.

Not only is vision our most important sense, but the visual system provides a good example of the organisation of a sensory system. The sensory receptor for vision is the eye, which is more than an optical system for producing an image on light-sensitive cells since it also forms the first stage in the nerve network for feature detection. There are 130 million light receptors in a human retina, the layer of cells which covers the interior of the eye. These receptor cells contain a pigment, which chemically decomposes in the presence of light, producing the equivalent of a nerve impulse. Also found in the retina are neurons which process the information received from the receptor cells and then transmit it to the brain.

We are all familiar with the fact that in relatively bright light we see colours but in dim light we see only black and shades of grey. This is because there are different types of receptors in the eye. One type called rods, because of their shape, respond non-selectively to colour and are found mainly in the periphery of the eyeball. Thus they only provide information about light intensity. There are three types of cone receptors which are concentrated in the centre of the retina and these respond selectively to three different colours of light: red, green and blue. By a process of mixing the outputs from these three types of cones, the brain is able to produce the range of colours we see. Because the rods are more sensitive than the cones, we can see shades of grey in dim light, but not colours.

Feature extraction

Some of the most important and fascinating experiments on brain research in the last few years have been those of David Hubel and Torsten Wiesel (1962) of Harvard University. Their experiments have shown how neurons in the visual system extract pattern features. In their experiments, an anaesthetised cat is placed in a rigid frame facing a screen. A microelectrode is inserted into the cat's eye or brain to record activity from single nerve cells. The electrode is moved until the firing of a nerve cell is clearly displayed on a cathode ray oscilloscope. Then a pattern of light is moved about the screen in front of the cat. If an appropriate stimulus for the cell being recorded is moved into what is called the 'visual field' of the cell, then the baseline activity of the neuron will be changed either by an increase or by a decrease in firing rate. Using different stimuli, Hubel and Wiesel found what were the optimal stimuli for neurons at different stages in the visual system, and Fig. 5.8 shows what were appropriate stimuli for activating neurons in the eye, the relay centre in the visual tract, and in the visual cortex.

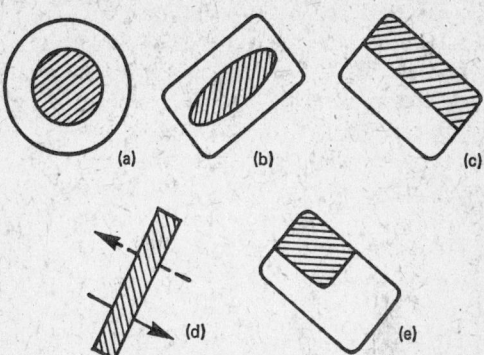

Fig. 5.8 Arrangements of visual fields. Except for (d), the hatched areas indicate either an area of lightness or an area of darkness; the unhatched area is the opposite of the hatched area. In the retina and the relay area in the visual tract are found cells with fields as shown in (a), and in the visual cortex are found cells with visual fields of type (b), (c), (d) and (e). In (d) is shown the visual field of a cell which responds to a bar of light which moves in one direction only. Each type of cell has many orientations.

To summarise their findings very briefly, it appears that the appropriate stimulus to activate cells in the visual pathway becomes progressively more complex as information passes deeper into the visual system. The system is extracting information about the edges and contours of objects, accounting for our ability to identify objects by contour rather than by texture. This also explains why outline drawings such as cartoons are so readily recognised.

There have been some rather interesting experiments recently performed by Blakemore and Cooper (1970) of Cambridge University, using the techniques of Hubel and Wiesel. They brought up kittens with their mothers in darkness, except for a brief period each day when they were individually exposed to black and white vertical *or* horizontal stripes. Collars were fitted to prevent the kitten seeing its own body and each kitten saw only one orientation of stripe. After several months' exposure, the visual response characteristics of neurons in visual cortex of the kittens were investigated. In normal cats the cell population in the visual cortex shows no overall preference for particular orientations of slits of light. Individual cells show a preference for a particular orientation of a slit of light, but other cells show different preferences and, overall, all orientations of slits of light are found in different cells. But cells in the visual cortex of Blakemore's deprived kittens responded mainly to horizontal or vertical slits depending on previous exposure. The importance of this finding for the development of perception is profound. It appears that we are probably born with a malleable visual system which becomes tuned to the type of stimuli we see in the early months of life.

Purposive behaviour

In our everyday use of language we discuss our own and other people's behaviour as if it were goal-directed or had purpose. For example, we might say, 'I am going to lunch because I am hungry', or, 'Joe is acting foolishly because he wants to get that girl to bed'. These examples demonstrate that something in the future has an effect on our present behaviour, but we know the future cannot affect the present. The question we must resolve is how the future can *seem* to affect the present, or how purposive behaviour is implemented by the nervous system.

Most people have had experience of what are called negative feedback systems. Such a system is found when a thermostat controls central heating. The desired temperature is set by adjusting the thermostat, which is usually a simple temperature-sensing device. If the air temperature is too low the thermostat switches on a boiler which heats up the air until it is warm

Physiological Psychology 71

enough, when the thermostat will switch the boiler off again. In this way a desired condition is maintained and the system as a whole gives the impression of purposiveness. Negative feedback systems in biology have been given the name homeostatic systems. In these there is an optimum condition which has to be maintained, and deviations from this initiate processes for re-attaining the optimum. Again, the systems appear purposive. The control of feeding provides a good example of such a regulatory system, and this section outlines some of what is known about it. The requirements of the feeding system are that it monitors the level of nutrients in the body. When this level is too low, food-seeking and feeding behaviour will be initiated. This should cause the level of nutrients in the body to rise and produce the termination of feeding.

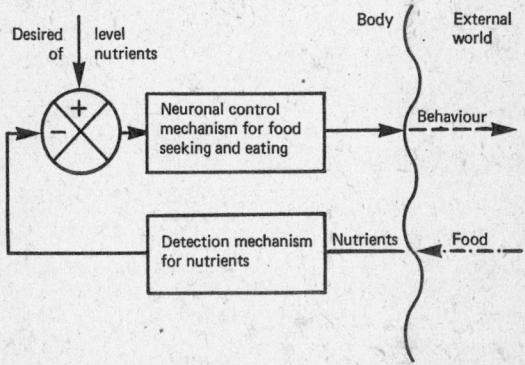

Fig. 5.9 A block diagram using control system symbols of the hunger control system. When the level of nutrients in the body drops below a threshold value, a signal initiates food-seeking and feeding behaviour. As the nutrient levels in the body rise during feeding, a feedback signal switches off the feeding behaviour.

Two important techniques of physiological psychology have been used to investigate brain processes involved in feeding. The first is called lesioning, and in this a piece of wire, an electrode, is inserted deep into the brain of an anaesthetised animal and through its tip is passed a current. This causes *local* tissue destruction. Inferences can be made about the function of the destroyed tissue by observing the behaviour of animals with such brain damage. The second technique is called electrical stimulation of the brain (ESB) and again involves inserting an electrode into the brain, but in this case the electrode is left in place. When the animal has recovered from the operation, it is possible by passing a small electric current through the tip of the electrode to initiate local activity in the brain; this sometimes produces behavioural activity. Using ESB in conjunction with lesioning it is possible to map out brain functions.

Lying at the base of the brain is a structure called the *hypothalamus* which forms a junction between the CNS and the ANS.

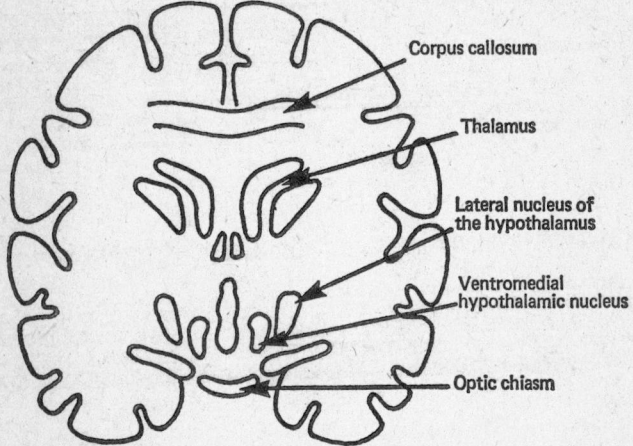

Fig. 5.10 A section taken through a human brain at the hypothalamic level. The front of the brain would lie above the plane of the diagram. (Adapted from Netter, F. H., *CIBA Collection of Medical Illustrations*, Vol. 1.)

The hypothalamus consists of several distinct groups of cells called *nuclei* and it has been shown that a pair of these, the *ventromedial nuclei*, control the cessation of eating. Lesioning these nuclei in rats and other animals causes voracious eating of quantities of food far greater than bodily requirements. Electrically stimulating these nuclei in hungry animals that are eating causes this behaviour to stop immediately. When the stimulation ceases, eating starts again. The ventromedial nuclei have been called the 'satiety centre'.

Adjacent to the ventromedial nuclei lie the paired lateral *hypothalamic nuclei*, which control the onset of feeding. Destruction of these nuclei causes a dramatic and total abolition of eating and drinking. Such animals, if force fed, will recover some control of feeding and drinking, but would otherwise die.

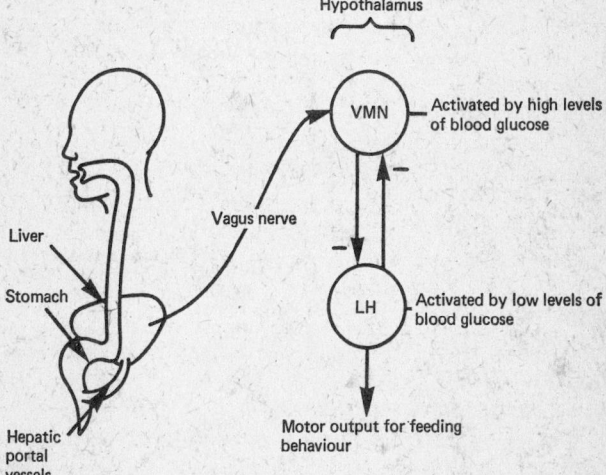

Fig. 5.11 An adaptation of Stellar's model of feeding control. A fall in blood glucose reduces activity in the VMN (ventromedial nucleus) thereby releasing LH (lateral hypothalamus) from inhibition—this produces eating. Some of the food entering the stomach is digested, absorbed as glucose and transported to the liver. Glucoreceptors in the liver inform the hypothalamus of the raised glucose level, producing greater activity in the VMN which inhibits LH, so stopping feeding.

Electrically stimulating the lateral hypothalamic nuclei causes food-sated animals to eat. Thus the lateral hypothalamic nuclei appear to be the centre that initiates eating. Eliot Stellar, an American psychologist, proposed that the lateral hypothalamic and ventromedial nuclei are reciprocally connected in the manner shown in Fig. 5.11.

These two sets of nuclei appear to be the equivalent of a thermostat switch in a negative-feedback model of feeding behaviour. However, while a thermostat also measures temperature, do the hypothalamic nuclei 'sense' or measure the nutritional state of the animal? Current evidence indicates that the level of a nutrient, glucose, in the blood is being monitored by the hypothalamus. It has been shown that neurons in both the ventromedial and the lateral hypothalamic nuclei are activated if minute quantities of glucose are placed near them. But it has also been recently shown that the level of glucose in the liver affects the activity of hypothalamic neurons.

Thus the ventromedial nucleus appears to monitor the level of glucose in the blood flowing through the brain. When the blood glucose level drops the ventromedial nucleus becomes *less* active, thereby releasing its inhibitory influence from the lateral hypothalamus which starts the animal feeding. It has been suggested that the lateral hypothalamus facilitates (increases the activity of) the nerve pathways involved in food-seeking and ingestive behaviour. As the animal eats, one of the first products of digestion will be glucose, which will be taken, because of the organisation of blood supply of the stomach, to the liver. Glucose receptors in the liver will register the increased glucose level and signal this to the ventromedial nucleus, which will become more active, thereby inhibiting the lateral hypothalamus. The animal will then stop eating.

Memory

Sensory experiences can produce long-term changes in behaviour which we talk about as learning and/or memory. These two processes, although intimately linked, should be considered as being independent, and in this section, only the problems of memory will be discussed.

If some experience causes an alteration of behaviour, we would expect a change to have occurred in the nervous system. This we call a memory trace or *engram*. A search for the engram has occupied the time of many researchers for the past century. Their diligence, however, has gone unrewarded, for we still do not know where memories are stored. But this failure did cause Karl Lashley, an American psychologist, who has probably had the greatest influence on current ideas in this field, to propose the principle of equipotentiality. Lashley and others have shown that it is not possible to produce a total loss of memory for a task by removing a discrete area of cerebral cortex in an animal which has been trained on the task. The principle of equipotentiality is that learning or memory produces modification of activity of diffuse and widespread neural pathways.

Even if memories are not stored in discrete areas of cerebral cortex, nevertheless permanent memories must still exist as a structural change in the nervous system. An appropriate structural change would be at the synapse between neurons, as it is not possible to alter the transmission characteristics of neurons, i.e. the all-or-none law of action potentials. Such a change would make it more or less likely for a neuron, or set of neurons, to be active under certain stimulus conditions. Synaptic alterations could be in the rate of production of neurotransmitter substances, or a change in the quantity of neurotransmitter released, or a change in the post-synaptic membrane to make it more or less receptive to neurotransmitters. Whatever the physical basis of memory, proteins must be involved at some stage. This is because all cell processes are dependent upon *enzymes* (organic catalysts), which are protein based, and also the cell membrane is made of a protein-lipid (fat) sandwich. It is therefore not unreasonable that it has been shown that intracerebral injections of potent protein-synthesis inhibitors like puromycin or actinomycin affect memory. Animals which have such brain injections before being trained on a task fail to form new long-term memories for its solution. Also, injections given within a few hours of training on a problem cause a retrograde amnesia (forgetting) for it.

The problem of the physical basis of memory is only one aspect of this complex subject. Others of equal importance are those of consolidation,* filing and retrieval. In a lifetime we store so much information that it is a wonder that we recall anything at all. Memory involves not only laying down new traces of events but also the appropriate filing of information which makes retrieval possible. But investigators into memory have not always made clear the distinction between these three processes, and this has been further hindered by the design of memory experiments. It is usual in such experiments to train an animal on a task and later to test for retention. A memory-disrupting treatment is given either just before or soon after training. Even if the animal fails to recall, it cannot be definitely concluded that the treatment affected consolidation (prevented an adequate trace forming), or disrupted the process of filing the new information, or even disturbed the retrieval mechanism.

This is in reality a genuine clinical problem, since many people suffer from head injury in motor-car and other accidents. The traumatic event leading up to the blow to the head and loss of consciousness is often forgotten, as also are incidents in the minutes, hours and sometimes even days prior to the accident. This is called retrograde amnesia, but it is not in fact a permanent loss of memory as the lost memories are progressively recovered, although not usually the event causing the head blow. Retrograde amnesia may be explained as a failure to consolidate new memories or the disruption of filing of the new memories. But these explanations are not necessarily exhaustive or correct. A head blow could also damage the retrieval mechanism, which then takes time to recover.

* Consolidation is the term given to the process of forming a new long-term memory trace as a structural as opposed to a neurotransmission event.

A head blow would be a clumsy and unreliable way of producing amnesia in animals, so physiological psychologists use treatments which they can control more exactly. In one of these, electroconvulsive shock (ECS), an electric current is passed across the brain, producing unconsciousness and convulsions. If a rat experiences a single nasty event like a footshock after stepping down from a small platform, it will, on the next trial, remain on the platform. However, if ECS is given to the rat within about five seconds of stepping down and receiving footshock, it will 'forget' the nasty event and, on the following trial, quickly step down from the platform. It has been argued that ECS—and, by analogy, head blows—prevents a long-term memory being formed. But it has recently been shown that ECS can disrupt memory even if given thirty seconds after a stepdown footshock, but the animal must be 'rehearsing the response', i.e. being given a second footshock at the time. Possibly ECS not only blocks consolidation but also disrupts the filing and/or retrieval mechanisms.

Although we do not know where memories are stored, because of the work of Wilder Penfield, a neurosurgeon, and Brenda Milner, a psychologist, we do have some idea of the mechanisms involved in filing and retrieval. During the 1950s Penfield attempted to cure patients with temporal lobe epilepsy by removing their malfunctioning temporal lobes. The postoperative behaviour of these patients has been studied over many years by Brenda Milner. Unfortunately for the patients, the cure was more damaging than their initial illness, for they suffered a dramatic impairment in memory. Just after their operation the patients showed a retrograde amnesia, which sometimes went back over several months. The amnesia was, however, temporary, as most of these memories came back. A more damaging impairment they suffered from was an inability to store new information in long-term memory. For example, they could be introduced to someone and have a conversation with him, but on the following day they would deny having seen the person before.

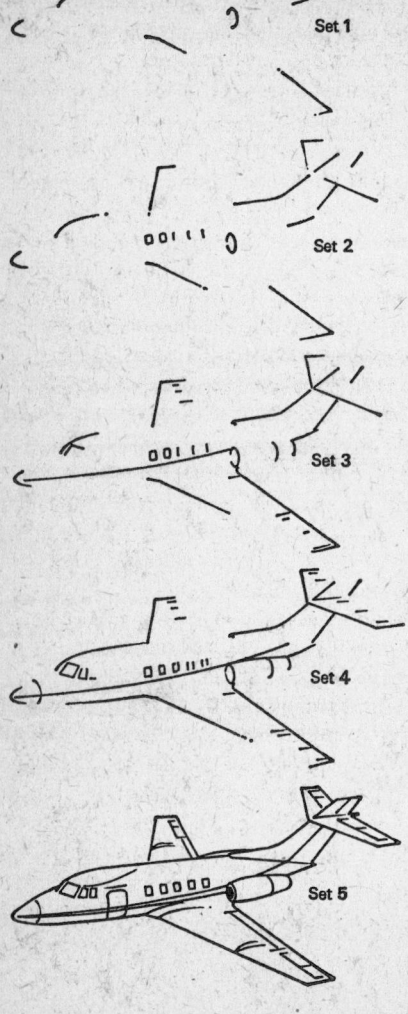

Fig. 5.12 An example of the fragmented stimuli used by Warrington and Weiskrantz to show that patients with temporal lobe damage are able to recall new information. The figures of Set 1 are shown first, then those of Set 2 and so on until the patient recognises the object.

Additional operations have shown that the memory impairment in these patients was, in fact, caused by damage to a structure deep in the temporal lobe called the *hippocampus* and/or in the adjacent cortical tissue. More recent studies by Elizabeth Warrington and Lawrence Weiskrantz (1968) in London have shown that patients with similar brain damage are not totally impaired in storing new information. In a conventional recognition memory test ('Which of these figures did I show you yesterday?') these patients were impaired. But when presented in order with a series of decreasingly fragmented stimuli which finally formed a recognisable figure, the patients improved with repeated testing of the same set of stimuli; that is, they showed retention for the fragmented stimuli. Warrington and Weiskrantz argue that these amnesic patients are disturbed in filing and/or retrieving new information, but by presenting partial recall cues the patient was able to retrieve poorly filed material.

From this brief survey of memory it is obvious that research has provided few answers and many more problems. If we are to understand the processes involved in memory it will require the combined skills of psychologists, physiologists, biochemists and neurologists.

This brief review of some topics of interest in physiological psychology should have made it apparent that, even at the point where elusive mentalistic events join with biology, there is still much to be discovered. There is a useful corpus of knowledge on some aspects of many areas like nerve transmission, vision and so on, but as to how the brain as a whole functions our understanding is still very primitive. However, as physiological psychology is a dynamic subject with a constant stream of new evidence coming from laboratories in America, Europe and Russia, we are continually gaining new insights into the functions of the brain.

References

Blakemore, C., & Cooper, C. F. (1970), 'Development of the brain depends upon the visual environment'. *Nature*, 228, 447-8.

Hodgkin, A. C., & Huxley, A. F. (1939), 'Action potentials recorded from nerve fibre'. *Nature*, 144, 710-11.

Hubel, D. H., & Wiesel, T. W. (1962), 'Receptive fields, binocular interaction and functional architecture in the cat's visual cortex'. *J. Physiol.*, 160, 106-54.

Lashley, K. (1929), *Brain Mechanisms and Intelligence*. Chicago: Chicago Univ. Press.

Milner, B. (1966), 'Amnesia following operation on the temporal lobes'. In Whitty, C. W. M., & Zangwill, O. L. (eds), *Amnesia*. London: Butterworth.

Penfield, W., & Roberts, L. (1959), *Speech and Brain Mechanisms*. Princeton, NJ: Princeton Univ. Press.

Stellar, E. (1954), 'The physiology of motivation'. *Psychol. Rev.*, 61, 5-22.

Warrington, E., & Weiskrantz, L. (1968), 'New method of testing long-term retention with special reference to amnesic patients'. *Nature*, 217, 972-4.

Recommended further reading

Grossman, S. P. (1973), *Essentials of Physiological Psychology*. New York: John Wiley.

Milner, P. (1970), *Physiological Psychology*. London: Holt, Rinehart & Winston.

Oatley, K. (1972), *Brain Mechanisms and Mind*. London: Thames & Hudson.

Schwartz, M. (1973), *Physiological Psychology*. New York: Appleton-Century-Crofts.

6

Social Psychology

G. M. Stephenson

Social psychology is about relationships between people. It is everyman's concern, for we all have to cope with other people, sum them up after very short acquaintance and gauge their intentions towards us. People thwart and deny us, and we try to dissuade them. Circumstances change, in families, at work, at the club, at church, and new ways of behaving are called for; shared beliefs are challenged, and new aims and concerns created to take their place. Social psychology examines such processes in its attempt to elucidate the principles of social interaction.

Social behaviour is a relatively new field of experimental psychology. Of course, religious thinkers, social philosophers, politicians and lawyers have sought for centuries to say what is appropriate conduct for man with man, and the recent growth of social psychology owes much to the work of social anthropologists, who demonstrated how a culture plays an important part in the development of personality. Moreover, it is not possible to exist in society without having an immediate working knowledge of the way people respond to one another, and some social psychologists in the sociological tradition would claim that man's intuitive understanding of situations defines the legitimate boundaries of their subject. The experimental psychologist, however, although last on the scene, accepts the risk that he may be accused of discovering the obvious, or of confirming common sense. He will protest that to examine the theories man spontaneously engenders it is necessary to create new situations in which the implications of our ideas can be systematically explored. It is the aim of this chapter to illustrate some products of this belief.

Experimental enterprise in social psychology started in the 1920s with studies of 'social facilitation'. The mere presence of others was shown to affect individual behaviour by encouraging people to work harder, though not necessarily better, at various tasks. It was thoroughly established in the United States, however, with studies by Kurt Lewin in the 1940s of certain socially and politically explosive topics. Lewin—an Austrian refugee from Nazism—showed how group processes could be exploited in order to change people's cherished beliefs, and he demonstrated how different styles of leadership—'autocratic', 'democratic' and 'laissez-faire'—could drastically affect the work and social behaviour of children. The production of reliable conclusions on matters of social importance ensured the immediate and continuous success of the experimental study of social behaviour. In this chapter, I hope to indicate something of the flavour of more recent work in this area. There are two main sections. In the first, entitled 'Roles and role relationships', the interplay of behaviour and attitude is explored. How does the way we are required to behave affect the sort of people we become? In the second part—'Relations within and between groups'—we explore primarily questions of how people affect each other in face-to-face situations, and how our loyalties to different groups influence social behaviour.

Roles and role relationships

1 Introduction—People as actors
To some extent people in society are like actors following a script. We all have parts to play, rules to follow which are dictated by the positions we occupy. More important than the

formally written script, or rules, however, are the unwritten expectations attached to positions. Having just watched three party leaders fight a General Election campaign (February 1974), one may reflect that nothing forbids them saying what they really think about their opponents and being equally rude back to very rude interviewers. Yet none of them did these things—despite considerable provocation—for it is part of their 'position-role' at least to *appear* to be patient and civil, however untrue to character the performance may be.

One of the problems that people as actors in society have to face is to reconcile the conflicting expectations that others have of them. The public performance of a prospective Prime Minister has to satisfy his party workers, members of the public who hold opposed views, as well as his colleagues, whose confidence he will need to maintain. The expectations of each of these groups almost certainly conflict, which accounts partly, no doubt, for the vagueness of speeches at election time. *Intra-role* conflict of this type, in which an individual is faced with conflicting demands arising from his occupancy of just *one* position, is common enough. Let us take a different, less flamboyant, everyday example. The school teacher frequently faces contradictory demands from pupils, parents and other teachers, and must attempt to reconcile such demands without appearing inconsistent or underhand. This intra-role conflict is sometimes contrasted with *inter-role* conflict, arising from an individual's conflicting commitments to two or more position-roles. The teacher's role may conflict with that of father, husband or church official. Such conflict is frequently minimised by separating the performance of the different parts in time and place, a strategy that cannot be applied in the case of intra-role conflict. In such cases, where the dilemma cannot easily be evaded, there is evidence that people usually take a more or less expedient line, satisfying those parties whose power and influence is greatest.

2 Consequences of role-playing—Striving for consistency

How we manage to cope effectively with conflicting role requirements is one problem. Another concerns the consequences of playing a role. When people respond to role requirements and start behaving as schoolboys, fathers, doctors, miners, politicans or golf-club members, they do not remain as professional actors presumably do—more or less untouched, unmarked by the experience; they come to take on the attitudes that typify such people. There is a wealth of evidence to suggest that when a person publicly indicates by his behaviour just where his sympathies lie, those beliefs will henceforth be strengthened. So true is this that a number of psychologists have suggested that a most effective way to change established beliefs and habits is to have people act out the opposite viewpoint. One experiment concerned confirmed cigarette smokers. How could they be induced to stop smoking? The technique employed was role-playing. They were asked to play the role of a lung-cancer patient. A cigarette smoker would be asked to believe that the white-coated person he was to meet in the 'surgery' was a doctor, who had in his possession the results of tests and X-rays which would confirm or not confirm the diagnosis of lung cancer. The diagnosis was duly 'confirmed' in the course of a half-hour interview with the doctor, who spared no details of the condition, nor of the likely path the disorder would follow. The results of this experience were dramatic. Nearly all the subjects who played the patient role at least cut down their consumption of cigarettes, a number gave up altogether. On the other hand, comparable subjects who merely *observed* the role-playing sessions were barely influenced at all. They were subjected to the same information but failed to show the same beneficial response as those who had acted out the cancer-patient role: active participation was necessary (Janis and Mann, 1965).

If we pledge ourselves at the behavioural level, then our attitudes and beliefs will follow suit. The way we are led or induced to behave will determine the way we want to behave. Action according to that principle is hardly new. Fanciful, embarrassing initiation ceremonies are the hallmark of certain religious and secret societies for whom wholehearted commitment is a matter of faith. Recently, psychologists have demonstrated that 'severe' initiations, if voluntarily undertaken, do, indeed, more effectively indoctrinate prospective members of a group than do milder ceremonies. For example, young women induced to undergo embarrassing sexually provocative 'tests' before being allowed to join a discussion group on sex, subsequently rated members of the group and the highly boring discussion as much more intelligent and entertaining than did others whose initiations were milder or non-existent. Acceptance of these humiliating procedures had to be justified in terms of increased belief in the purpose of the group (Gerard and Mathewson, 1966).

All too frequently we are induced to act in flagrant opposition to our principles. What happens then to our beliefs? Much experimental work indicates that the critical issue is the amount of incentive that is necessary to induce the violation of belief. If the incentive, say to tell a lie, is sufficiently high, then we will excuse ourselves the wickedness. If we lie without any guaranteed payoff, on the other hand, we will need to justify such action, perhaps by coming to believe in the untruth we have told. A number of experiments have demonstrated this effect. Subjects have been asked to assist the experimenter by telling new subjects that they are due for an exciting experience, when in fact they will be required to perform a very boring task. Those paid a relatively large amount of money to tell the lie maintain their private belief in the dullness of the experiment; those paid a miserly sum come to believe in the lie they have told. The payment alone is not sufficient to justify the lie: belief has to change as well (Carlsmith, Collins and Helmreich, 1966).

This suggests that a sound way to change people's attitudes and beliefs is somehow to ensure that only a change in attitudes could justify the way in which they have been induced to behave. If the inducement is too strong, then no change of attitude will be demanded. Those of us who are parents know it is better to try to avoid bribes and punishments in our dealings with children. The 'technique' is to induce willing co-operation and obedience, and that will not be done if greed or fear is a sufficient inducement. A series of experiments clearly demonstrated this fact (Freedman, 1965). Children left alone in a playroom were asked not to play with a most attractive toy—a mechanical robot—under conditions of *mild* or *severe* threat. In the severe-threat condition, children were left in little doubt that the experimenter would be very angry if he were disobeyed, whereas in the mild-threat condition, the experimenter's wishes were stated without any suggestion that disobedience might produce unpleasant repercussions. In the event almost all the children obeyed; they did not yield to temptation. Opinions about the robot, however, underwent a marked change amongst subjects in the mild-threat condition. They began to think less of the robot. There was no such 'sour grapes' mentality in the severe-threat condition. The children subjected to severe threat knew very well why they had not played with the robot, and they still wanted to play with it. They had no need to justify their behaviour by denigrating the toy, as did children in the mild-threat condition. The principle suggested is that a child who *behaves* morally will only *become* moral if the incentives are barely sufficient to induce his compliance with parental demand. He will then need to develop his own, conscientious reasons for compliance.

3 Informal role relationships

David Hargreaves observed this incident in a secondary modern school some ten years ago: 'One day in the spring term the Youth Employment Officer visited the school to speak to the boys in the fourth. As he left the Hall at the end of the speech, someone began to cheer. The Deputy Head Teacher, who was standing on the platform, pointed down to the boys and shouted "You! go to my room!" The boy who had cheered was a prefect, but Don of 4D stood up, even though he had not cheered. It was as if he expected to be rebuked even when he had committed no crime.' Don is here obligingly acting out his role as a notorious troublemaker. When trouble is evident, Don lays claim to it almost possessively, regardless of guilt, as if he can think of himself only in terms of his nuisance value.

Teachers soon come to know who have responsible attitudes, who the 'clowns' and who the 'louts' are; and once established, such roles are exceptionally difficult to throw off, for only behaviour appropriate to the role is permitted. By and large the 'responsible' pupils receive responsible jobs, the clowns are always good for a laugh and the louts are consistently provoked. Some psychologists have recently given a great deal of attention to the process whereby 'labelling' of this kind tends to become self-fulfilling (Rosenthal and Jacobson, 1968). The technique has been to mislead teachers about the latent intellectual potential of particular children in their care. It is suggested that psychological tests have indicated that those children are due for a sudden spurt in intellectual growth. There is no basis for this suggestion, but teachers do tend to believe it, and in a number of investigations the selected children have performed consistently better than their classmates, about whom no such suggestions have been made. They do better in examinations and perform better on some tests of intelligence. It happens because the teacher's relationship with his pupils comes to be built around the information he has received about them. More is expected of the 'spurters', more attention is given them, they receive more encouragement and are given more difficult work to do. The children change too. Their behaviour is more amenable, they don't fool about so much compared with their unselected fellows. The teachers also admire the 'late-bloomers' more, for both their personal and their academic qualities. This is essentially because the children are living up to expectations. The better a designated late-bloomer performs, the higher he is rated by the teacher. This contrasts with the treatment meted out to the remaining children. With them, the better a child does, the *less* he is admired by the teacher; it is as if he's acting 'out of place' by doing well. A number of investigations support the statement that pupils who do better than they are expected to do may come in for criticism from the teacher. Rogues must continue to misbehave and dullards to be stupid if they wish to be liked! A recent naturalistic investigation (Seaver, 1973) has confirmed the results of these experiments. The subjects were children whose older siblings had attended the same school. Would the reputation of the older child affect the progress of the younger? This happened, as predicted, only when the younger child was taught by the same teacher. If the older child had done especially well at school, then the younger child taught by the same teacher did better than if he was taught by a different teacher, who would have no clear idea of the elder's ability and character. Similarly, a poor performance by the older child adversely affected the younger child's progress when taught by the same teacher.

4 The 'what?' and 'how?' of social behaviour

How is the quality of a relationship expressed? How do we know if someone feels friendly or hostile towards us? Partly it must be because of what they say and do to us, but more important is the way they do it. There is some evidence in the experiments described above that the expectations of the teacher are communicated to the child as much by his manner as by what he actually says. In fact, people tend to judge others with whom they converse not so much on the content of speech as on the manner of delivery. Imagine you have arrived at a university department of psychology to take part in a psychological experiment and are greeted with these words: 'These experiments must seem rather silly to you and I'm afraid they are not really concerned with anything very interesting and important. We'd be very glad if you could spare us a few minutes afterwards to tell us how we could improve the experiment. We feel that we are not making a very good job of it, and we feel rather guilty about wasting the time of busy people like yourself.' Reading this I'm sure you'd judge the speaker to be a meek soul, lacking in self-confidence or sparkle and plagued with feelings of inferiority. If, on the other hand, you knew that he delivered this speech with head held high, shoulders squared, a loud clear voice and looking at you unsmilingly straight in the eyes, then your judgement might be different! A number of experiments have been performed which have deliberately put verbal and non-verbal indications into opposition in just this way. The results are quite clear-cut, and show that it is the non-verbal cues that people mostly use when making judgements. In the example just given, the 'inferior' speech delivered in a 'superior' way led to the speaker's being judged 'superior'; an 'inferior' delivery (nervous, hesitant speech, looking down a lot) of a distinctly 'superior' speech leads, on the other hand, to judgements of 'inferiority'.

Non-verbal cues like posture, gesture and looking may frequently indicate something of the nature of a relationship between two people. People in love do not—as is commonly supposed—necessarily gaze more into one another's eyes. Nearly all gaze is simultaneous gaze for couples in love—one looks towards the other when the other looks towards him. There is now some reliable evidence to support the view that for any relationship there is a desirable level of intimacy which is signified by such factors as 'eye-contact' (mutual gaze) and the distance between two persons. If distance between strangers is uncomfortably close, as in a crowded underground train, then eye-contact may be reduced in order to keep the relationship at an appropriately formal level. Laboratory studies have shown that as the distance between two persons increases, so also does the degree of eye-contact and mutual gaze (Stephenson and Rutter, 1973).

Relations within and between groups

1 Acting together

People may come together in groups in pursuit of common goals, for example as members of a cricket or golf club; or their association may have a distinctly more fortuitous basis, as with members of a family or work group. What are the consequences of repeated association? A main effect is that people who interact frequently come to like each other more. The faintly depressing fact is that sheer proximity to another, and hence ease of association with him, will increase the chances of friendship. Alphabetical seating arrangements in school ensure that friendships develop between those with alphabetically adjacent initials. Persons on the ground floor of a block of flats will have more friends within the block than those who live on the first or second floors, especially if the former live next to the staircase and so increase the chances of accidental encounters.

People highly value the esteem of others, and experiments have shown that they are more likely to yield to the wishes of others who like them than those about whom they have no information. In the interests of maintaining a valued relationship, differences of opinion will be minimised and emphasis placed on matters of agreement. Hence it is found that persons who interact frequently become more *similar* in time. They develop common attitudes and ways of behaving. This development of group standards or 'norms' brings with it a concern for conformity's sake. Norms come to have moral force and deviation is offensive. An interesting experiment looked systematically at what happens to different kinds of 'deviate'—in particular, contrasting the fates of those who, having started by deviating, decide to 'slide' into safe conformity with those who stoutly maintain their deviant stand. Certain members of groups formed to discuss issues of human relations and public policy were persuaded to adopt a line contrary to the majority opinion. Initially the remaining members of the group paid them a great deal of attention. Clearly the others were concerned to secure the deviate's support for their views. If he turned into a 'slider' and began gradually to switch his allegiance, he was befriended and welcomed by the others. If, on the other hand, his deviation was maintained, then in various verbal and non-verbal ways the others indicated their rejection of him—by not talking to him and ignoring his contribution, by turning their backs on him and in general excluding him from interaction (Schachter, 1951).

Interaction may lead to liking, and liking to similarity, but the opposite sequence also holds. We tend to seek out those whose attitudes are similar to our own, to like them and to wish to associate with them. People *expect* their friends to have similar attitudes and may feel angry and hurt when expectations are confounded. A particularly good investigation by Newcomb (1965) demonstrated the reverse sequence of events. He twice studied groups of some eighteen young male college students who, in exchange for subsidised accommodation in a large house, agreed to take part in his investigation. He was able to show that initially friendships were formed on accidental grounds. Some factor—chance arrival at the same time for meals or a lecture, for example—would bring people together. In these early friendships people believed, often quite erroneously, that their new friends largely shared their political and social beliefs. Those early friendships in which beliefs happened not to be shared tended, however, to break up in time. By the end of one year, it was discovered that people had so rearranged things that those they associated with most frequently had similar attitudes.

2 *The authority of the group*

The interdependence of interaction, liking and belief suggests that attitudes and opinions originating in a group context will have considerable stability. Kurt Lewin, some thirty years ago, demonstrated this using a technique—group decision—which has still to be fully exploited by various professionals, for example doctors, whose job it is to advise and persuade. Lewin showed, and others have confirmed, that lecturing to people or individually advising them to follow a particular course of action—like adhering to therapeutic advice—is not a very effective means of securing co-operation. It is far more effective to let a group of people discuss the issues, themselves seek advice and guidance from the expert, and then to come to a common decision on an issue (see Ley and Spelman, *Communicating with the Patient*, 1967).

It has become clear that we rely greatly on others whom we

admire and respect, to confirm or validate our opinions and beliefs. What happens when we find ourselves at variance with them? It is an uncomfortable experience, and one which, by and large, people tend to avoid. For example, politics and religion are by tradition virtually taboo topics in the classic drawing-room conversation, for disagreement on such uncomfortable topics can only be eliminated by an impossibly elaborate procedure for the selection of guests. Some well-known experiments have been conducted in which avoidance of conflict of opinion has been rendered impracticable. In one such series (Asch, 1956) perceptual judgements were at issue. Eight people sitting in a room were asked to say which of three comparison lines was the same length as another standard length line. The judgements were easy to make because the difference between the comparison lines was never less than $\frac{1}{4}$ inch, and went up to $1\frac{1}{2}$ inches. After a few easy trials, one of the eight would find his judgement enormously contradicted. All the others would agree that a palpably longer or shorter line was the same length as the standard. In fact, the experimenter had primed the others to behave in this way. Only the one 'subject' was genuine, and he usually found the experience distinctly uncomfortable, sweating, looking anxious, apologising and acting generally in a confused manner. This conflict between the evidence of one's senses and the evidence (normally trustworthy) of one's fellows induced about two-thirds of the subjects on at least one of twelve comparisons to make a faulty judgement, i.e. to yield to the false majority. How do those who yielded to such pressure excuse their conduct? A few people genuinely came to believe in the truth of the group's judgement and fancied that they saw the lines the same way as the others. Other naive subjects knew that their judgements were contradicted by the others, could not explain it and yielded for the sake of peace. The majority who yielded arrived at some formula which reconciled the discrepant judgements—'perhaps the others were subject to some illusion' or 'perhaps my eyesight is faulty' are typical examples. The physical presence of the disagreeing others was not essential, but greatly increased the ability of the false judgements to influence the deceived subject. Clearly a subject's acceptability in the sight of others was a powerful factor inducing conformity.

The desire to be acceptable at the expense of independent judgement is most aptly conveyed in the controversial experiments of the psychologist Stanley Milgram (1965). Here the unacceptable pressure arose not from a silent majority but from a recognised authority, the experimenter himself. If ordered to do so, would you torture an innocent person in the interests of science? This is what Milgram asked his subjects, adult US citizens, to do. He asked them to 'teach' other subjects a task by giving electric shocks whenever a wrong response was made by the 'learner'. On successive trials the intensity of the shocks increased up to a level of 450 volts, labelled 'dangerous'. In fact, the 'learner', who made many mistakes, was the experimenter's accomplice, but very few 'teachers' realised or even suspected that fact. Frightened, agonised screams from the victim failed to deter many subjects from giving the maximum shock, even when the 'learner' was known to have a heart complaint, and even if the 'teacher' was required to hold the learner's hand firmly on a supposedly electrified terminal. With the experimenter in the same room as the 'teacher', and with the 'learner' audible in an adjacent room, more than 60 per cent of the subjects gave the maximum shock. The task was not relished, and many 'teachers' protested violently about the job they would rather not do but felt obliged to perform. But disobedience was somehow felt to be improper, and interestingly it was found that obedience occurred equally when the experiment was conducted in a city-centre back-street as when the venue was an experimental laboratory on the university campus. The immediate relationship with the experimenter was critical, as indicated by a lowered rate of compliance when orders were given to the subject from a distance by telephone.

3 Social progression and social competition
Individual change is an almost inevitable consequence of joining

a group. To be acceptable one must first accept and conform to tradition. Newly appointed leaders of groups usually find it to their advantage to demonstrate their acceptance of things as they are before suggesting how differently things ought to be organised. But no member of a group remains completely passive and accepting of its dictates. Traditions do change as a result of mounting pressures from individuals and factors within the group. Mainly this arises because people like to establish the distinctiveness of their beliefs and attitudes. If a number of people decide to form a club for the pursuit of a particular goal—say, a disco club or a tennis club—then how will their attitudes towards music or tennis change as a result of their increased association together? We know already that they will become more *similar* in attitudes; but how? It is most unlikely that unanimity is achieved by some people becoming more enthusiastic and others less enthusiastic, i.e. by an *averaging* process. They are more likely to justify their coming together by increasing their dedication to the purposes of the club. Their attitudes will become more extreme in defence of what is seen to be the interests of the group. Recently, other research has shown that even temporary discussion groups formed for experimental purposes in psychological laboratories tend to become more extreme in their attitudes as a result of their discussions together. This occurs especially if some challenge or threat to the group is perceived (Stephenson and Brotherton, 1974).

In fact, groups tend to perceive threats very readily. Competition, at least in our society, is so deeply ingrained that the formation of in-groups leads inexorably to the rejection of out-groups. Members of groups tend to exaggerate the qualities of their own group to the detriment of others, even when no actual competition exists between the two. When competition does exist, as between rival churches, or between managements and unions, then the mutually hostile stereotyping and discrimination is intensified; unrealistic conflict is engendered to the detriment of common interests. An interesting recent experiment demonstrated just how easily both defensive and hostile reaction will be invoked. A French psychologist (Doise and Sinclair, 1973) asked a group of college students and a group of engineering apprentices to rate members of their own group and members of the other group on various personal qualities and interests. How a subject did this was shown to depend on whether or not he knew that a comparison was being made. If a college student knew when rating his own group that he would later be rating the apprentices, he tended to exaggerate the virtuous qualities of his own group and to denigrate the others. No such differences occurred when the first ratings were made without his knowing that the rating of the other group would be required. It has even been shown that discrimination against members of another group will occur when subjects have been divided at random into two groups 'x' and 'y' and the individual does not even know who else is in each group!

The reduction of inter-group rivalry in international, industrial and race relations has preoccupied too few psychologists. Muzafer Sherif is a notable exception, and he stressed the importance of 'superordinate goals' in the process of reconciliation. In situations of inter-group conflict the search must be for goals, or interests that will necessitate the active co-operation of both sides for their successful pursuit. 'In considering group relations in the everyday world,' Sherif stated, 'it seemed that the most effective and enduring co-operation between groups occurs when *superordinate goals* prevail, superordinate goals being those that have a compelling appeal for members of each group, but that neither group can achieve without participation of the other' (Sherif, 1966, p. 89). Sherif demonstrated how successful such a technique could be with two groups of schoolboys between whom mutually hostile and violent relationships had been experimentally created on a camping holiday. For example, on one occasion an outing had been arranged to a lake some distance away. A large truck was to go for food, but when everyone was hungry and ready to eat, the staff ensured secretly that the truck would not start at the bottom of a hill. The boys got a rope—one they had used previously in an acrimonious tug-of-war—and all needed to pull together to start the truck. 'Joint efforts in situations such as this did not *immediately* dispel hostility. But gradually, the series of activities requiring interdependent action reduced conflict and hostility between the groups—new friendships developed, cutting across group lines.'

In real situations, the removal of perceived differences between groups, the eradication of truly conflicting interests and the creation of common interests are not so readily achieved, but must surely be attempted. There are good indications that increasingly the experimental skills of social psychologists can and will contribute to the understanding of social problems and the formulation of social policy (Stephenson, 1971; Streufert, 1973).

References

Asch, S. E. (1956), 'Studies of independence and conformity. A minority of one against a unanimous majority'. *Psychol. Monogr.*, 70, 9 (whole No. 416).

Carlsmith, J. M., Collins, B. E., & Helmreich, R. L. (1966), 'Studies in forced compliance: 1. The effect of pressure for compliance on attitude change produced by face-to-face role playing and anonymous essay writing'. *Jour. of Per. and Soc. Psychol.*, 4, 1–13.

Doise, W., & Sinclair, A. (1973), 'The categorisation process in intergroup relations'. *European Jour. of Social Psychology*, 3, 145–57.

Freedman, J. L. (1965), 'Long-term behavioral effects of cognitive dissonance'. *Jour. of Experimental Social Psychology*, 1, 145–55.

Gerard, H. B., & Mathewson, G. C. (1966), 'The effects of severity of initiation on liking for a group: A replication'. *Jour. Exp. Soc. Psychol.*, 2, 278–78.

Hargreaves, D. H. (1967), *Social Relations in a Secondary School*. London: Routledge & Kegan Paul.

Janis, I. L., & Mann, L. (1965), 'Effectiveness of emotional roleplaying in modifying smoking habits and attitudes'. *Jour. Experimental Research in Personality*, 1, 84–90.

Ley, P., & Spelman, M. S. (1967), *Communicating with the Patient*. London: Staples Press.

Milgram, S. (1965), 'Some conditions of obedience and disobedience to authority'. *Human Relations*, 18, 57–75.

Rosenthal, R., & Jacobson, L. F. (1968), *Pygmalion in the Classroom*. New York: Harper & Row.

Seaver, W. B. (1973), 'Effects of naturally induced teacher expectancies'. *Jour. Per. Soc. Psychol.*, 28, 333-42.

Schachter, S. (1951), 'Deviation rejection and communication'. *Jour. of Abnormal Social Psychology*, 3, 1-5.

Sherif, M. (1966), *Group Conflict and Co-operation*. London: Routledge & Kegan Paul.

Stephenson, G. M., & Brotherton, C. J. (1974), 'Social progression and polarisation: a study of discussion and negotation in groups of mining supervisors'. *Jour. of Social and Clinical Psychology* (in press).

Stephenson, G. M., Rutter, D. R., & Dore, S. R. (1972), 'Visual interaction and distance'. *Brit. J. Psych.*, 64, 251-57.

Stephenson, G. M. (1971), 'Intergroup relations and negotiating behaviour'. Chapter 16 in Warr, P. B. (ed.), *Psychology at Work*. Harmondsworth: Penguin Books.

Streufert, S. (1973), 'How applied is applied social psychology?' Editorial. *J. App. Soc. Psychol.*, 3, 1-5.

Recommended further reading

There are many good textbooks of social psychology, of which those by Aaronson, Argyle, Brown, Hollander, Kelvin and Newcomb are especially readable. Newcomb's textbook is particularly good on the topics included in the section entitled 'Roles and role relationships'. In addition, Erving Goffman's book *The Presentation of Self in Everyday Life* elucidates the concept of role, and is a good introduction to a predominantly sociological viewpoint. Leon Festinger's *A Theory of Cognitive Dissonance* has been a potent influence on attitude research in the last twenty years. Rosenthal's *Pygmalion in the Classroom* discusses the effect of teacher expectations on the performance of pupils, and Argyle's textbook emphasises the importance of non-verbal communication in social interaction.

Hollander's and Newcomb's textbooks are perhaps the most appropriate for 'Relations within and between groups'. George

Homans' book *The Human Group* is an excellent description of the development of relationships within groups; Davis' short book is a comprehensive account of studies on group pressures; and Sherif's *Group Conflict and Co-operation* remains the most useful account of work in that area. Hargreaves' *Social Relations in a Secondary School* is a compelling contribution to the same subject. Finally, two books of readings—those edited by Hollander and Hunt on the one hand, and Doob and Regan on the other—portray accurately the flavour of past and present contributions respectively to the study of social psychology.

Full details of these books, listed alphabetically by author, are given below.

*Aaronson, E. (1972), *The Social Animal*. San Francisco: Freeman.
*Argyle, M. (1972), *The Psychology of Interpersonal Behaviour*. (2nd edition) Harmondsworth: Penguin Books.
Brown, R. (1965), *Social Psychology*. New York: Macmillan.
Davis, J. H. (1969), *Group Performance*. London: Addison-Wesley.
Doob, A. N., & Regan, D. T. (1971), *Readings in Experimental Social Psychology*. New York: Appleton-Century-Crofts.
Festinger, L. (1957), *A Theory of Cognitive Dissonance*. London: Tavistock.
Goffman, E. (1971), *The Presentation of Self in Everyday Life*. London: Penguin Press.
Hargreaves, D. H. (1967), *Social Relations in a Secondary School*. London: Routledge & Kegan Paul.
Hollander, E. P. (1971), *Principles and Methods of Social Psychology*. (2nd edition) New York: Oxford Univ. Press.
*Hollander, E. P., & Hunt, R. G. (1972), *Classic Contributions to Social Psychology*. New York: Oxford Univ. Press.
Homans, G. C. (1968), *The Human Group*. London: Routledge & Kegan Paul.
Kelvin, P. (1970), *The Basis of Social Behaviour; an Approach in Terms of Order and Value*. London: Holt, Rinehart & Winston.
Newcomb, T. M., Turner, R. H., & Converse, P. E. (1966), *Social Psychology; the Study of Human Interaction*. (2nd edition) London: Tavistock.

* Particularly recommended for introductory reading.

Newcomb, T. M. (1961), *The Acquaintance Process*. New York: Holt, Rinehart & Winston.

Rosenthal, R., & Jacobson, L. F. (1968), *Pygmalion in the Classroom*. New York: Harper & Row.

Sherif, M. (1966), *Group Conflict and Co-operation*. London: Routledge & Kegan Paul.

7
Psycholinguistics and the Psychology of Communication

D. J. Wood

Since the widespread acceptance of the theory of evolution, we have constantly been made aware of the essential continuity underlying the capacities of different species. Animals, even quite lowly ones, do learn; they will benefit from experience so as to adapt their behaviour more effectively to the demands of a changeable environment. All species, from the single cellular organism to man, share certain common characteristics in chemical and genetic structure. However, one of the most striking of man's abilities—his capacity to develop and exploit language—represents an essential *discontinuity* in evolutionary development. Although other species do communicate with each other—the singing of birds, the hoot of the ape, the growl of the dog, the 'dances' of the bee—none, so far as we are aware, display what can properly be called a *language*, in which abstract symbols—words, print and so on—are put together in lawful, conventional ways and in a variety of contexts for the purpose of communicating knowledge. Thus, the cry of the bird as a signal for danger is a set of reactions which, though perhaps *learnt*, occur only in specific contexts. The bird, it seems, cannot recount in the safety of its nest the fear which it felt some time ago in a hazardous situation. Its cries are discrete, repetitive and evoked only under certain conditions. Man, on the other hand, will utter quite arbitrary sounds and perform 'conventional' gestures, like winking, forelock touching and so on, whenever occasion demands. He need not have the object of his communication present. Furthermore, his language displays a structure or 'syntax', which is a unique characteristic and not naturally evidenced in animal communication. He puts words together into phrases, phrases into sentences and these into tales. His language is structured, and it is the nature of this structure which will concern us at some length in this chapter.

The central question in what we are considering is: 'How does a listener understand a speaker?' What information does he use and how does he use it when he achieves comprehension of the spoken word? A related question, which concerns us more briefly towards the end of the chapter, considers in general terms what we know about the *development* of our capacity to understand language.

We begin, in effect, with patterns of sound waves, disturbances of the air created by a speaker. These impinge upon the ear drums of his listener and the remarkable process of verbal communication begins.

Phonetics and distinctive features

At some time or another, most of us try to master a foreign language. We soon learn, alas, that a variety of difficulties lies in wait for us. Vocabulary, tenses, genders, conjugations, all provide their share of trouble. There is also the problem of achieving 'good pronunciation'—producing not only the right word but also the right 'sound'. To an Englishman, all but the most proficient Frenchman, however fluent in vocabulary and grammar, have a distinctive accent when speaking English. So too have the German, Swede and Italian, though theirs are different again. Even within a culture we find variety in accent and dialect—compare the Yorkshireman and the Cockney.

All these variations indicate that the fundamental 'building blocks' of language—the elementary units out of which speech patterns are produced—are different from language culture to language culture and even within those cultures. Traditionally, these hypothesised units of language are called 'phonemes' and their study 'phonetics'. Remarkably enough, even given such tremendous variability in the sound patterns produced by different speakers of a language, they still manage to *understand* each other. Since there are these differences, it must follow that when we listen and understand speech we do not do so simply by comparing each word with some 'ideal sound pattern' or 'template' in our heads. Every voice produces a different sound. Indeed, speech analysis reveals that every sound, like a fingerprint, is unique—albeit in fine detail. How, then, do we manage to recognise words? This is just one part of the more general problem raised above—'How does a listener understand a speaker?' Clearly, the actual speech patterns carry most of the message (supplemented, perhaps, by gestures and facial expressions), but just what *aspects* of the speech pattern are important?

One interesting idea to emerge from psycholinguistics (as the psychological study of language is usually termed) is the theory of 'distinctive features' produced and developed by Roman Jackobsen and his colleagues (Jackobsen and Halle, 1956). According to Jackobsen, all human speech sounds can be thought of as a pattern of features, and each of these can be traced back to some part of the anatomy of the voice production system. So, for example, when you produce a sound, you may or may not have your lips apart; you may or may not let your tongue contact the roof of your mouth; you may or may not let the vocal cords vibrate for some time after the initial production, and so on. Essentially, then, Jackobsen attempts to specify the elementary vocal actions underlying human sounds. According to his view, the phonetician can characterise any speech *sound* in terms of the presence or absence of these various distinguishing features, and any *language* in terms of the sets of features which make up its characteristic sound patterns.

Another branch of Jackobsen's theorising is that the human

infant—wherever he is found—produces and explores in the babbling stage all the distinctive features in human sound. A similar view has been elaborated by a number of other researchers (see, for example, Lieberman, Cooper, Harris and McNeilage, 1962). It is argued that the infant produces a sound when babbling by moving certain vocal muscles in a particular way, and he hears what the effect is. He thus discovers the relationships between speech *production*—patterns of movements in the vocal tract—and *acoustic* patterns—neural activity created by movements of the ear drum.* So, the argument continues, when the child hears someone else speak—a particular pattern of ear drum movements—he can recognise and identify what the person has said by examining the correlated self-produced muscle patterns which would be necessary to create such sound features. Thus, the prediction is that the child will only recognise and discriminate a sound if he himself has produced one with the same distinctive feature patterns at some time in the past.

Some doubts have been raised, however, as to whether the infant *does* produce all speech sounds in babbling, and, more important, evidence is accumulating which suggests that infants and children can perceive, recognise and discriminate sounds *before* they can produce them for themselves (see, for example, Shvachkin, 1966).

Despite such difficulties with the more specific aspects of the theory, there have been studies which provide evidence for the general value of Jackobsen's main idea—that distinctive feature analysis is a useful way of conceptualising the structure of human sound. In one study, for example, Nakazima (1962) examined the speech sounds produced by two groups of infants, one being reared in Japan and the other in the USA. Basically, the question she asked was whether the sounds produced by these two groups would be similar to each other, or whether they would tend to differ and resemble instead the sound structure of their own

* The discerning reader may well have noticed a striking similarity between this view and the more general theory of perception by Piaget outlined in Chapter 2.

language cultures. The question is an important one for a number of reasons. In the first place, it asks whether the early development of speech is universal to all mankind. Intuitively, there should be such a basis of commonality since, presumably, any infant could be taken from his own culture and transplanted to another and learn that language phonetically perfectly. Nakazima found, in fact, that the repertoire of elementary sounds (basically, the sets of features which define vowels and consonants) for the two groups was similar, even up to the time when both groups were producing true words and phrases. The second important finding lay in the discovery of a definite pattern in the emergence of different features. This suggests a maturational or 'innate' basis for the development of speech sounds. The similarities in Nakazima's study, however, related only to the 'segmental' features of the sound patterns produced— the elementary units of vowels and consonants. Other studies have shown that when one examines more 'molar' aspects of infants' sound patterns—aspects such as the pitch of the utterance, its intonation, stress pattern and duration—*then* one finds that, even in the first months of life, the infants' utterances begin to sound like those of their own adults. So, it would seem, the overall *shape* or *contour* of the child's vocalisations (sometimes called the 'prosodic' or 'supra-segmental' features) soon begins to take on the properties of the host language (Tonkova-Yampol'skaya, 1969). Very early in life, then, the form of our language is shaped by an interaction between universal patterns of maturation, which constrain the production of the elementary sound units or features, and the general 'shape' or 'pattern' of the sounds around us in our own language culture.

Syntax and grammar

The systematic relationships between the distinctive feature system of analysis and empirical observation suggest strongly that the analysis is a psychologically meaningful one—it does relate to aspects of human behaviour. So there are at least some grounds for the assumption that the listener decodes speech by extracting from it patterns of distinctive features.

But is this extraction of features sufficient to characterise human *understanding* of spoken languages? What is the relationship between *speech* and *meaning*? It might be argued, for example, that we simply learn associations between different sets of sound features on the one hand, and things, events and qualities of the world on the other, decoding speech *through* these associations to discover a speaker's meaning. But is this analysis sufficient to explain the achievement of understanding? Quite simply, it is not. Consider the following list of sentences:

Jane's coat was put on the peg by John.
John put Jane's coat on the peg.
The coat belonging to Jane was put on the peg by John.
The peg was occupied by Jane's coat which had been put there by John.

The sound pattern produced by each of these sentences is quite different. Although certain key items figure in each one—the peg and coat, John and Jane—the number and arrangement of words, the tense and the mood all vary. And yet they all have a similar fundamental *meaning*. It would seem, then, that the actual arrangement of sound features—though clearly important in *carrying* meaning—is not all that is involved. Consider next the following sentences:

They were eating apples.
I know more important people than Bill.

Both these sentences are ambiguous—most of us could think of more than one meaning for them, even though only one word pattern may be involved. Thus, on the one hand, we have sentences which sound quite different yet mean very similar things and, on the other, we have those which sound similar but can be interpreted very differently. Chomsky, a leading American linguist, points out that any adequate theory of our *competence* to use and understand language must take account of and explain such phenomena, and in 1957 he formulated the first version of such a theory. This holds that when a listener understands a speaker he is not working simply at the level of phonetic features in the auditory signal. He also gains knowledge of the message from the overall structure of the sentence spoken; from its 'syntax' as it is more technically called.

One of the most important ingredients of the theory which describes this structure is the notion of 'transformational rules'. A couple of examples should provide a basis for a brief discussion of these. Consider the sentence 'John kicked the dog'. The fundamental idea being expressed concerns a relationship (kicking, being kicked) between an *agent* (John), who is the subject of the sentence, and an *object* (dog). A number of elaborations can be made around this fundamental notion. For example:

Sentences	*Transformational markers*
John did not kick the dog.	Negative
The dog was kicked by John.	Passive
John *did* kick the dog.	Emphatic
Did John kick the dog?	Question
Didn't John kick the dog?	Question, negative

Two types of transformational rules are supposedly involved in these sentences: obligatory ones, which are involved in *any* utterance and hence in all the sentences, and *optional* ones, which are used only in specific circumstances. The obligatory transformations will always yield sentences of the basic type 'John kicked the dog'. This is a simple, active sentence which makes a declaration about an event; it involves agent and object in a quite simple relationship. Chomsky called these 'kernel' sentences. Complex sentences—those involving negatives, questions, emphatics, auxiliaries and so on—are the result of both obligatory and further optional transformations. So, for example, a negative transformation applied to negate the idea involves (amongst other things) the inclusion of the word 'not' and the auxiliary verb 'did' in a suitable place. A passive transformation would involve the rearrangement of the object and agent (in each other's position) and the inclusion of the auxiliary verb 'was'—'The dog was kicked by John'.

If one takes this initial analysis by Chomsky as the basis for a psychological theory (which many psycholinguists have done), one accepts that we derive meaning from speech by applying rules to the phonetic pattern. Where an understanding is achieved between a speaker and a listener, each of them has supposedly used a common set of transformations—one to translate his knowledge ultimately into a set of muscle programmes for his vocal tract, and the other to decode the resultant air-wave patterns to reveal the message.

In the 1960s a number of attempts were made to assess the psychological reality of various aspects of the theory by trying to relate the theoretical analysis to actual performance in experimental situations. One such experiment was performed by Savin and Perchonock (1965). It was designed to test the implication that more 'memory space' is required to comprehend and remember sentences with complex, optional transformation structures than those with simpler ones. Eleven different sentence types, each based on the same kernel idea, were read to subjects. One was a simple, active declarative (The boy has hit the ball), while each of the others contained a larger or smaller number of extra, optional transformations. One, for example, was 'Has the boy not hit the ball?' (negative question) and another, 'The ball has been hit by the boy' (passive). The listener was told to expect a list of eight unrelated words after the delivery of each sentence. His task was to remember this verbatim and then remember as many of the unrelated list of words as possible.

Basically, what they found appeared to confirm transformational theory: the more complex a sentence in terms of proposed number of transformations, the *fewer* the unrelated words recalled. Thus, subjects recalled a mean 5·27 of the words given after the active declarative sentence, but only 4·55 after the passive and 4·39 after the negative question (even though this contained fewer *words* than the passive).

On the basis of this and other studies one might hypothesise that the simple, active, declarative sentence—the kernel— represents a first and necessary step in the production and comprehension of any sentence. Thus, when a listener listens and extracts the features of the auditory signal, he analyses the message in terms of its sentence structure, transforming this back to kernel form, remembering too the various 'markers' for the optional transformations used (negative, emphatic and so on)—thus ultimately decoding the speaker's intended meaning.

Although several experiments based on similar lines provide some support for Chomsky's early ideas, each of them suffers from a number of drawbacks which render their generality questionable. In every case, the subject of the experiment is passively listening and waiting for a 'disembodied' sentence. He has little opportunity to display any more sophisticated or complex cognitive abilities and it is debatable whether performance in such situations really reflects what goes on in everyday discourse (though it is interesting that the theory should fit even the limited situation). In fact, it became increasingly clear in the later sixties that neither the distinction between 'obligatory' and 'optional' transformations nor the view that the generation of the kernel sentence occurs prior to the production and comprehension of more complex sentences* fits the facts. One rather obvious question which springs to mind is that, if certain types of sentence construction are more complex and difficult than others, even though they may communicate the same basic message (e.g. an active and passive statement of the same idea), why are they employed at all? Are human beings so systematically irrational that they produce unnecessary sources of difficulty for themselves? The answer, of course, is that the linguist's 'disembodied' grammars do not do full justice to the complexities

---

* This supposition, though apparently adopted by many researchers, is not necessarily implied by the theory.

of language *use*, nor to the relationships between the *form* of an utterance and the more general needs and consequences acting upon the speaker/hearer.* A number of experimental studies have shown quite convincingly that transformationally more 'complex' material, such as that involving negative statements and passive forms, may well be as easy to comprehend as the 'kernel' form, depending upon the *context* in which the statement occurs and the expectancies of the listener. Turner and Rommetviet (1968), to cite but one example, have shown that when the attention of the listener is directed to the object of the action (e.g. 'the ball' in 'The ball was hit by John') passive sentences are rendered relatively easy to comprehend. In 1965 Chomsky reformulated his theory (not, one should add, to meet psychological criticisms but to make the theory more linguistically elegant). He removed the distinction between the two types of transformation, thus lessening the theoretical importance of the kernel sentence. He introduced a distinction between 'deep' and 'surface' structures in linguistic organisation. The actual sound patterns in speech are based on the 'surface structure' of an utterance, while the underlying meaning or knowledge expressed in the message is based on the 'deep structure'. Thus, sentences which sound different may be judged equivalent if they can be derived from similar deep structures, while a sentence will be considered ambiguous if its surface structure can be derived from more than one deep structure. As in the earlier theory, transformational rules specify how the deeper level of analysis is transformed to produce the actual structure of the surface form. However, all transformations in this second theory are of the same type; they are all specified in the deep structure.

Although the revised theory incorporates a number of important new ideas, most of these lie beyond our present concern. For our purposes, the most important points to note are that the distinction between different levels of linguistic organisation

* In fact, Chomsky himself anticipates this conclusion and is careful to emphasise that 'knowledge of a language . . . is only one of the many factors that determine how an utterance will be understood in a particular situation' (Chomsky, 1972, p. 26).

remains, as does the notion of transformational relationships between these levels.

The position since Chomsky's reformulation of his theory has become increasingly complex and technical. On the whole, experimental studies have tended to confirm the hypothesis that language must be analysed in terms of a number of levels—deep versus surface structure (e.g. Bever, 1971; Levelt, 1970). However, the more detailed assertion that these levels are related by a small number of transformational rules has not been corroborated.

In the last decade or so a number of other theories have been proposed. Many of these accept the distinction between surface and deep structure, but suggest alternatives to the transformational rules. Some deny any necessity for a distinction between different levels at all and seek, instead, to describe and explain language use in terms of one level only. (For a critical review of these various theories, see Greene, 1972, and Lyons, 1970.)

All these and any other theories, however, must take due note of Chomsky's analysis of the *competence* we display in using language. They must say how we generate and understand an indeterminate number of sentences, explain how we appreciate and remove ambiguity, achieve paraphrases, and so on. He has made it clear that any psychological theory of language must explain the *structural* and *generative* aspects of language use.

So, to sum up the points made so far: it is argued that the hearer uses a variety of sources of information in achieving comprehension: the features of the actual sounds, the syntax or structure of the sentence, and such factors as intonation, expectations, gestures and so on, which serve to isolate, highlight and relate the various aspects of the message; all these play a part in the establishment of shared meanings.

Achieving an understanding of what someone is saying is far from a passive or simple process, then. Rather, it is a dynamic affair, in which a wealth of information may be used to uncover the intended meaning. Where the message is structurally simple and refers to familiar objects in well-known relationships (e.g.

John hit the ball) there is usually little trouble in reaching this understanding. However, where the message contains unfamiliar, abstract or ambiguous material, there may be considerable 'effort after meaning' by both the speaker and the listener in establishing agreement as to what the message is. It is these active, creative and interactive aspects of linguistic competence which have been somewhat neglected to date in the study of language.

Language acquisition

Psycholinguists are interested not only in how adult, skilled users of language achieve an understanding of each other but also in explanations of how infants develop, acquire or learn those abilities in the first place.

Before the advent of Chomsky's transformational theory and the various ideas and sub-theories to which it gave rise, the prevalent psychological theory of language acquisition rested mainly on the notions of 'shaping', 'reinforcement' and 'imitation' (Skinner, 1957). It was argued that the child learns to speak much as he learns any other system of 'responses'. He makes various sounds in the context of an object, event or circumstance and some of these are 'reinforced' by the adults around him. Thus, if the child utters any sound resembling the word 'dog' in the presence of the appropriate quadruped, his parents and others will praise him or reward him in some other way, thus 'shaping' and 'reinforcing' his 'verbal behaviour'. In this way the child gradually picks up the elements of his language. He also supposedly 'imitates' the words and sentences of adults as he gets older and is further reinforced for doing so.

This view of language acquisition presents a number of fundamental problems. In the first place, the view of language as combinations of discrete words fails to do justice to all the syntactic factors outlined above. Ambiguity, paraphrase and a number of other structure-dependent aspects of language cannot be handled economically by such simple ideas. The whole concept of imitation as it stands is also unacceptable. To begin with, many of the sentences one hears spoken by children are hardly likely to have been taken from adults—'Daddy all gone', for example. In fact, the results of a number of studies make it appear unlikely that the child acquires his language simply by imitating the sound patterns or 'surface structures' that he hears. What he takes from adult speech is systematically selective and characteristic of his level of development. So, for example, suppose the two-year-old is told, 'Your daddy is coming home'. It is almost certain that he will not, and indeed cannot, repeat the string of words heard. However, he may well say something like 'Daddy come'. What he repeats of what he hears is a précised version, which contains the most important ingredients of the original more complex message—what Roger Brown and Colin Fraser (1964) have called 'telegraphic speech'. Another crucial aspect of the child's linguistic development lies in its apparent *generativeness*; it embodies rules. Having heard and said for the first time that many examples of the thing 'box' are called 'boxes', he may well go on to 'foot' as 'footses' and 'hand' as 'handses', even though he may have been pluralising some of these other words correctly earlier on in development (Ervin, 1964). What the child takes from adult speech is apparently used productively in a rule-following fashion. He is not simply imitating blindly patterns of sounds but making complex inferences about systems of rules or regularities underlying speech and constantly extracting the crucial idea or 'deep structure' from complex verbal information.

A number of contemporary psycholinguists argue, then, that the baby and child are not passive agents who are 'shaped' linguistically by adults but extremely active, self-determining agents who display language structures of 'their own'; structures which could not possibly have been devised and communicated by adults. Their view is, in fact (Chomsky, 1972; Lenneberg, 1967; McNeill, 1970), that all the major characteristics of language are innate and not determined by experience at all. They argue that all languages share certain fundamental characteristics—'linguistic universals'. Thus, it is claimed, all languages embody a distinction between deep and surface structure, and all discriminate between relations, objects, feelings and qualities (Lenneberg, 1967). Other evidence, like the work of Nakazima mentioned earlier, stems from observational and experimental studies. Lenneberg, for example, develops a number of lines of evidence in support of the claim that linguistic competence is a unique human characteristic, which is not 'learned' or 'taught' as, say, mathematics or physics might be but is *acquired* as the nervous system matures. In support of this assertion, he proposes that language acquisition is to a large extent independent of even major environmental upheavals which markedly disrupt the process of more 'conventional' learning. He has studied the language development of children reared by deaf parents, children reared in institutions, those with retarded parents, and children with various forms of retardation themselves. In every case, he claims, some linguistic development along 'normal' lines takes place. He also suggests that there are critical periods in the development of language. So, for example, if the basis for language is not acquired by the teens (due, perhaps, to some form of temporary deafness or other handicap), then there is no possibility of later development, even though the original handicap may disappear.

Essentially, then, the argument is that all languages share certain common elements and that fundamental aspects of linguistic development are based on maturational processes. However, many of the criticisms levelled above against the view that the syntax of an utterance conveys its meaning are relevant here too. A variety of other theories have been proposed. each of which has different implications for a theory of language development. Indeed, it may well be that detailed studies of development may prove one of the best testing grounds in the evaluation of these different ideas. However, leaving aside the assertion that many of the structural aspects of the child's language are innately determined, it is clear that much more than syntax is involved in the acquisition of competence in communicating ideas: the sensitivity to non-verbal factors (which precedes truly linguistic development); recognising when one is not getting the message across; being able to simplify and paraphrase utterances to meet the needs of another, and so on. All these are skills—communicative skills—which the child must develop and which may well act back to shape the structure of his utterances.

A really detailed and testable psychological theory of the relationships between these many factors in the determination of our linguistic abilities has yet to be formulated. However, work in the psychology of language and communication over the past two decades indicates that such a development may not be too far away.

References

Bever, T. G. (1971), 'The integrated study of language behaviour'. In Morton, J. (ed.), *Biological and Social Factors in Psycholinguistics*. London: Logos Press.

Brown, R., & Fraser, C. (1964), 'The acquisition of syntax'. *Monographs of the Society for Research in Child Development*, 29, 43-79.

Chomsky, N. (1957), *Syntactic Structures*. The Hague: Mouton.

Chomsky, N. (1965), *Aspects of the Theory of Syntax*. Cambridge, Mass: MIT Press.

Chomsky, N. (1972), *Language and Mind*. (Enlarged edition) New York: Harcourt Brace Jovanovich.

Ervin, S. M. (1964), 'Imitation and structural changes in children's language'. In Lenneberg, E. H. (ed.), *New Directions in the Study of Language*. Cambridge, Mass.: MIT Press, 163-90.

Greene, J. (1972), *Psycholinguistics: Chomsky and Psychology*. Harmondsworth: Penguin Books.

Jackobsen, R., & Halle, M. (1956), *Fundamentals of Language*. The Hague: Mouton.

Lenneberg, E. H. (1967), *Biological Foundations of Language*. New York: John Wiley.

Lieberman, A. M., Cooper, F. S., Harris, K. S., & McNeilage, P. F. (1962), 'A motor theory of speech perception'. *Proc. of the Speech Communication Seminar*. Speech Transaction Laboratory, Royal Institute of Technology, Stockholm.

Levelt, W. J. M. (1970), 'A scaling approach to the study of syntactic relations'. In Flores d'Arcais, G. B., & Levelt, W. J. M. (eds), *Advances in Psycholinguistics*. Amsterdam: North-Holland.

Lyons, J. (1970), *New Horizons in Linguistics*. Harmondsworth: Penguin Books.

McNeill, D. (1970), *The Acquisition of Language: The Study of Developmental Psycholinguistics*. New York: Harper & Row.

Nakazima, S. (1962), A comparative study of the speech developments of Japanese and American English in childhood'. *Studia Phonologica*, 2, 27-39.

Savin, H. B., & Perchonock, E. (1965), 'Grammatical structure and the immediate recall of English sentences'. *J. Verb. Learn. Verb. Behav.*, 4, 348-53.

Shvachkin, N. K. (1966), Reported in Smith, F., & Miller, G. A. (eds), *Genesis of Language*. Cambridge, Mass.: MIT Press, 381-2.

Skinner, B. F. (1957), *Verbal Behaviour*. New York: Appleton-Century-Crofts.

Tonkova-Yampol'skaya, R. V. (1969), 'Development of speech intonation in infants during the first two years of life'. *Soviet Psychology*, 7, 48-54.

Turner, E. A., & Rommetveit, R. (1968), 'Focus of attention in recall of active and passive sentences'. *J. Verb. Learn. Verb. Behav.*, 7, 543-8.

Recommended further reading

Chomsky, N. (1972), *Language and Mind* (enlarged edition). New York: Harcourt Brace Jovanovich.

Greene, J. (1972), *Psycholinguistics: Chomsky and Psychology*. Harmondsworth: Penguin Books.

Oldfield, R. C., & Marshall, J. C. (eds) (1968), *Language*. Harmondsworth: Penguin Books.

Slobin, D. (1971), *Psycholinguistics*. Glenview: Scott, Foresman.

8

Mathematical Psychology

R. B. Henry

The names of most of the specialisms that are introduced in other chapters of this book describe particular psychological content areas. Thus developmental psychology is concerned with psychological aspects of individual development, animal psychology with the behaviour of animals, and so on. Within each of these content areas psychologists carry out both empirical and theoretical work. On the one hand, observations are made and experiments performed and, on the other hand, attempts are made to explain the data that has been collected. Naturally, workers in each area have developed their own research methodologies appropriate to the particular problems that they encounter. It remains true, however, that it is content and not method that is generally taken to be the defining characteristic of an area of study. Cutting across this system of classification comes the present chapter and also the chapter on experimental psychology. Both are primarily concerned with method rather than content, but whereas experimental psychology is part of the empirical side of activity, mathematical psychology is part of the theoretical side. In both cases, the methods that have been developed can be applied to the study of a wide range of behaviour.

The underlying approach is to use mathematics as a language in which to express psychological theories. The aim is to produce an abstract mathematical system that represents, or models, the psychological system under investigation. There are many varieties of mathematics and correspondingly many varieties of mathematical model. A short introductory chapter such as this cannot do justice to them all or convey the breadth of application that this method now enjoys. Instead, one particular kind of model is illustrated by its application to one particular area of psychology. Any misleading impression that is created as a result of this will soon be corrected by reference to the recommended further reading.

Probabilistic mathematical models

A consistent objection to the use of mathematics as a tool for psychological theorising has arisen from the conviction that the precision of mathematics is inappropriate to the description of human behaviour. Individuals are not like pieces of matter, always behaving in exactly the same way under identical external conditions. A prediction of what an individual will do under given circumstances can always be falsified by his freedom to choose his course of action. (Note that this is particularly true if the individual is informed of the prediction.) In the 'real world' of psychological experiments, however, the situation seems to be even worse than this. It is impossible to hold all the psychologically relevant external conditions constant while manipulating the experimental variables. Both known and unknown factors will influence the values of the dependent variables that are observed. At best we can only design our experiments in such a way that all such extraneous variables operate without any consistent bias between different experimental conditions. We can never eliminate them completely.

The use of mathematics does not, however, limit the student of behaviour to an entirely deterministic approach. There are overall consistencies in behaviour that are reflected in numerical descriptions of the data collected in experiments—statistics such as the average value of a dependent variable or the proportion of trials on which a subject makes a certain kind of decision. Although we are unable to predict the exact response of a subject on any one trial, quite precise statements may be made about the statistics of a set of responses. It is indeed the case that probabilistic and statistical concepts are fundamental to the majority of mathematical models in psychology.

Many of the important characteristics of mathematical modelling in psychology are well illustrated by theories of sensory discrimination. The ability to detect the presence of low-intensity sound or light sources, and to discriminate small differences in intensity, is studied by psychologists as part of a wider study of psychophysics—the relation between psychological quantities such as brightness and the corresponding physical quantities such as intensity. The classical theory of detection, developed by one of the earliest mathematical and (experimental) psychologists G. T. Fechner is based upon the concept of 'sensory thresholds'. It is supposed that the physical stimulus (i.e. the sound or the light) produces an internal activity, the strength of which is a direct function of the strength of the stimulus. However, the internal activity must equal or exceed a critical value before the observer becomes aware of the stimulus. This critical value is known as the *absolute threshold* or *limen*. The corresponding value of the stimulus intensity is used as a measure of the absolute threshold and is sometimes referred to as being itself the threshold. We will consider just one of the classical methods developed to determine this value.

In the *method of constant stimuli*, a number of narrowly spaced stimulus intensities are selected to span the approximate value of the absolute threshold. On successive trials, one of these intensity values is selected at random, the stimulus is turned on and the subject is asked to report whether or not he can detect it. The data are recorded as the proportion of trials on which a positive response is made for each intensity value. A typical result of such an experiment is illustrated in Fig. 8.1 in the form of a graph known as a *psychometric function*. There it can be seen that as intensity increases there is at first a slow rise in the proportion of positive responses, followed by a faster rise over the middle range and finishing with a slow rise at the higher intensities. Where is the stimulus intensity corresponding to the absolute threshold?

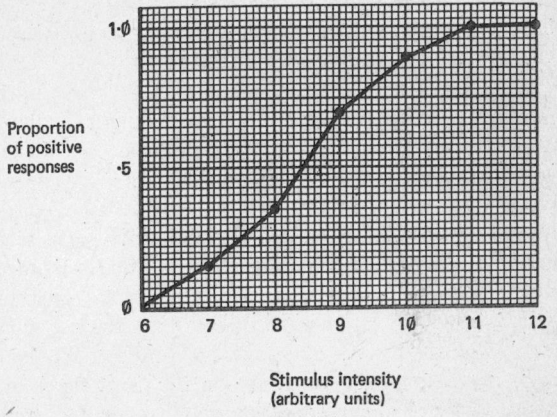

Fig. 8.1 An empirical psychometric function.

If the absolute threshold was a fixed value, and the internal effect of a particular stimulus intensity was always the same, then the psychometric function would appear as in Fig. 8.2. The absolute threshold would then be located as somewhere in between intensities 8 and 9. With more closely spaced stimuli the position of the threshold could be located to any required degree of accuracy. A simple mathematical model, that allows for variation in the threshold, or in the internal effect of a stimulus, can, however, be developed to explain the results that are actually observed.

Once we admit the possibility of variation in the sensory threshold it becomes a matter of probability, rather than of certainty, as to whether a given stimulus will be seen or not. For the mathematical model, it is not necessary to specify the reasons for the variation but only to specify the form of the variation. The assumption that is made is that the value of the threshold follows a *normal distribution*. The reader can gain an appreciation of the approximate shape of a normal distribution by carry-

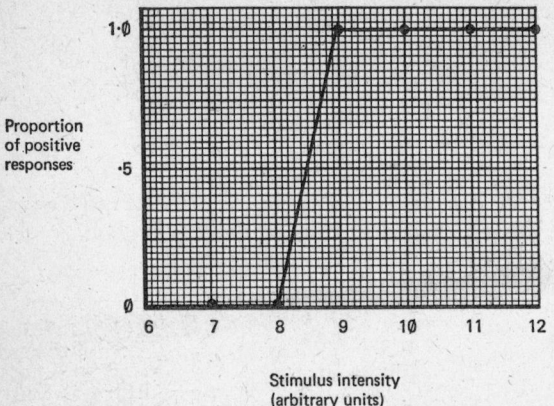

Fig. 8.2 A theoretical psychometric function for a fixed threshold.

ing out the following exercise. Take a coin and spin it six times, scoring 1 for a tail and 2 for a head, so as to obtain a total in the range 6 to 12. Repeat this a large number of times, keeping a record of the number of times each of the possible totals occurs, as in Table 8.1. If you then draw out your results graphically, as proportions of the overall number of totals, you should see something similar to Fig. 8.3. The majority of totals lie close to the central value of 9. Progressively fewer totals lie further away from this central value, but there are about as many above 9 as below 9. Now, assuming that the coin is fair, the binary events heads and tails are equally likely to come up on each throw. The totals, however, are not equally likely. There is only one way in which a total of 6 can occur (tails each time); there are six ways in which a total of 7 can occur (any of the six heads and the rest tails); and so on. Table 8.2 gives the complete list. If these

Mathematical Psychology 121

Total score	Observed frequency
6	1
7	10
8	22
9	31
10	25
11	11
12	0
Number of totals:	100

Table 8.1 Observed frequencies of occurrence of each possible total obtained by spinning a coin six times, scoring 1 for a tail and 2 for a head.

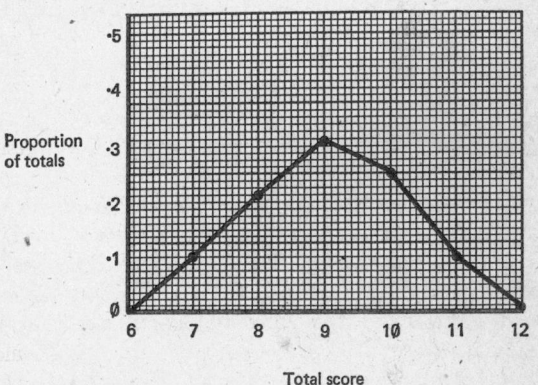

Fig. 8.3 Typical outcome from the coin-spinning experiment. Each total is obtained by spinning a coin six times, scoring 1 for a tail and 2 for a head.

numbers of ways are plotted graphically, as proportions of the total number of ways that six coins can be thrown (64), then the theoretical distribution of Fig. 8.4 is obtained. The empirical distribution departs from this only because of chance variation

Total score	Number of ways
6	1
7	6
8	15
9	20
10	15
11	6
12	1
Total number of ways:	— 64

Table 8.2 Number of ways in which each total may be obtained.

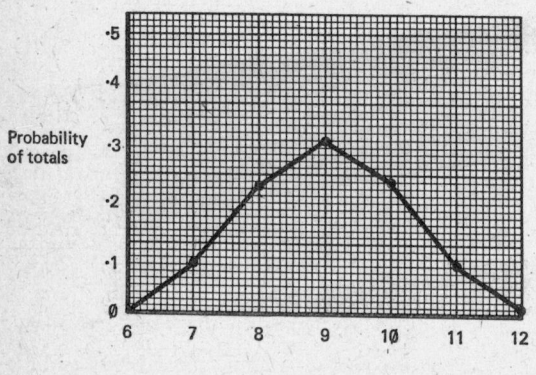

Fig. 8.4 Theoretical outcome for the coin-spinning experiment.

in the way the coin comes up. The theoretical distribution shown here is only an approximation to a true normal distribution. Better approximations can always be obtained by increasing the range of the component variables (e.g. throwing a dice instead of a coin) or by increasing the number of components (the number of times that the coin is thrown to obtain a total). Many of the quantities measured in psychological experiments are found to be normally distributed, and this is to be expected if they are determined by the sum of a number of independent random variables.

An impression of the shape of the psychometric function predicted by the model can be obtained using the approximate normal distribution of Table 8.2. The totals represent the magnitude of the internal activity produced by the set of external stimuli. For each total, the distribution gives the number of times that the threshold is less than or equal to that value but greater than the value of the previous total. Out of 64 trials, the predicted frequency with which the threshold is less than or equal to the internal activity corresponding to the lowest stimulus is just 1. The next stimulus should be seen on $1+6 = 7$ trials, the next on $1+6+15 = 22$, and so on. The theoretical psychometric function is shown graphically in Fig. 8.5. The

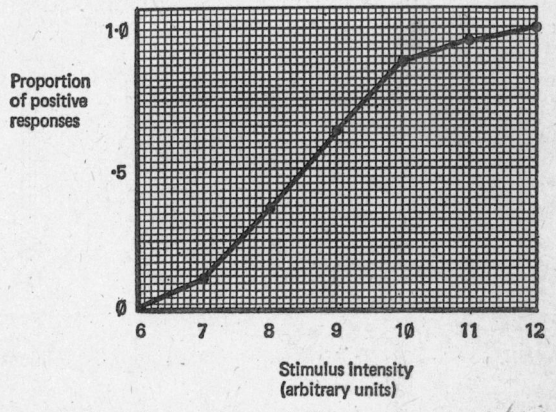

Fig. 8.5 A theoretical psychometric function for a threshold that varies according to an approximate normal distribution.

shape closely resembles that of the empirical function obtained by experiment (Fig. 8.1). Such curves are called *ogives*.

We can now give an answer to the question of what value of stimulus intensity to take as a measure of the absolute threshold. At the central or average value of the threshold, the corresponding stimulus will be seen on 50% of the trials. We therefore take the intensity that is estimated to lead to a positive response on half the trials as the measure of the threshold. Note that none of the intensities at which observations have been made will give exactly this value. Also, empirical results will differ from the smooth theoretical curve because of the operation of chance. (A typical empirical result could be produced by using Table 8.1 instead of 8.2 to produce the psychometric function.) The mathematical psychologist is therefore forced to use statistical techniques to find the ogive that fits the data better than any other. These techniques then indicate whether or not the observed results are within the bounds of chance departures from the theoretical curve. If acceptable, the 50% point can be read off from the curve. The data from experiments using the method of constant stimuli are usually well fitted by normal ogives.

The classical theory of sensory discrimination involves a very simple mathematical model, but the same principles are used when this method of thinking is applied to more complex situations. The assumptions on which the model is based are precisely stated in mathematical terms. Their implications are then worked out mathematically. Finally, statistical tests are carried out to determine whether the predictions provide a satisfactory fit to experimental data. As we have seen already with the introduction of the assumption of threshold variability, if the data do not conform to expectations, then simple extensions will be made to the model if at all possible. Old theories are continually updated and modified until some fundamentally new approach provides a better explanation of the data. To illustrate this process it is instructive to continue with our consideration of theories of sensory discrimination.

The early psychophysicists were not slow to realise that the measured value of the absolute threshold is influenced by a variety of non-sensory factors such as the readiness of a subject to make a positive response. After all, the subject expects some stimulus to be present on every trial. He may therefore be wary of making negative responses. As a check on this, *blank trials* are given on which the stimulus intensity is set at zero. It is usually found that subjects do occasionally report the presence of a stimulus on blank trials. The proportion of positive responses obtained on blank trials is known as the false alarm rate, FAR. If the threshold theory is to be maintained, false alarms must be accounted for by some process other than that which determines true positive responses—a zero intensity stimulus cannot lead to above-threshold internal activity. Traditionally, false alarms were treated as the result of guessing behaviour on the part of the subject. These guesses must, however, contribute to the observed proportions of positive responses when a stimulus is in fact present. If $P'(Y)$ is the true proportion of 'yes' responses (i.e. the proportion due to above-threshold internal activity), then $1 - P'(Y)$ is the true proportion of negative responses. On a certain proportion of these below-threshold trials the subject guesses that a stimulus is present. This proportion is estimated by the false alarm rate, FAR. The observed proportion of positive responses, $P(Y)$, is given by the sum of the true positive responses and the guesses:

$$P(Y) = P'(Y) + FAR(1 - P'(Y))$$

A little algebraic manipulation gives the traditional *correction for chance success*:

$$P'(Y) = \frac{P(Y) - FAR}{1 - FAR}$$

This correction was applied to the observed response rates before fitting the normal ogive. On the classical model, this gave an estimate of the absolute threshold that was unaffected by guessing behaviour on the part of the subject.

As has frequently been the case in the history of psychology, a development in another discipline eventually led psychophysicists to take a different approach to the study of the detection of weak stimuli. In the early 1950s, W. P. Tanner (1961) led the modification of mathematical analyses of optimal physical detection of electrical signals in noise into a psychophysical theory. This rival of classical theory is known as the theory of *signal detectability* (TSD). As applied to absolute threshold situations, it is supposed that a combination of external and internal random processes leads to a normal distribution of internal activity even in the absence of a stimulus. (There is some physiological support for this in the spontaneous firing of neurons, but again the exact mechanism is irrelevant to the mathematical theory.) For illustration, we will represent this so-called *noise* by the distribution of Table 8.2. The effect of a stimulus (or *signal*) is to raise the general level of internal activity. Suppose that the effect of a signal of given intensity is to raise the internal activity by one point on our arbitrary scale. The resulting distribution for signal+noise can be compared with the noise alone distribution in Table 8.3. Now envisage an experimental situation slightly modified from the method of constant stimuli. Instead of a range of intensities, a single intensity is chosen. On approximately half the trials the signal is given, but on the remaining trials it is not. The choice signal/no signal is made at random and the subject's task is to say whether or not a signal is present on each trial. The information upon which the subject bases his decision is the strength of the internal activity. The only consistent way in which a subject can make such a decision is to select a criterion value of the internal activity. The response 'no signal' is made if the activity is less than or equal to the criterion, and the response 'signal' is made if it is above.

Internal activity (arbitrary scale)	6	7	8	9	10	11	12	13
Frequency given:								
noise alone	1	6	15	20	15	6	1	0
signal+noise	0	1	6	15	20	15	6	1

Table 8.3 Example distribution of internal activity given noise alone and signal+noise.

The question of the selection of a criterion value may be postponed until after we have considered the implications of the sort of process described above. There are two kinds of positive responses: correct detections (*hits*) and false alarms. In terms of classical theory these arise from separate processes and are independent. According to TSD, they arise from the same process—it is just a matter of chance whether an internal activity that is above criterion arises from noise alone (leading to a false alarm) or from signal+noise (leading to a hit). Furthermore, if a high criterion is adopted in an attempt to reduce the number of false alarms, there will necessarily be a drop in the number of hits. If a low criterion is used so as to increase the number of hits, then the number of false alarms must also increase. To use our illustration (Table 8.3), if a criterion value of 12 were operated, then out of 64 signal trials we should expect 1 correct detection and out of 64 noise trials there should be no false alarms. With a criterion value of 11 the number of detections goes up to 7 but the number of false alarms goes up to 1, and so on. This relationship can be seen graphically in Fig. 8.6, which is known as an *operating characteristic* curve. The predictions of the two theories are thus quite different.

If the subject wishes to maximise his number of correct responses, then he must compromise between a high hit rate and a high rate of correct rejections. In the example, a criterion value of 9 will lead to the maximum number of correct responses: 42 hits and 42 correct rejections. Under different circumstances, however, a different criterion may be optimal. The subject may be paid the sum of 2p for each correct detection but fined 1p for a false alarm. He would do better by shifting his criterion to a lower value to take advantage of this. The optimal value would, in fact, be 8. Similar changes in the optimal criterion follow from changes in the relative frequency of signal and noise trials. If signals only occur infrequently, then it is appropriate to require a higher internal activity before making a positive response.

In the above discussion we enter the realm of *decision theory*, which is another important area of mathematical psychology. As

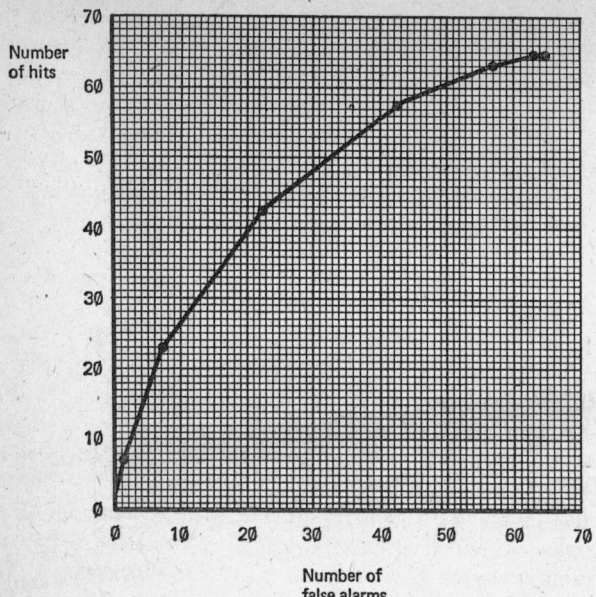

Fig. 8.6 Operating characteristic for the distributions of Table 8.3. Each point on the graph represents the use of a different criterion in deciding 'signal' v. 'no signal'.

our interest is primarily with sensory processes in this illustration of mathematical psychology, the relationship between optimal criteria and those operated by human subjects need not be discussed. Suffice it to say that experimental investigation has shown that manipulation of the values placed on correct and incorrect responses does indeed lead to changes in hit rates and that false alarm rates vary accordingly, as predicted by TSD. This has brought into serious question the very existence of a sensory threshold below which there can be no effect upon performance.

In its treatment of optimal decision criteria, TSD has normative implications. The mathematical analysis indicates what people ought to do, given the assumptions upon which the theory is based. This is a characteristic of much of mathematical psychology. Optimality of behaviour, in this restricted sense, is not crucial to the theory as the mathematical model may still be adequately descriptive of behaviour when it is operating suboptimally. The normative or prescriptive approach does, however, provide a useful baseline against which to compare human performance.

Computer simulation

A crude mathematical model of the distribution of the hypothesised sensory threshold was presented in the previous section. The treatment was entirely numerical. The theoretical distribution was derived by explicitly considering the number of different ways in which the various values could be obtained. Equally well, the development could have been algebraic. It is quite a simple matter to derive an equation to give the distribution as a function of the value of the threshold. This approach has the advantage of generality. The equation could easily be extended to allow for a variable number of binary events, whereas in the example of spinning the coins we were limited to just six. Furthermore, mathematical analysis can be applied to equations so that the implications of the theoretical assumptions can be deduced. For these reasons the full presentation of such theories is carried through algebraically and the mathematical model is embodied in a system of equations.

There is another kind of approach that was touched upon in the previous section. The crux of the simplified model of the threshold discussed there was the combination of equally likely binary events. A true mathematical model treats these in the abstract. We saw, however, that it is possible to give these abstract events concrete embodiment in a physical system that has the required properties. Spinning a fair coin is equally likely to lead to heads coming up as to tails coming up. We can therefore *simulate* the value of the theoretical threshold by actually spinning a series of coins and combining the results. A typical sequence of responses in an experiment using the method of constant stimuli could be produced by someone obeying a set of rules such as the following:

1. Obtain the next value in the random sequence of stimulus intensities (from the list of values prepared by the experimenter).
2. Obtain the current value of the varying (stimulus) threshold (spin a coin six times, scoring 1 for each tail and 2 for each head).
3. If the threshold value is less than or equal to the stimulus intensity, then respond 'yes'; otherwise respond 'no'.
4. Go back to rule 1.

The model is now embodied in a set of rules and the predictions of the model can be generated by following the rules in a literal fashion.

Simulation seems at first sight to be a poor alternative to the mathematical method. Not only is it laborious to generate the predictions but, once generated, they only apply to the particular stimulus intensities and to the particular average and range of threshold values embodied in the model. In the case of the probabilistic models such as the present one, a large number of simulation runs would be needed to obtain information on the variability of the results so as to allow a comparison with experimental data. In addition to all this, it may prove impossible to find a physical system (corresponding to the coin) that has the properties required of it for the simulation. On the other hand, the equations for a complex mathematical model may not be amenable to mathematical analysis, thereby enforcing the use of an alternative method.

Fortunately, there is a way out of this impasse. A general-purpose digital computer can be programmed so that it operates according to the rules of the model. The rules must be written out in great detail because such a machine has very few functions. This process can be tedious and is subject to error but, once the computer program has been written, many powerful advantages accrue. The predictions of the model can then be generated automatically. As each basic function takes only a few millionths of a second to operate, it becomes feasible to undertake many simulation runs over a range of conditions. It is also relatively easy to modify the program, to implement small changes in the model and then to repeat the simulation runs to observe any consequent changes in behaviour.

Although the digital computer is a deterministic machine, it is possible to program it so as to produce an acceptable simulation of probabilistic behaviour. This is done using sections of program that generate pseudo-random sequences of numbers. One way of using such a sequence to replace the coin spinning of our example simulation would be to take the property odd/even to correspond to heads/tails.

Computer simulation has been introduced here as an alternative technique to mathematical analysis as a method of generating the predictions of a mathematical model. This is one reason for including the topic in a chapter on mathematical psychology. The technique of simulation is, in fact, much more general than this. It is possible to generate a set of rules that embody a psychological theory without deriving any corresponding equations. Such equations may not even exist. The task of expressing these rules as a program, which must be capable of being run on a computer, can then replace mathematical analysis as a method of testing the internal logical consistency of the theory.

Like mathematics, computer simulation as a theoretical tool is neutral with respect to the content of a theory. The use of these techniques should not predispose the psychologist to any particular theoretical standpoint. Thus previously existing theories have been embodied in computer programs with fruitful results in the way of increased precision of expression and accuracy of prediction. From such work it has become clear that it is difficult for us to intuit the behaviour of even quite simple systems. We cannot rely on the use of verbal descriptions and appeals to common sense. With the increasingly widespread use of mathematical modelling and computer simulation, theoretical psychology has come of age.

References and recommended further reading

Extracts from Fechner's *Elements of Psychophysics* are reproduced in *Mathematics and Psychology* (see below).

Miller, G. A. (ed.) (1964), *Mathematics and Psychology*. New York: John Wiley. A useful collection of readings interspersed with expert commentary from the editor.

Restle, F. (1971), *Mathematical Models in Psychology*. Harmondsworth: Penguin Books.

Swets, J. A., Tanner, W. P. Jr., & Birdsall, G. J. (1961), 'Decision processes in perception'. *Psychol. Rev.*, 68, 301–40. Extracts are reproduced in *Mathematics and Psychology*.

9
Animal Behaviour
T. R. Cox

Introduction

Man has always been interested in the behaviour of other animals. This interest was once reflected in the popularity of the Christian bestiaries, the natural history books of the Middle Ages, which contained descriptions not only of the forms and shapes of animals but also of their behaviour. Unfortunately, much of the information contained in these books was mere speculation and without any reasonable foundation; for example, their authors variously recorded that snakes suck milk from cows and that bears lick their offspring, born as formless masses, into shape. Many of the animals which existed in the pages of the bestiaries were purely fictitious; the unicorn, the dragon and the mermaid are perhaps some of the best known. In Anthony Barnett's book *Instinct and Intelligence* it is said that those who wrote the bestiaries described fabulous animals which never existed, or attributed to real animals characteristics and virtues that they never possessed. Typically, the books were written as collections of stories describing animals' habits and characteristics in terms of human attributes, and were laced with moral comment. Common language is still full of expressions which reflect the moral characters that the bestiaries assigned to various species: brave as a lion, greedy as a pig, cunning as a fox, and so on. Although they stimulated much interest, the bestiaries embodied two of the most fundamental mistakes made in reporting on animal behaviour. First, they failed to present systematic or objective observations; each book was a conglomeration of explanations in terms of human feelings, of exaggerations and of folk lore. Secondly, they passed judgement on the behaviour of the animals they described, judgement based on human values and attitudes. However, there was a more practical and more realistic side to the early studies of animal behaviour, which came about because farmers and hunters had to develop a working knowledge of their animals. This manifested itself in the domestication of animals useful to man, and in their subsequent inbreeding for specific characteristics. Both had very early beginnings. For example, we know that the domestication of the dog began in the age of Neanderthal man, and that from this early companion and guardian have been bred the hundreds of varieties of thoroughbred dogs which exist today. All are probably descended from one or possibly two species, the jackal and the wolf. Despite man's early involvement with animals, however, the science of animal behaviour has lagged far behind the general progress of scientific method and thought, and it was not until late in the nineteenth century that, under the moving influence of Darwin's theory of evolution, man seriously began to search in a scientific manner for an understanding of behaviour. With the acceptance of Darwin's views on the origin of the species, it became apparent that man could look for the roots of his own behaviour in that of lesser animals.

The importance of modern studies

There are several reasons why the modern psychologist is interested in studies on animal behaviour. There is an intrinsic interest, a curiosity about the natural history of animals. This curiosity is not merely the expression of an academic whim, but has provided data and manpower useful in the struggle to conserve our existing wildlife in the face of industrial expansion. Such studies are also of immediate applied value. Advances in agricultural science, in the development of drug therapy and surgery, and in many other areas have relied heavily on the investigation of how animals behave under certain conditions and after certain treatments. For example, the understanding of the sexual behaviour of insects has led to more efficient pest control, whilst the study of the social and feeding behaviours of domestic animals has led to greater milk and meat yields, and to the production of improved grain feeds. The development of psychoactive drugs and of organ transplant surgery has likewise benefited from animal research. Such research is of inestimable value and cannot be replaced by the currently available alternatives to experimentation with living animals. In many ways the psychologist concerned with the behaviour of animals is just as much an applied psychologist as his industrial or occupational counterpart. A third reason for the interest in animal behaviour is the attempt to understand in greater depth man's own behaviour by analogy to and generalisation from that of lesser animals. Such a concern usually follows the accepted scientific practice of experimentation with the generation of testable hypotheses, which are extended from the infra-human to the human situation. Although this is the ideal approach to this type of study, the truly 'phylogenetic' comparison (the comparison of behaviour across species) is rare.

It is interesting to observe that the pre-scientific studies are characterised by their explanations of infra-human behaviour in terms of human attributes, while scientific studies are the embodiment of the reverse situation.

The methods of study

The reasons why psychologists study animal behaviour have been outlined, and it is important to discuss how they conduct their studies. The point that the scientific approach was slow to develop has been made, and equally, it is hoped, it has been stressed that this is the only valid way in which animal behaviour can be studied. There are essentially two different types of person engaged in this area of research: one is the ethologist and the other is the comparative psychologist. The ethologist is the 'field' scientist; his methods are those of the systematic observation of animals in their natural habitats with little restriction placed on their behaviour. Generally the ethologist refrains from interference in the situation which he is studying, and is content to record what is happening. He is usually trained to make these recordings in an objective way, although still liable to error, and then to interpret his results in the light of other findings and current ideas. The origin of the modern meaning of the word 'ethology' can be traced back to a nineteenth-century French biologist, Isodore Geoffrey-Saint-Hillaire. Previously, it had been used in a completely different context by philosophers, such as John Stuart Mill, to mean the study of ethics.

The comparative psychologist is the 'laboratory' scientist; his methods are those of planned and controlled experimentation. However, in the execution of these methods, he removes his subjects from their natural surroundings and imposes much restriction on the types of behaviour that they can express. Experimental techniques permit extreme control to be exercised over the behaviour of the animals under test and give rise to situations in which the effects of particular manipulations, for example the presentation of shock, different schedules of feeding or the administration of drugs, can be usefully measured. The extent to which these techniques provide information about 'spontaneous' or 'normal' behaviour is a matter of argument. In the experimental situation animals are usually trained to make one, or at the most two, very specific responses. These responses have a certain simplicity and are easy to measure. We have common examples of rats running in mazes and pressing levers, and of pigeons pecking at keys, and it is obvious that such responses are not the most natural for the particular species, although animals cannot be trained to make responses for which they are not 'prepared'. Pigeons cannot be trained to run across a cage to avoid shock, and it is difficult to train cats to press levers. It is a statement of the obvious to say that experimental techniques interfere with the normal course of behaviour, but this is often forgotten.

Both the ethological and comparative approaches have their advantages and disadvantages, and much time and effort can be wasted arguing which is the better. As is common, the sensible compromise is the most acceptable solution. Three examples are worth noting. First, in the study of population control in rodents, and in the study of overpopulation stress, artificial colonies of animals have been established in natural surroundings, the experimenter exercising control of the colony's initial population size and its physical limits. Within these restrictions, observations of behaviour have been made without further interference, apart from post-mortems on animals which have died. Secondly, in the study of the effects of drugs on unconditioned behaviour, Hall's open field test for emotionality has been developed as a useful screening method. The open field is essentially a large circular arena, which is placed under a gantry housing sources of light and noise. Animals are placed in the arena and certain of their behaviours measured under known lighting and noise conditions. Easily recognisable and easily scored behaviours are recorded, and, although simple, this test can detect psychoactive drugs with great reliability. Thirdly, in the study of the acquisition and retention of learned behaviour, the operant technology developed around the Skinner box (an animal 'test' chamber) has become popular. However, the criticisms made of comparative psychology in general are especially true of operant studies, which tend to concentrate on the investigation of highly restricted and 'unnatural' responses. Fortunately, this can be overcome to some extent by combining orthodox operant practice with a more general observation of the behaviour which accompanies the chosen operant response. The widespread use of videotaping equipment, especially with the development of low-light cameras, has greatly helped in combining the ethological and the experimental analyses of behaviour.

Psychology is an umbrella term which describes some common attribute of many different types of study. Studies on animal behaviour have ranged from those carried out by geneticists and zoologists into the genetic mechanisms controlling the inheritance of behaviour, through those of the pharmacologists and physiologists concerned with the elucidation of drug action and of the relationship between physiology and behaviour, to the experiments carried out by comparative and developmental psychologists and by cyberneticists on the formulation of models of problem-solving behaviour and learning. However, despite this wide and increasingly large area of interest, the number of species investigated in the laboratory has been remarkedly small. Several lower vertebrates, fish, amphibians and reptiles, have attracted attention, but most experimental animals have been birds or mammals. Most of the birds studied are passeriformes, or perching birds, the most popular example of which is the pigeon. Of the large number of mammalian orders that exist, the rodents, rats and mice, the carnivores, cats and dogs, and the primates, monkeys and man, have received most attention. However, field studies have been far wider ranging in their subjects, and there are few creatures which have not been scrutinised by the ethologist.

In general, animal experimentation is concerned with one of three questions. First, what do animals do? This question produces descriptions of behaviour by way of answer. There are two types of description which are possible; both have their advantages, as well as their inadequacies. The first is description by motor pattern; that is, in terms of the actual movements of the body and of the limbs. For example, the movement of the earthworm (*Lumbricus sp.*) can be analysed in terms of the contractions of its circular and longitudinal muscles, and of the role of the coelomic fluid, septa and setae. Likewise, locomotion in the laboratory rat (*Rattus norvegicus*) can be described in terms of a series of movements involving the flexion, extention, protraction and retraction of its limbs. Such descriptions are precise but lengthy, and more economical terms such as creeping and walking are usually employed. However, the major disadvantage arising from description by motor pattern is its failure to make obvious the 'ends' of particular behaviours, especially as several different 'means' may be used to accomplish those 'ends'. For example, a rat may be trained to run down a maze to receive a food reward. If the maze is flooded the rat will swim down the maze, or if its legs are tied it may roll down the maze. A description in terms of the movements made by the rat would class all these variations as widely different activities, although they obviously have much in common. The alternative is description by consequence. The rat, in the above example, would be described as negotiating the maze to receive a food reward, or more simply as approaching the food. How it achieves this is not considered. This type of description is most economical, but in its economy glosses over much possible detail. Again, the sensible compromise is the best solution, and will be determined by the requirements of the particular study under consideration. The second question is, 'How do they do it?' This is usually answered by the physiologists with descriptions of the relevant neuromuscular or glandular apparatus. The third question is, 'Why do they do it, and when?' This stimulates study of the internal and external factors controlling behaviour. Two such factors are instinct and learning.

Innate and acquired behaviour

Most of the behaviour that we observe in animals is adaptive. They respond to their environment in such a way that they can find food and shelter, mate, and protect their offspring. Occasionally they may behave maladaptively, and this can lead to the death of the individual, and even to the extinction of the species. However, such cases are not common and usually result from an interference with the animal's normal environment. In the past, such interference has been mainly climatic, but it is now increasingly due to man's influence; Darwin saw fit to call man the 'arch-destroyer'. Despite this interference many species survive, and their survival is primarily due to two mechanisms by which the individual animal's behaviour becomes fitted to its normal environment. First, the animal can be born with the potential for adaptive behaviour 'built into' its nervous system, as part of its inherited structure, much in the same way as it inherits its height, colour, sex and so on. The stickleback, for example, inherits the complex behaviour which is involved in its nest-building and mating. Such behaviour has been termed innate or, more popularly, instinctive. However, the concept of instinct has been much abused and, although still used by the ethologist and the zoologist, has been avoided by the comparative psychologist for several decades. Innate behaviours develop slowly, again much as do the structural features, both within the individual (ontogeny) and within the species (phylogeny). In their evolution they are subject to environmental pressure and natural selection, and it is these agencies which shape the adaptiveness of inherited behaviour. Sometimes it is not immediately obvious how a particular behaviour which has developed is adaptive. For example, certain shore-living sponges (*Porifera*) squirt water out with some force, and it is difficult to understand the function of this behaviour until there is hot weather. In such conditions many of the sponges die, and usually those living in caves or in rock formations where there is stagnant water are the only ones to survive. Squirting water functions to remove the waste from the pools. The more efficient the squirting behaviour, the greater chance the sponges have of surviving and of producing the next generation. The total potential for innate behaviour forms a sort of 'species memory' and is stored in the complex double helix of the DNA molecule. One might draw a parallel with Jung's assumption of a 'racial subconscious'—a universal memory.

Much of the behaviour of the lower animals is innate, with little scope for flexibility or for the acquisition of new response patterns. Higher animals are born with far fewer behaviours programmed into their being, and as a result what they do is far less automatic and stereotyped, and is shaped in the light of their own experience. These animals learn which behaviours are the most effective for obtaining food and shelter and so on, and it is the processes of reward and punishment which ensure the adaptiveness of their behaviour. In order to study these processes, techniques of conditioning have been developed in the laboratory, by which the presentation of reward and punishment can be manipulated to bring about particular changes in behaviour. Learning occurs in a wide range of different animals and under a great variety of circumstances. It has been central dogma to some psychologists that there are general 'laws of learning', which apply with equal force wherever learning occurs. In the past it has been commonly assumed that contiguity plus reinforcement is all that is required to associate any stimulus with any response, but recently it has been suggested by Seligman that animals approach learning situations with a good deal of built-in bias or preparedness. This bias usually relates to the natural requirements which their behaviour has evolved to meet. Rats are 'prepared' to associate taste with sickness even after a single trial and a long delay, but will not connect visual stimuli and sickness. Conversely, they will readily associate light and electric shock if they occur together in time, but they will not associate taste and shock.

It is probably helpful to attempt to distinguish between different categories of learning. However, such distinctions are bound to be artificial, and must be recognised as but aids to thought. Thorpe has proposed a classification of learning which provides a starting point for discussion. Within this classification is the distinction between 'associative' and 'non-associative' learning. The classification is shown overleaf (Table 9.1). Unfortunately, there is not room in this chapter to record more than this brief outline of learning. The interested reader is referred to Thorpe's book, or to an excellent short text by Rachlin. The particular merit of Thorpe's book is that he provides complete coverage of the whole animal kingdom.

It has been suggested, by direct analogy to the biochemical mechanisms underlying innate behaviour, that information acquired during the life-time of the individual is stored in the RNA molecule and that it is expressed through altered protein synthesis.

Type	Subtype	Synonyms
Associative	Classical conditioning	Conditioned reflex, Type I or respondent conditioning
	Instrumental conditioning	Trial and error, Type II or operant conditioning
Non-associative	Habituation	
	Latent learning	
	Insightful learning	
	Imprinting	

Table 9.1   Classification of learning (after Thorpe)

The following topic, that of exploratory behaviour, cuts across the rather rigid distinctions of innate and acquired behaviour. For although when stated as they have been there is a clear dichotomy, this is unrealistic, and when actual examples are studied it is often difficult to decide where genetic influence ends and learning begins. The nature versus nurture controversy is far from easy to settle.

Exploratory behaviour

If a cockroach (*Blatella germanica*) is allowed access to a vertical column it will climb it, and after reaching the top it will descend. A short time later it will climb the column again, and descend once more. With repetition the rate at which the cockroach 'ups and downs' will decline. If it is now offered another column it will immediately climb up and down this new one. The creature's behaviour appears to be governed by novelty; the animal is exploring its surroundings. Likewise, if a rat is placed in a simple T maze it will first enter one arm, leave it and enter another, and so on. This situation has been structured to produce a phenomenon common throughout the mammalian order, that of spontaneous alternation. The rat is placed in the stem of the simple T maze; it moves forward to the intersection and chooses to enter one of the two arms. It is then withdrawn from the maze, and after a short time replaced in the stem. Once again the rat moves forward to the intersection, but this time it chooses the arm which was not entered last time. The animal has alternated its response, and has chosen the novel as opposed to the more familiar arm. If the procedure is repeated a number of times it will be seen that the rat will more often than not alternate responses. Spontaneous alternation has been demonstrated in most mammals, but it has been studied most extensively in the rat.

Many different types of theory have been put foward to explain why animals alternate responses in certain situations, but perhaps the most widely accepted is that advanced by Glanzer in the 1950s. Glanzer has suggested that alternation is a stimulus-controlled behaviour, in that satiation of the perception of a stimulus reduces the tendency for the animal to respond to that stimulus. Familiarity with a stimulus reduces an animal's interest in it. In a two-choice situation the alternative stimulus, which is more novel, therefore becomes more effective in evoking the response. Careful research led Glanzer to state that in the presence of the stimulus, satiation increases as a negative function of time; while in the absence of the stimulus, satiation decreases as a negative function of time. Kirkby has investigated alternation in invertebrates, birds and mammals of various ages, and under several different physiological conditions. From the results of his studies he concluded that alternation was an exclusively mammalian phenomenon, and that the rate at which rats and hamsters alternated increased with maturation. However, Darchen has shown that spontaneous alternation can occur in the cockroach, and thus the hypothesis that the phenomenon is limited to mammals may be mistaken. The control of this behaviour in mammals appears to reside in areas of the limbic system of the brain, for lesions of the striatum and hippocampus have been shown to impair alternation.

Perhaps the most important point to note about spontaneous

alternation is that it is a response to the familiarity, or conversely the novelty, of the situation. In mammals, in particular, temporal and spatial stimulus changes, which present novelty, elicit exploration. Animals given access to a novel environment will approach and explore it with whatever sensory equipment is available to them. In this way they may learn the character of their surroundings, and it is during exploration that escape routes and general pathways, food sources and objects within the novel area become familiar. However, within any particular species, the types of behaviour which may be described as exploratory are diverse, which means that a definition of exploration should be no more precise than 'a response to novelty'. It has been suggested by Hinde that in this response to novelty can be distinguished an orientating response, which is associated with immobility and which involves the animal turning towards the novel stimulus, and active exploration, which involves full body movement. Research with both monkeys and young children has shown that if confronted with a strange object they may vacillate between passive staring (orientation) and active exploration.

In addition to novelty, exploratory behaviour seems to be influenced by two other important factors, memory and fear. Consider the rat in the simple T maze alternating its responses. It has been argued that information processing is an essential part of the control mechanism (Cox, 1970), and without doubt the retention of information from one trial to another must play some part in that processing. Dember (1956) allowed rats to explore the stem of a T maze, one arm of which was painted black and the other white. Entry into these arms was prevented by transparent glass screens. The rats were briefly removed from the maze and were replaced after the arms had been made the same colour and the screens removed. The rats immediately entered the arm that had changed colour. To respond in this way to the change in stimulation they must have remembered what they had previously experienced. Memory is obviously implicated in exploration, and indeed exploration can lead to learning (latent learning). Several studies have shown that fear inhibits exploration; rats that are shocked explore less than animals that are not shocked. But the situation is more complex than this simple formulation at first suggests. It appears that small changes in the environment elicit investigation, while larger changes elicit fear and perhaps avoidance. Small birds, such as chaffinches and tits, will avoid owls but will approach objects with only a few owl-like characteristics. The movement of a strange object precipitates withdrawal and avoidance behaviour, but the movement of a more familiar object elicits exploration. At intermediate degrees of strangeness, animals vacillate between approach and avoidance.

The internal state of the animal also affects whether it will approach and explore or avoid an unfamiliar object. At a few weeks of age chaffinches and tits will approach and explore a stuffed owl, but a few weeks later they will keep away from the object. Their internal state changes with age, and this affects their threshold for the expression of fear. Wild rats are more likely to avoid strange objects than laboratory rats, and this difference is correlated with the larger adrenal glands of the wild forms. This increased wariness, a manifestation of the dominance of the fear response over exploration, is of adaptive value. In the wild state the brown rat (*Rattus norvegicus*), from which the laboratory rat is derived, is a notorious pest. Colonies of these animals often reside and flourish near farm buildings. Every night they tread well-worn paths to the buildings in search of food. In an attempt to rid himself of these pests the farmer places food mixed with an odourless and tasteless poison along the path. This immediately stops the rats from following this path, but no rats die, and they eventually establish a new path. The food is an unfamiliar object on the path and simply elicits withdrawal and avoidance. If the same procedure could be followed but with laboratory rats instead of wild rats, then the results would be very different. Many rats would explore and eventually eat the food. As a result they would die. Their behaviour would be maladaptive, but they would have been placed in what would be an unnatural environment for them.

It has been shown that animals will work for access to novelty, that is they will work so that they can explore. It has been shown that rats will cross electrified grids to gain entrance to mazes containing novel objects, and that monkeys will learn if it results in an opportunity to look out from their dim-lit test chamber into a room full of novel objects. They will learn faster if these objects are in motion. Through this brief discussion, it can be seen that exploration is obviously a powerful force in guiding animal behaviour, and the study of exploratory activity is essential to the understanding of behaviour.

Concluding remarks

Behaviour consists of the activities by which animals survive and reproduce. The more animals are required to search through their environments, the more complex and flexible their behaviour. The development of elaborate behaviour patterns is thus related to the demands of the animal's environment. Both are shaped by evolutionary pressures. To understand this fully it must be remembered that behaviour is as much a biological process as digestion or respiration. It has a structure for expression, the muscular and exocrine systems, and has a genetic basis. The potential range of an animal's behaviour is wholly controlled by those parts of the DNA responsible for this function. The development of an animal's behaviour, within the limits set by this genetic potential, are part a function of maturation and part a function of learning. Learning is most important in the higher animals.

Behaviour is, however, not limited to the animal kingdom, nor is it necessarily complex. Certain carnivorous plants are able to make sudden directed movements to catch their prey. The Venus flytrap (*Dionaea*), for example, clamps its modified leaves around insects, while certain fungi are able to snare nematodes (e.g. threadworms) by tightening hyphal loops around their bodies. The sensitive mimosas are able to fold and partially retract their leaves when touched. Obviously these plants accomplish these movements without benefit of special nerves or muscles, and they rely on sudden changes in cell turgor. Within the animal kingdom, the most primitive forms of behaviour are displayed by groups which, like plants, lead a wholly sedentary existence. Adult corals and barnacles do little more than extend and retract their bodies, move their feeding arms and ingest the small organisms captured as prey.

Perhaps the most important point on which to conclude is that behaviour, of whatever species and including that of man, is a biological process and is most easily understood if examined systematically by the application of scientific method.

References

Barnett, S. A. (1967), *Instinct and Intelligence*. Harmondsworth: Penguin Books.

Cox, T. (1970), 'The effects of caffeine, alcohol and previous exposure to the test situation on spontaneous alternation'. *Psychopharmacologia (Berl.)*, *17*, 83-8.

Darchen, R. (1955), 'Stimuli nouveaux et tendance exploratrice chez Blatella germanica'. *Z. Tierspsychol.*, *12*, 1-11.

Dember, W. N. (1956), 'Response by the rat to environmental change'. *J. Comp. Physiol. Psychol.*, *49*, 93-5.

Glanzer, M. (1953), 'Stimulus satiation, an explanation of spontaneous alternation and related phenomena'. *Psychol. Rev.*, *60*, 257-68.

Hinde, R. A. (1970), *Animal Behaviour*. London: McGraw-Hill.

Kirkby, R. J. (1967), 'A maturation factor in spontaneous alternation'. *Nature (Lond.)*, *215*, 784.

Rachlin, H. (1970), *An Introduction to Modern Behaviourism*. London: Freeman.

Seligman, M. E. P. (1970), 'On the generality of the laws on learning'. *Psychol. Rev.*, *77*, 408-18.

Recommended further reading

Barnett, S. A. (1967), *Instinct and Intelligence*. Harmondsworth: Penguin Books.

Hinde, R. A. (1970), *Animal Behaviour*. London: McGraw-Hill.

Rachlin, H. (1970), *An Introduction to Modern Behaviourism*. London: Freeman.

Thorpe, W. H. (1963), *Learning and Instinct in Anima's*. London: Methuen.

10

Psychopathology

W. E. C. Gillham

One popular view of psychology—although less prevalent than it was—is that it is mainly concerned with the study of abnormal behaviour and has as its principal techniques and theories those deriving from the work of the psychoanalyst Sigmund Freud.

In fact, as this book amply demonstrates, abnormal psychology (or psychopathology) is just one area of study within the overall framework of behavioural science. It does, however, overlap with the related discipline of medicine. Millon and Diesenhaus (1972) emphasise this joint interest in their definition of psychopathology as that 'field of medicine and psychology concerned with the study of maladaptive behaviour, its aetiology, development, diagnosis, and therapy'. The medical specialism in psychopathology is normally referred to as 'psychiatry'. Psychiatrists and psychologists are generally lumped together in the popular mind as being essentially the same profession, but there are important differences stemming from their basic disciplines. This fundamental distinction goes some way to explaining their different approaches to the study of psychopathology. The psychiatrist's first degree is in medicine, which is traditionally concerned with the study of human anatomy, physiology and biochemistry; the psychologist's first degree involves the study of the nature and development of human behaviour and experience. Although both subjects employ the scientific methodology and philosophy of the natural sciences, medical studies are, from the first, oriented towards clinical applications; by comparison the study of psychology is oriented more in the direction of research.

The different emphases in the basic disciplines mean that the psychological and the medical study of abnormal behaviour differ, to some extent, in what is regarded as 'significant'—due to the way in which they explain the behaviour; and because of these differences in explanation (or *theorising*) different descriptive terms may be used and, of particular importance, different remedies proposed.

The sorts of explanations one prefers and the sorts of terms one uses form the basis for conceptualising the behaviour of others and, to a degree, *determine how one sees them*. One of the great practical (and ethical) problems in psychopathology is deciding when behaviour *is* abnormal and considering the consequences—in terms of a person's perception of himself as well as how he is perceived by others—of attaching a label indicative of abnormality. Consider, for example, how you would be influenced if you were told that someone you knew was 'neurotic' or 'schizophrenic' or 'had had a breakdown'; it would almost certainly lead you to interpret his behaviour differently and to notice as 'significant' things that you would normally disregard. These sorts of considerations have been a matter of great concern during the past decade or so (see Szasz, 1962)—hence the importance of scrutinising the theoretical systems employed by psychologists and psychiatrists and the terminology which they use. Millon (Millon and Diesenhaus, 1972) has proposed an analysis of the main theoretical approaches to psychopathology along the lines given in Table 10.1 (p. 151).

Of the four broad groupings of theoretical systems that Millon proposes, in very approximate terms the first two—biophysical and intrapsychic—reflect the medical approach to psychological disturbance and the last two—phenomenological and behavioural—the psychological approach. These different approaches are not so much concerned with different types of

Basic model	Biophysical	Intrapsychic	Phenomenological	Behavioural
	Disease	Adaptation	Dissonance	Learning
Definition of pathology	Biological dysfunctions and dispositions	Unresolved conflicts, repressed anxieties	Self-discomfort	Maladaptive behaviour
Types of pathology	Traditional psychiatric disorders	Symptom disorders, character patterns	Impoverishment, disorganisation	Numerable specific behavioural symptoms
Causes of pathology	Heredity, constitution, defects	Instinct deprivation, childhood anxieties	Denied self-actualisation	Deficient learning, maladaptive learning
Types of concepts	Operational definitions, intervening variables	Hypothetical constructs, intervening variables	Hypothetical constructs, intervening variables	Intervening variables, operational definitions
Major concepts	Genes, temperament, constitution, defects	Instincts, ego, unconscious defence mechanisms	Self, self-regard, Eigenwelt	Conditioning, reinforcement, generalisation
Data	Heredity, anatomy, physiology, biochemistry	Free association, memories, dreams, projective tests	Interviews, self-reports of conscious attitudes and feelings	Overt behaviour observed and recorded objectively

Modified from Millon (1969)

Table 10.1 From Millon and Diesenhaus, 1972

psychological disorder—although that is true to some extent—as with different ways of explaining and treating the problems. Note also that all approaches are related to treatment, to 'clinical' applications: this distinguishes abnormal psychology from other branches of psychology. As Millon and Diesenhaus (1972) observe: 'In contrast to many of his colleagues in general psychology research, whose interests centre on "abstract" or "basic" scientific problems, the researcher in psychopathology must always keep in mind the clinical significance of his work.'

The biophysical tradition is strong in psychiatry, particularly in this country. In this sort of system psychological disorders are seen as 'illnesses' like more obviously physical disorders; 'diagnosis' is important, and diagnosis indicates the appropriate treatment, or range of treatments—and these are primarily physical, i.e. drugs, electro-shock treatment, brain surgery and so on. Some of the reasons for this approach have already been indicated; it is not surprising that doctors think in terms of the physical constitution and the physical functioning of the individual. Of great significance also, however, are the traditional psychiatric systems of classifying disorder, most of which are derivatives of the system elaborated in the last century by Emile Kraepelin (1856–1926) which was dominated by concepts of genetic and organic factors in causation.

During the past fifteen years or so the biophysical approach has been greatly strengthened by the demonstrated effectiveness of drugs in controlling the behaviour and 'symptoms' of a wide range of disorders. But this improvement in 'management' is, of course, 'cure' at one level only. A standard exposition of physical methods of treatment, and the assumptions underlying them, is that of Sargant and Slater (1972).

The intrapsychic model is largely the construction of one man, Freud, although the related theories of his contemporaries, Jung and Adler, and the modifications and reformulations of their successors include much of importance. Freud's influence has extended far beyond the boundaries of abnormal psychology, and the extent of this influence has probably been a factor in

Psychopathology 153

establishing and supporting psychoanalysis and psychoanalytic therapies as valid and acceptable methods of treatment. Freud was a physician, and psychoanalysts are physicians who have undergone a 'training' analysis—that is, they have themselves been psychoanalysed; 'psychiatrist' is an alternative title for them. Psychoanalytic psychiatry is less well established in this country than it is in other parts of Europe and, especially, the United States. Full-scale psychoanalysis—treatment sessions several times a week for a period of years—is a comparative rarity; psychoanalytic therapy—weekly or twice-weekly treatment sessions for a period of months—is more common and is often provided by other professionals than psychiatrists, e.g. 'lay' (non-medical) psychotherapists and social workers. Perhaps the greatest influence of 'depth' psychology on psychopathology, however, is not in the form of treatment but in terms of psychoanalytic *understanding*. Freud's major contributions in this direction were: the importance he attached to unconscious motivation; his emphasis on the covert meaning of some behaviours; his conceptualisation of anxiety in the development of psychoneurosis; and the significance he gave to early childhood experiences for the development of the normal personality as well as later personality disorder. The influence of these ideas has been very great even on those who would in no way consider themselves as 'psychoanalytic'. A concise summary of the work of Freud and the 'neo-Freudians' is contained in Brown (1964).

The view that personality development and, therefore, the development of personality disorder depends on an individual's view of himself and his world—that is, his concept of 'self' and his habitual ways of thinking about his experience—has as its major exponents Carl Rogers (Rogers, 1961) and George Kelly (Bannister and Fransella, 1971). Although there are significant differences between their approaches they have much in common. They both reject 'diagnosis', that is deciding what is 'wrong' with somebody else so that a 'treatment' can be applied. Those seeking help are assisted in the examination of their 'constructs'—to use Kelly's term—change coming from the results of such scrutiny in a non-directive, accepting, empathetic relationship. The 'democracy' of such approaches makes them particularly acceptable at this point in time since they emphasise that psychological problems are 'individual'—depending upon subjective 'phenomenological' experience (i.e. our own relatively unique perception of the world and ourselves)—and solutions are also individual since they involve changes in terms of this same phenomenological experience.

Rogers and Kelly are both psychologists; so also, but of a very different kind, is B. F. Skinner, the 'father' of behaviour modification or behaviour therapy approaches to psychopathology. Skinner's most influential work *Science and Human Behavior* (1953) initiated a range of new techniques and new applications of the concepts of learning theory. A central concept was that of 'operant' conditioning, the main principle of which is that learned behaviour (the operant) is controlled, in the sense of whether or not it is likely to recur, by its *consequences*, i.e. the presence, or absence, of 'reinforcement', be it positive (desirable) or negative (undesirable). Skinner's theories are, of course, derived from the earlier work of learning theorists, particularly Clark Hull (1884-1952), but he has been the most able and effective exponent of the significance of the behaviourist viewpoint in any situation where changes in patterns of learnt behaviour are sought. Ethical concerns have been aroused because, on this basis, if you can control the *consequences* of a person's behaviour you can control his *behaviour*. In fact, the opportunities for exercising such control are extremely limited and, in any case, there are considerable technical and practical problems in maintaining a reinforcement schedule even in advantageous circumstances. Behaviour modification techniques have been extensively used, with varying sophistication and with a wide range of subjects but mainly the profoundly disturbed or the mentally retarded (Mikulas, 1972; Blackham and Silberman, 1971). Since the co-operation of the subject is not required, psychologists and others have been able to alleviate the behaviour problems of children and adults who, not being amenable to an approach at the level of personal relationships, could otherwise only have been 'damped down' by drugs. On the more positive side, more or less elaborate, hierarchical, programmes of reinforcement known as 'shaping' have permitted the development of quite complex behaviours, including speech. Learning theory techniques can also be used to modify one's own behaviour—for example, such 'problem' behaviours as smoking and sexual impotence; this normally occurs in the context of a counselling relationship (see, for example, Jehu, 1972). Such an approach is valid if one takes the behaviourist view that subjective psychological discomfort is the consequence of being unable to control one's own undesirable behaviours—or achieve desirable ones (Mowrer, 1966).

The different theoretical standpoints which have been outlined determine, amongst other things, what is seen as a psychological disorder, and this in its turn influences estimates of the incidence of psychological disorder in the population. Mechanic (1970) comments: 'In viewing various results from epidemiological investigations in psychiatry, it is obvious that investigators, *depending on their theoretical perspectives*, have played a "numbers game" that either maximises or minimises the amount of mental illness that allegedly exists by changing the criteria used' (my italics). Mechanic refers to a review by Plunkett and Gordon (1960) surveying studies up to 1960 and which reports incidence rates of from less than 2% to 33%. However, when more limited (and more precisely agreed) descriptive categories are used there is greater concordance; thus, for example, internationally the incidence of the schizophrenias is reported as occurring in $\frac{1}{4}$% to $\frac{1}{2}$% of the population (Wing, J., 1967)—but even here there is a significant variation due to international differences in diagnostic classification (Kendell *et al.*, 1971). Probably the major reason for the great variation in incidence rates is the essentially subjective, relativistic status of the concept of 'neurosis'. Neurosis, which conventionally encompasses anxiety states, 'hysteria', compulsive/obsessional states and some forms of depression, is the major 'mental health' problem in adults. Neurotic conditions affect personal relationships and 'efficient' functioning to a greater or lesser degree and are distinguished from psychosis largely by the amount of 'reality' distortion involved. The major forms of psychosis are the schizophrenias, characterised by withdrawal and gross disorders of thought processes; the most common of these, paranoia, is characterised by delusions of persecution and a sense of personal danger. Other traditional categories are of the 'affective' or 'mood' psychoses, of which depression is by far the most common but with manic, or manic-depressive, states also in evidence, and 'organic' psychoses, which, in the main, accompany the physical deterioration of old age. Psychopathy, a lack of feeling—and guilt and anxiety—in personal relationships, fits no other category; the epilepsies, significantly associated with psychological disorder, and mental retardation are two further groups conventionally the province of psychopathology—the latter being mainly concerned with abnormality of cognitive functioning.

The foregoing descriptive groups—and incidence rates—apply to adults. Children manifest less psychological disturbance and it takes somewhat different forms; it is also more transitory and less severe, hospitalisation being rarely required (Robins, 1970). Psychosis is very rare and, pre-puberty, does not seem to be related to adult schizophrenia. The most common form of psychosis in children, infantile autism (a condition marked by impairment and abnormality of language development, bizarre 'ritualistic' behaviour and gross disturbance of the ability to relate to others), has a prevalence rate of 4/5 per 10 000 and follow-up studies suggest neurological involvement (Rutter, 1966).

One of the problems of assessing disorder in children is deciding when behaviour is abnormal for a particular age level; indeed, some of the traditional clinical signs of psychological disturbance in children, for example, nail-biting and restlessness, are so common at all ages that they can hardly be relied upon as differential indices (Shepherd, Oppenheim and Mitchell, 1970). In very general terms, however, psychological disorder in children can be conceptualised in a similar form to adult disorder. Rutter (Rutter, Tizard and Whitmore, 1970) defines 'psychiatric' disorder in children as 'an abnormality of behaviour, emotions, or relationships . . . sufficiently marked and sufficiently prolonged to cause handicap to the child himself, and/or distress or disturbance in the family or community'.

The more limited rights of children make epidemiological surveys easier than with an adult population, although they remain a very difficult practical exercise, which accounts for their relative rarity. An epidemiological survey must take into account the whole of the population group concerned, or at least a representative sample of it, and cannot rely upon data from hospitals, clinics, etc., to whom referral might be made, since that would almost certainly underestimate true prevalence (not everyone is referred) and, of equal importance, would be a selected, *biased* sample of those who actively sought help. The two major recent surveys of childhood disorder in this country are those of Shepherd, Oppenheim and Mitchell (1970), and Rutter, Tizard and Whitmore (1970). The latter was a comprehensive survey of many aspects of the development of children applied to the entire population in the age range ten to eleven years in the Isle of Wight. Children were screened for 'psychiatric disorder' by means of a questionnaire completed separately by teachers and parents. Children scoring above a certain level on either questionnaire were then seen individually by psychiatrists and a further selection was made. The final 'corrected' prevalence rate was 6·8%. A number of interesting facts emerged. Parents and teachers were approximately equal in their accuracy of detecting 'disturbed' children but, in the main, they selected *different* children: this emphasises the importance of situational factors in psychological disturbance in children. Shepherd, Oppenheim and Mitchell (1970) in their similar, but longitudinal, survey found that changes in disturbed behaviour in children were usually associated with situational changes.

Rutter used seven 'diagnostic' categories: (i) neurotic disorder (anxiety disorders, depression, etc.); (ii) conduct disorder (anti-social behaviour); (iii) mixed neurotic and conduct disorders; (iv) developmental disorder (enuresis); (v) hyperkinetic syndrome (overactive, distractible); (vi) child psychosis (infantile autism); (vii) personality disorder (fixed abnormality of personality).

The results of the survey showed that there were almost twice as many boys 'psychiatrically disturbed' as there were girls. This imbalance was almost entirely due to the greater prevalence of anti-social behaviour in boys. The absolute numbers (126 children in all from a total population of 2199) are as follows (Table 10.2):

Disorder	Boys	Girls
(i) Neurotic disorder	17	26
(ii) Conduct disorder	34	9
(iii) Mixed neurotic and conduct disorder	22	5
(iv) Developmental disorder (enuresis)	7	1
(v) Hyperkinetic syndrome	1	1
(vi) Child psychosis	1	1
(vii) Personality disorder	0	1
	82	44

Table 10.2 From Rutter, Tizard and Whitmore, 1970.

Prevalence rates of the order presented by the Isle of Wight study—and these are by no means as high as some that have been reported—may seem to offer a pessimistic picture. But, in children, 'symptoms' are soon remitted: Shepherd *et al.* (1970) followed up 400 'deviant' children (as classified by their survey) and found after three years that 50% were 'deviance free'. Furthermore, long-term follow-ups have shown little connection between disturbance in childhood and disturbance in adult life (Robins, 1970). This is most true for neurotic disorders;

Robins concludes that 'psychosis and anti-social behaviour along with severe mental retardation . . . are the childhood psychiatric categories for which serious adult difficulties can be predicted.' The relationship between behaviour in childhood and adulthood is a subtle and complex one (see, for example, Kagan and Moss, 1962); it would be overly simplistic to expect a manifest and straightforward continuity. What does seem likely is that childhood experiences and patterns of behaviour have some influence on the range of reactions possible in adult life; but it is impossible to predict what experiences an individual will go through as an adult. The cumulative significance of psychologically adverse circumstances is difficult to appraise, but since single events, for example bereavement (Stein and Susser, 1970), can bring about breakdown, it is likely to be considerable.

It also seems probable that the extent and quality of relationships open to a person as an adult may be affected by the quality and security of early relationship experiences, particularly *mothering*. Bowlby (1946) was impressed by the separations experienced early in life by a group of adolescent thieves he investigated; in particular, he noted their 'affectionless' character. He proposed profound and irreversible effects following on from separation of the child from its mother in early life (Bowlby, 1953). Later work suggested that, although separation could be very distressing and disruptive, it was the opportunities for forming relationships and the *quality* of these that mattered most. Rutter (1972), reviewing the research, concluded that a failure to develop 'bonds' with another person before three years of age would seem to be the main factor in the development of psychopathy and that after that age the situation is probably irreversible. There are obviously degrees of 'bonding', and presumably this has varying effects on personality development and the capacity for relating.

Adolescence and the onset of puberty change the pattern of psychological disorder. The most dramatic difference is the increase in anti-social behaviour, of which formal delinquency is perhaps the most obvious manifestation; this is succinctly expressed in the following table for indictable offences committed by juveniles in England and Wales (Table 10.3):

Age	Male	Female
10	326	20
11	797	51
12	1486	156
13	2403	283
14	3797	448
15	4831	497
16	5199	525
17	6550	715
18	6055	681
19	4939	614
20	4352	549
21–24	3058	422
25–29	1925	326

Table 10.3 Number of persons found guilty of indictable offences per 100 000 of population of the age group. (From *Criminal Statistics for England and Wales 1972*. London: HMSO.)

Other changes are the appearance of schizophrenia of adult form (dementia praecox); abnormalities of sexual behaviour; and more overt neurotic disorders.

Adolescence is normally an unstable period—as one might expect when established relationships are loosened and modified and new ones sought and developed; when the demands of new roles in school or employment, in sexual relationships, and in society at large, have to be met; when the self-concept is undergoing rapid, continuous revision. It is clearly a testing time for the quality of the personal development that the adolescent has been enabled to achieve through his earlier history; it is also a test of the quality of the situation in which the adolescent finds himself. It is hardly surprising that when breakdown does occur it is often 'out of the blue'—for example, a sudden refusal to attend school for no 'reason'. However, almost all the problems are transitory even if, when at full expression, they appear very dramatic.

Adulthood is marked by a considerable and progressive decrease in anti-social behaviour in men and a progressive increase in neurotic conditions in women, which reach a peak in middle age. Thus, although boys are seen by psychiatrists more often than girls, the reverse is true in the case of men and women.

The incidence of psychological disorder is correlated with social class and environmental conditions—although this is less true in the case of psychotic disorders (Mechanic, 1970). Rosenthal (1971), in a review of genetic factors in the aetiology of psychopathology, concludes that there is little evidence for such implications except in the schizophrenias and manic-depressive psychosis; to these one can add epilepsy and mental retardation. Eysenck (1960) proposes, however, that there are genetic differences in conditionability which, for example, at one extreme would lead to the easy establishment of phobic conditions or anxiety states and, at the other, to great difficulty in achieving 'inner' controls over behaviour, i.e. the psychopathic personality. Although an attractive and plausible hypothesis, the available evidence is limited and inconclusive.

Differences in the pattern of psychological disorder between children and adults are paralleled by differences in types of treatment. Treatment with drugs (chemotherapy) is much less common with children, except in the case of epilepsy. Individual verbal therapy is limited by the cognitive development and verbal abilities of the age group; play therapy, with a verbal component but which permits symbolic expression through play, is more often used with pre-adolescents. Straightforward behaviour modification is quite often employed with children, partly because of their 'naive' status but also because they are more often in standard, controlled environments like schools where reinforcement schedules have a possibility of being maintained. The direct manipulation of situational variables—including attempts to influence the attitudes and understanding of others (e.g. parents and teachers)—is relatively common in the treatment of children, relatively rare in the treatment of adults.

There is very little evidence as to the effectiveness of these treatments, with the exception of chemotherapy and behaviour modification where the variables are more tangible and the goals more precise. Long-term follow-up of 'treated' as against 'untreated' children, all of whom were diagnosed as disturbed but where the untreated group refused child guidance help, showed no difference in outcome (Levitt, 1957). This does not mean, of course, that during the crisis time when disorder was manifest that treatment did not relieve anxiety and facilitate readjustment.

The uncertain effectiveness of verbal therapies is also apparent in the follow-up of treated adults (see Rachman, 1971, for a pessimistic reading, and Meltzoff and Kornreich, 1970, for a more optimistic one), although there may be subjective impressions of improvement (Rogers and Dymond, 1954) without overt changes in behaviour. Physical methods of treatment are empirically successful but lack a sufficient theoretical basis (Sargant and Slater, 1972). Behaviour therapy has also demonstrated its effectiveness but is restricted in the range of disorders to which it has been applied—simple phobic conditions, for example (Eysenck and Rachman, 1965).

The result of scrutinising and evaluating the 'treatment' of psychological disorder, once it has arisen, is not an optimistic one. Real solutions to such problems must lie, to a major extent, in the organisation of society as a whole. To the degree that individuals are subjected to continued stress, are deprived of self-esteem, security and opportunities for making satisfactory relationships, they will be likely to develop psychological disorder; this is true even if genetic factors are allowed a role because, except in rare cases, they are predisposing factors only. In a very real sense, then, the disorders of the individual are the disorders of society at large; and in broad terms preventive measures must be social and economic—ultimately, political.

Epilepsy

Epilepsy is a physical disorder—or rather a group of physical disorders—with important behavioural consequences, as the following definition by Kolb (1973) indicates: 'a symptom complex characterised by periodic, transient states of alteration in the state of consciousness which may be associated with convulsive movements or disturbances in feeling or behaviour, or both.'

In physiological terms epilepsy can be considered as a heightened disturbance in activity of the discharging cells of the brain, presumably due to irritative stimuli. Electroencephalogram (EEG) recordings of the electrical activity on the surface of the brain show characteristic patterns and foci of abnormal activity in the great majority (approximately 85%) of individuals suffering from epilepsy but also in 5% to 10% of those who are not. The relatives of epileptic patients have abnormal EEGs in about 60% of cases, which suggests that genetic factors play a major role, at least in predisposal to the disorder (data from Kolb, 1973).

In approximately three-quarters of all cases there is no known cause for the epilepsy (so-called 'idiopathic' epilepsy); in the remainder there is more or less evidence of acquired brain injury (so-called 'symptomatic' epilepsy).

Lennox (1960) gives a prevalence rate of 5 per 1000 for the general population, basing his figures on data obtained from the medical examination of military recruits, which are unlikely to be exactly representative. The same author (Lennox, 1953) estimates that 5% to 7% of all children may have had one or more convulsive seizures prior to the age of seven years, usually when their temperature was abnormally high ('febrile convulsions').

Conventionally, epileptic attacks are classified as:

1. Grand mal—a major fit accompanied by loss of consciousness, muscular spasms, etc.

2. Petit mal—minor attacks, characterised by brief 'blank spells' and occurring almost entirely in children.
3. Psychomotor epilepsy (also known as temporal lobe epilepsy)—very slight overt symptoms, for example a brief slurring of speech.

It is the latter group which is most prone to manifest psychiatric disturbance—50% according to Gibbs and Gibbs (1964) as against 10% in other epileptic patients.

The concept of the 'epileptic personality' is almost certainly a fiction—in any case, epilepsy is not a unitary disorder. However, as Schmidt and Wilder (1968) point out, 'epileptics as a group do have a higher incidence of intellectual impairment and of behavioural and personality disturbances than is found in the population at large'.

Many of the psychological disturbances of people suffering from epilepsy are undoubtedly due to the anxiety aroused by the subjective experience of epileptic attacks and the real or imagined significance of suffering from the disorder, and to the general attitude of society as well as the individual's specific experiences of the attitudes of others. Drug treatment has greatly eased the physical symptoms of epilepsy, but the problems just mentioned are psychosocial ones, which means that solutions are in the psychological terms of personal relationships and social attitudes.

Mental retardation

The mentally retarded are an ill-defined group and, even when some specific, empirical definition is employed, such as IQ level, they remain heterogeneous in other terms. Certainly their main characteristic is a level of cognitive attainments very much below the average for the relevant population group but, especially in the most severe cases, there are often additional physical handicaps. Furthermore, and this is particularly true of the intellectually borderline adolescent or adult, many are classified as mentally retarded more on the basis of social than cognitive competence—that is, on their ability to manage their lives effectively rather than their ability to reason and solve 'intellectual' problems; indeed, the British Mental Deficiency Act of 1913 (superseded in 1958) was couched almost entirely in such terms.

The severely mentally retarded—in approximate terms those with an IQ of 50 or less—make up about ½% of the population. A large proportion of this group show manifest signs of neurological damage or other neurological abnormality (e.g. microcephaly); others have chromosomal abnormalities—the most well known, and the largest, group being those with Down's syndrome (mongolism); there is also a rare group with biochemical disorders (e.g. phenylketonuria), but the largest single group is unclassified in aetiological terms. Medical research into the aetiology of mental retardation has had some spectacular successes in recent years. The cause of mongolism (an extra chromosome) was identified as recently as 1959 (Lejeune, Gautier and Turpin, 1959). But as Clarke and Clarke (1973) point out, mental retardation is essentially a *behavioural* deficit and must therefore be conceptualised—and remediated—in behavioural terms. Remediation should obviously be based on a knowledge of the cognitive characteristics of the mentally retarded, and implemented in terms of clearly defined objectives approached by stages suited to their learning capacity as well as the logical demands of the skill or task concerned. But Clarke and Clarke (1973) observe that 'The question of whether the mentally subnormal is qualitatively deficient, due to general CNS impairment, or a retarded normal, remains to be resolved . . .' Much of what one can say about the mentally retarded compared with the average could be said about the average compared with the mentally gifted. The most evident difference, however, is probably in the area of language skills which, even within their own group, are markedly inferior to other, nonverbal, performance skills. Luria, the Russian psychologist (Luria, 1963), sees mental retardation as largely a failure to integrate language and motor skills.

Unlike the mildly mentally retarded (IQ range approximately

50 to 70), who are almost entirely from social classes IV and V (in terms of parental occupational status), the severely mentally retarded are fairly representative of all social classes. This may mean that genetic and constitutional factors are mainly responsible for their condition; it does not mean that they are not influenced by environmental factors, that they cannot learn, or that their condition cannot be ameliorated in cognitive terms.

This very brief account of mental retardation cannot do justice to the importance of the subject; nor is it possible to plot the massive need for sophisticated research to investigate the complexities of the problem. Suffice it to say that the major contribution of psychologists to the study of mental retardation in this century—namely, the more systematic appraisal of 'intelligence'—is largely redundant since 'intelligence' tests merely provide normative information and say nothing about *why* the individual is unsuccessful (or successful) at the tasks with which he is presented. Elsewhere I have pointed to the need to develop techniques of assessment directly referenced to remediation (Gillham, 1974a, 1974b).

References

Bannister, D., & Fransella, F. (1971), *Inquiring Man*. Harmondsworth: Penguin Books.

Blackham, G. J., & Silberman, A. (1971), *Modification of Child Behavior*. Belmont, Wadsworth.

Bowlby, J. (1946), *Forty-four Juvenile Thieves: Their Characters and Home Life*. London: Baillère, Tindall & Cox.

Bowlby, J. (1953), *Child Care and the Growth of Love*. Harmondsworth: Penguin Books.

Brown, J. A. C. (1964), *Freud and the Post-Freudians*. (Revised edition) Harmondsworth: Penguin Books.

Clarke, A. D. B., & Clarke, A. M. (1973), 'What are the problems? An evaluation of recent research relating to theory and practice' in Clarke, A. D. B., & Clarke, A. M. (eds), *Mental Retardation and Behavioural Research*. Edinburgh & London: Churchill Livingstone.

Eysenck, H. J. (ed.) (1960), *Behaviour Therapy and the Neuroses*. Oxford: Pergamon.

Eysenck, H. J., & Rachman, S. (1965), *The Causes and Cure of Neurosis*. London: Routledge & Kegan Paul.

Gibbs, F. A., & Gibbs, E. L. (1952), *Atlas of Electro Encephalography*. Reading, Mass.: Addison-Wesley.

Gillham, W. E. C. (1974), 'The British Intelligence Scale: à la recherche du temps perdu'. *Bull. Brit. Psychol. Soc.*, 27, 313-17.

Gillham, W. E. C. (1974), 'A language programme for young mentally handicapped children'. *Spec. Educ.: Forward Trends*, 1, 1.

Jehu, D. (1972), *Behaviour Modification in Social Work*. London: John Wiley.

Kagan, J., & Moss, H. A. (1962), *Birth to Maturity*. New York: John Wiley.

Kendell, R. E., Cooper, J. E., Gourlay, A. J., Copeland, J. R. M., Sharpe, L., & Gurland, B. J. (1971), 'Diagnostic criteria of American and British psychiatrists'. *Arch. Gen. Psychiat.*, 25, 123-30.

Kolb, L. C. (1973), *Modern Clinical Psychiatry*. (8th edition) Philadelphia: W. B. Saunders.

Lejeune, J., Gautier, M., & Turpin, R. 'Les chromosomes humains en culture de tissus'. *C.R. Acad. Sci.*, 248, 602-3.

Lennox, W. G. (1953), 'Significance of febrile convulsions'. *Pediatrics*, 11, 341-57.

Lennox, W. G. (1960), *Epilepsy and Related Disorders*. Boston: Little, Brown & Co.

Levitt, E. E. (1957), 'The results of psychotherapy with children'. *J. Consult. Psychol.*, 21, 189.

Luria, A. R. (1963), 'Psychological studies of mental deficiency in the Soviet Union' in Ellis, N. R. (ed.), *Handbook of Mental Deficiency*. New York: McGraw-Hill.

Mechanic, D. (1970), 'Problems and prospects in psychiatric epidemiology' in Hare, E. H., & Wing, J. K. (eds), *Psychiatric Epidemiology*. London: Oxford Univ. Press.

Melzoff, J., & Kornreich, M. (1970), *Research in Psychotherapy*. New York: Atherton Press.

Mikulas, W. L. (1972), *Behavior Modification: An Overview*. New York: Harper & Row.

Millon, T. & Diesenhaus, H. I. (1972), *Research Methods in Psychopathology*. New York: John Wiley.

Mowrer, O. H. (1966), 'The basis of psychopathology: malconditioning or misbehavior?' in Spielberger, C. D. (ed.), *Anxiety and Behavior*. New York: Academic Press.

Rachman, S. (1971), *The Effects of Psychotherapy*. Oxford: Pergamon.
Robins, L. N. (1970), 'Follow-up studies investigating childhood disorders' in Hare, E. H., & Wing, J. K. (eds), *Psychiatric Epidemiology*. London: Oxford Univ. Press.
Rogers, C. R. (1961), *On Becoming a Person*. Boston: Houghton Mifflin.
Rogers, C. R., & Dymond, R. F. (1954), *Psychotherapy and Personality Change*. Chicago: Univ. of Chicago Press.
Rosenthal, D. (1971), *The Genetics of Psychopathology*. New York: McGraw-Hill.
Rutter, M. (1972), *Maternal Deprivation Reassessed*. Harmondsworth: Penguin Books.
Rutter, M. (1966), 'Prognosis: psychotic children in adolescence and early adult life' in Wing, J. K. (ed.), *Early Childhood Autism: Clinical, Educational and Social Aspects*. London: Pergamon.
Rutter, M., Tizard, J., & Whitmore, K. (1970), *Education, Health and Behaviour*. London: Longman.
Sargant, W., & Slater, E. (1972), *An Introduction to Physical Methods of Treatment in Psychiatry*. (5th edition) Edinburgh & London: Churchill Livingstone.
Schmidt, R. P., & Wilder, B. J. (1968), *Epilepsy*. Philadelphia: F. A. Davis.
Shepherd, M., Oppenheim, B., & Mitchell, S. (1971), *Childhood Behaviour and Mental Health*. London: Univ. of London Press.
Skinner, B. F. (1953), *Science and Human Behaviour*. New York: Macmillan.
Stein, Z., & Susser, M. (1970), 'Bereavement as a precipitating event in mental illness' in Hare, E. H., & Wing, J. K., *Psychiatric Epidemiology*. London: Oxford Univ. Press.
Szasz, T. (1962), *The Myth of Mental Illness*. London: Secker & Warburg.
Wing, J. (1957), 'The modern management of schizophrenia'. In Freeman, H., & Farndale, J. (eds), *New Aspects of the Mental Health Services*. New York: Pergamon.

Recommended further reading

Engel, M. (1972), *Psychopathology in Childhood*. New York: Harcourt-Brace-Jovanovich.

Lowe, G. R. (1969), *Personal Relationships in Psychological Disorder*. Harmondsworth: Penguin Books.

Ulett, G. A. (1972), *A Synopsis of Contemporary Psychiatry*. (5th edition) St Louis: C. V. Mosby.

11

Behavioural Pharmacology

T. R. Cox

Introduction

This chapter concerns an expanding area of study that has been called both 'psychopharmacology' and 'behavioural pharmacology'. These terms have now been in common use for some time and are developing slightly different connotations. Broadly speaking, they refer to research towards one of two ends: either the administration of drugs is used as an instrument with which behaviour is investigated or, conversely, behaviour is used as a measure or assay for the analysis of drug action.

The term 'psychopharmacology' has been used to denote the investigation of drug effects on the various cognitive, emotional and perceptual states of man. The drugs chosen for study have tended to be those which have hallucinogenic properties, or which obviously affect interpersonal relationships. Such agents have been used in many societies, including our own, since time immemorial. Many are well known, for example alcohol, nicotine and caffeine, and opium, cocaine and marihuana. LSD_{25} is among the more recent synthetic additions to this group. These substances have been used for many purposes, but rarely for modifying or curing a disease state; usually they have been employed to facilitate social, religious and orgiastic functions. By and large, the methods used for studying these drugs have developed from those used by the early introspective psychologists, and only recently from those of the experimental psychologists. By comparison, the term 'behavioural pharmacology' has been used to describe a more controlled study of drug effects, which tends to make reference to animal (infra-human) behaviour. The term has also been adopted by operant (Skinnerian) researchers to denote studies which combine drug administration with their orthodox operant practice. The drugs chosen for study are usually of academic interest—those that interfere with the metabolism of brain transmitters—or of applied importance—those that have potential clinical application. Despite the important differences that have come to exist between behavioural pharmacology and psychopharmacology, the two terms are still used interchangeably by many authors.

The importance of studies on drugs

There are several good reasons why psychologists show interest in studies on the behavioural effects of drugs, most of which are of applied importance. First, such studies contribute to our understanding of clinically useful drugs; what changes they bring about in both normal and abnormal behaviour, when they should and should not be used, and in what doses they should be used. Secondly, this understanding aids the discovery and development of new drugs of value in the clinical situation. There is no need to emphasise the importance of safer and more effective drug therapy. The third reason why psychologists show interest in drug effects is that those effects provide them with a useful tool for investigating the structure and expression of behaviour. Conversely, knowledge of how a drug affects different types of behaviour can allow a more precise description of that drug's action.

In practice it is difficult to separate out these reasons. For example, consider the contribution that anticholinesterase drugs have made to pharmacology, to psychology and to clinical practice. These drugs prevent the acetylcholine released in the course of normal physiological activity from being destroyed. Acetylcholine is an important chemical 'cog' in the nervous mechanism. In pharmacology the use of these drugs has been central in demonstrating that the transmission of information between nerve cells, and between nerve cells and the various effector organs, is chemical in nature. One of the first chemical transmitters to be identified with certainty was acetylcholine. In psychology the use of these drugs has allowed an understanding of the contribution of acetylcholine-containing inhibitory mechanisms to the control of behaviour. It has been suggested by the author that there are two such mechanisms, one concerned with the accuracy of behaviour and the other with its activity. Clinically, anticholinesterases are used in the treatment of glaucoma, of myasthenia gravis and of paralytic ileus and related conditions. For the purpose of this example, it is sufficient to discuss just one of these conditions. Myasthenia gravis, a state of muscle weakness, is due to the lack of an effective concentration of acetylcholine at the junction between the nerves and the muscles. The rational treatment is to increase the amount of available acetylcholine, and this is achieved by the administration of an anticholinesterase. Physostigmine was used initially, but was soon replaced by neostigmine, which has remained the drug of choice. Neostigmine, unlike physostigmine, penetrates brain tissue with difficulty, and thus its effects tend to be limited to the periphery.

Because drugs are now such an integral part of everyday life, it is essential that psychologists fully understand what is involved in their use, and the relationship between their pharmacological action and their behavioural effects. These problems are real, and their study illustrates one of the important applications of psychology.

Sources of information

Our understanding of the effects of drugs is being pieced together from several widely different sources of information. Perhaps the oldest, and least reliable, are the anthropological sources. The drugs which have found use in rituals and ceremonials have formed a cardinal and recorded part of man's social evolution. However, the important effects of drugs in this role are essentially subjective and verbal, and there is therefore a basic difficulty in communicating information about such effects, and scientific analysis is likewise difficult. It is sometimes worth questioning the validity of historical records. Apart from the important questions already raised, it is impossible to be sure whether the drugs described in these records are the same as those used today. Many of the old sources of information tend to be legendary rather than factual, and it is an impossible task to trace out with precision the historical course of any particular drug.

More reliable sources of information became available during the late nineteenth century, with the development of institutions for the mentally ill. For the first time, physicians were able to make systematic observations of the behavioural aspects of drug action. Later, with the increasing use of drugs in the treatment of mental illness, clinical data became available from many other sources. However, much of the information now used in the development of new drugs and in further research on established drugs comes from the laboratory. For any particular attempt to gather data, the experimental method, most often used in the laboratory, provides the most controlled and reliable procedures. The application of the information gained through such studies to the clinical situation is, however, not always straightforward, and no matter how much laboratory data is available, drugs have to be tested in actual use before our knowledge is complete.

The psychopharmacologist, as defined in the introduction, could be said to be concerned with anthropological and clinical data, while the behavioural pharmacologist is involved in laboratory studies.

Laboratory studies

Most, but not all, studies on the behavioural effects of drugs that take place in the laboratory make use of the experimental approach, and perhaps the easiest way to provide a review of the work of the behavioural pharmacologist is by discussing the experimental methods that he uses.

1 Dosage considerations

Important in the design of drug experiments are dosage considerations. Drug concentration is the central dependent variable in pharmacology, and the need for exploration along this variable in behavioural studies cannot be emphasised too much. The logical impossibility of making any statement of drug action or any comparison between drugs on the basis of observations at a single dose level is well recognised. In experimental work on animals, it is usual to calculate the required dose of a drug on the basis of the individual animal's body weight. However, for man, drug doses are not always expressed in this way, and may be quoted as the weight of drug given to the individual, independent of his body weight. This is because differences in weight among human adults of the same sex and within the normal range of weights are mainly due to differences in the amount of fat they carry. The weight of non-fatty tissue remains almost constant, and thus differences in body weight only affect the required dose if the drugs are lipid (fat) soluble. Children, it should be noted, are more susceptible to some drugs than adults and normally require lower doses.

Consideration of the effects of different doses leads to the production of 'dose-response curves'. These are constructed by plotting the strength of the response to the drug (the change in behaviour) against the dose administered. Such curves will vary not only from drug to drug but also between behavioural measures, and it is unusual to obtain simple linear functions. For example, consider the sort of dose-response curve produced by drugs which in small to moderate doses increase the adaptiveness of some particular behaviour. It is interesting to do so, because all drugs, if given in sufficient doses, will disrupt behaviour, if only by killing the animal. The combination of these two effects produces a U-shaped dose-response function. This is

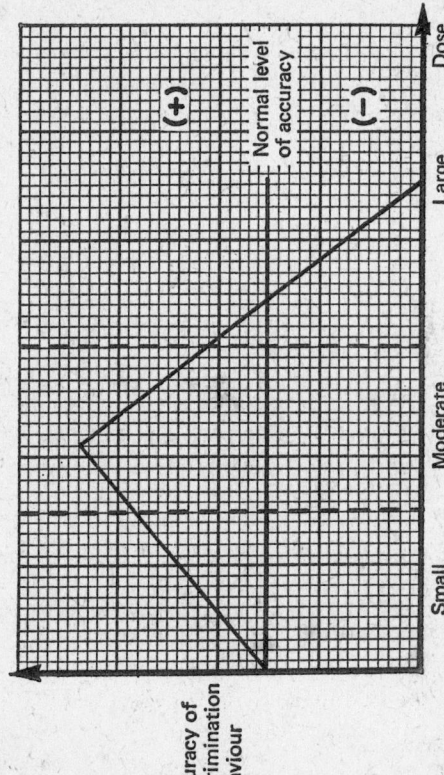

Fig. 11.1 The effects of physostigmine on the accuracy of discrimination behaviour in the rat. This dose-response curve is a typical U-shaped function.

exemplified by some studies by the author on the effects of the anticholinesterase physostigmine on discrimination behaviour in the rat (Cox and Tye, 1973; 1974). The pharmacological action of this drug has been described in an earlier section. In small doses (up to 0·06 mg/kg body weight) it produces an improvement in the accuracy of the rats' discrimination behaviour. In large doses (about 0·10 mg/kg body weight and above) it produces an impairment of accuracy which is probably due to the gross disruption of physiological function which such doses cause. Plotting the accuracy of the animals' discrimination against the drug dose produces an inverted U-shaped curve (see Fig. 11.1). Such a curve is obtained during both the acquisition and the maintenance of discrimination behaviour. The author has studied several discriminations of different discriminative difficulty.

2 Dominant and side effects

It is important for the psychologist to understand that all known drugs produce more than just a single effect and have more than one mode of action. Perhaps on any one occasion, one particular effect will be the most obvious, but which of the many effects it is will depend on the dose of the drug given, the situation in which it is given and how the response to the drug is being measured. This dominant effect will also vary from species to species, from strain to strain and between sexes. The other less obvious effects, the side effects, will similarly vary.

The central nervous system stimulant, amphetamine, has been shown from studies with rodents and with pigeons to have at least two important effects on behaviour. On the one hand, it produces a facilitation of responding in the operant situation and an increase in spontaneous activity; response times become shorter and the animals appear to be more active. However, on the other hand, it reduces the animals' interest in food (anorexia). If a hungry rat has been conditioned to press a lever for a food reward and is then injected with amphetamine, one of two things will happen depending on the dose administered. Doses up to 0·3 mg/kg of amphetamine will tend to increase the rat's rate of responding (due to the stimulation of behaviour), but doses of 1·0 mg/kg and above will decrease the rate of responding (due to the rat losing interest in the food reward). The dose-response curve is thus U-shaped (see Kelleher and Morse, 1968). If the 'anorexic' effect of amphetamine was not recognised, the 'rate depressant' action of this central nervous system stimulant might appear paradoxical.

3 Routes of administration

When a drug is being used for clinical or experimental purposes, it must reach its sites of action in a sufficiently high concentration to bring about the desired effect. The rate at which the drug arrives at those sites must balance the rate at which it is removed from those sites by the various processes of inactivation. The rate of arrival of the drug depends on the route and frequency of its administration: different routes mean different rates of drug absorption and different degrees of absorption.

Several other important aspects of drug action are immediately affected by the route chosen. The first is the minimum effective dose (and hence the limits of the dose-response relationship), and the second is the latency and duration of the onset of the maximum effect. Furthermore, with some routes it is difficult to state with any accuracy the 'effective' dose administered. Several instances are known of drugs being ineffective because of the use of unsatisfactory administration and dose schedules.

Three main types of route are commonly used in drug studies and drug treatment. The first is the oral route. For humans the drug is normally taken as a tablet or capsule, or in solution as a drink. In animals a tube is introduced down the throat into the stomach, and the drug then passed into the stomach in solution. Drugs can also be administered by inhalation: by smoking (as with nicotine and the tobacco alkaloids in cigarettes) or by the use of breathing and inhalation chambers. Perhaps the most common route is by injection. There are many ways in which drugs can be injected: into the muscles (intramuscular), under the folds of the skin (subcutaneous), into the peritoneal cavity of the abdominal region (intraperitoneal), into the veins (intravenous) or into the fluid-filled cavities of the brain (intraventricular). Among all the available routes of administration, the intraperitoneal route is probably the most widely used in laboratory studies, although it is unsuitable for use in man. After intraperitoneal injection, absorption of the drug is rapid, the minimum effective dose is relatively small and the latency of onset of the maximum effect is relatively short.

4 Site of origin of drug effects

Having administered a drug and shown that in certain doses it affects behaviour, it is necessary to know whether that effect is central or peripheral in origin. The drug could change behaviour by altering the normal activity of the central nervous system, or by affecting the peripheral nerves and the other organ systems of the body. There are several methods for deciding the answer to this question, most of which are based on the assumption of a blood-brain barrier.

There is reason to believe that some sort of physico-chemical barrier exists which protects the brain from chemicals circulating in the systemic blood. The barrier is selective and prevents certain of these chemicals from penetrating brain tissue. Pharmacologists have shown that drugs of a certain chemical structure easily pass this barrier, but others do not. Drugs which are tertiary nitrogen compounds penetrate brain tissue, while those which are quaternary nitrogen compounds do not. These two types of drug differ in the configuration and number of chemical groups around an important nitrogen atom in their structure. For example, atropine, which blocks the action of acetylcholine at certain sites in the nervous system, is a tertiary compound and readily enters the brain. Methyl atropine, which is a similar type of drug, is a quaternary compound and does not enter the brain. Hines, Lee and Miller (1970) have reported the effects of equal doses of these two drugs on the behaviour of thirsty rats trained to press a lever for a water reward. Atropine brought about a progressive reduction in the rate of responding, but methyl atropine had very little effect, except at very high doses. The following arguments can be advanced. Atropine affected this particular behaviour, and is also known to affect both central and peripheral mechanisms. Methyl atropine, on the other hand, did not affect behaviour, and is known only to affect peripheral mechanisms. Therefore, it can be reasonably concluded that the effect of atropine on this behaviour is central in origin. Another method for determining the site of action of drug effects makes use of the observation that certain drugs are able to reverse the effects of others. For example, anticholinesterases tend to reverse the effects of atropine. Bignami and Gatti (1966) have reviewed several studies which have shown that if the right doses of atropine and the tertiary anticholinesterase, physostigmine, are given together, then the anticholinesterase reverses the behavioural effects of the atropine. This reversal cannot be achieved using the quaternary anticholinesterase, neostigmine. Physostigmine readily penetrates brain tissue, but neostigmine does not. The behavioural effects of the atropine are therefore central in origin. Local application of quaternary drugs to parts of the brain can provide further proof. Warburton (1969) has shown that methyl atropine has no effect on behaviour unless injected into the brain (by intraventricular injection). Under these conditions it has similar effects to those of atropine.

5 Non-pharmacological effects

Although it is assumed that all drugs have some pharmacological action, it is relatively easy to demonstrate that their effects on behaviour may be brought about by the operation of 'non-pharmacological' processes, or that these processes may modify the pharmacological effects.

One important consideration concerns stress. When a stress is applied to an animal (man included), that animal tends to react in such a way as to minimise the effects of the stress. Behavioural, as well as physiological, activity alters to maintain the constancy of the 'milieu interieur' (internal environment). Drugs and the way in which they are administered obviously function as a stress and thus tend to evoke compensatory (non-pharmacological) reactions. Therefore, any drug may produce an indirect compensatory response in addition to its direct pharmacological action. This indirect effect may be peculiar to the particular drug, or a general reaction to the class of stress that drugs represent.

Many other 'non-pharmacological' factors can influence drug action, and while there is no clear-cut agreement as to what characterises such influences, commonly included in this rubric are age, sex and strain, experimental history, on-going behaviour and environmental control.

Fisher (1970) has outlined three general principles, which although discussed in a clinical context may equally well apply to the infra-human situation. First, the more a response system involves central (brain) processes, the greater will be the role of non-pharmacological factors influencing drug response. Second, many of the factors may be explained by simple physiological and pharmacological processes; and, third, the more 'potent' a drug is, the less sensitive it will be to such factors. There is every indication that in certain situations non-pharmacological factors dominate an animal's response to a drug. Thus similar effects may be obtained with dissimilar drugs, and may simply reflect the general disturbance that both cause when injected into the animal rather than their direct pharmacological actions. A related type of effect is that described as the 'placebo' effect. Essentially, this rests on the demonstration that pharmacologically inert substances may produce marked effects on behaviour. Such placebo effects are dealt with in some detail in Claridge's book *Drugs and Human Behaviour* (a paperback recommended for further reading).

One example will suffice. The author divided a large number of first-year psychology students into two equal groups, telling them that they were going to be asked to volunteer for an experiment on the effects of a 'metabolic stimulant' on time perception. None of the students refused. A one-hour lecture was then given on the pharmacology of 'd-aktizol' (apologies to any actual drug). It was stressed that this agent accelerated metabolic rate and thus the recipients' internal clocks. Time perception would thus be altered by the drug. The students were then screened for illness or pregnancy, which would prevent their taking part in the experiment, and were asked to sign a 'form of consent'. One group was given the 'drug' and the other group received a control substance. These were both administered by a medical practitioner, who was helping to conduct the experiment. The drug group were allowed by accident to see what they were receiving. In reality both groups received a small amount of sugar.

During the course of the experiment marked differences in time perception arose between the groups. The 'drugged' individuals consistently underestimated time intervals. Furthermore, they reported feeling dizzy and faint, and also sweating and having stomach pains. No such reports came from the control group. At the end of the experiment it was difficult to convince the 'drug' group that they had been given sugar and that the effects that they had experienced were due to a psychological process.

6 *Genetic variation*

Genetic differences provide one of several sources of variation in individual responses to drugs. Such variation is most easily recognised in species, strain and sex differences. Species differences are well known. For example, morphine has been shown to act as a central nervous system depressant in dogs, rabbits, rats, mice and birds, but as an excitant in sheep, pigs, goats and cats. An interesting example of strain differences is the response of rabbits to belladonna, the deadly nightshade. This plant is normally very poisonous, as it contains large amounts of atropine and atropine-like compounds. However, as early as 1852, it was reported that some rabbits could eat and survive, and actually thrive on belladonna leaves. This led to the postulation that they possessed an enzyme which broke down atropine and thus inactivated it. This enzyme was called 'atropinase'. Research showed that strains such as the Chinchilla possessed atropinase, while others such as Castle's A strain and the New Zealand White did not. The enzyme was shown to be determined by a single gene and to be linked to the colour of the rabbit's fur: black rabbits have the enzyme, others do not.

How do drugs affect behaviour?

The behavioural and pharmacological effects of most of the drugs in which psychologists have shown interest are thought to be due to their effects at the *synapse* and to their interference with the transmission of information between nerve cells.

1 Synaptic transmission

There are two basic processes involved in the functioning of the nervous system: one is the *conduction* of information along the nerve cells, and the other is the *transmission* of information across the gap (or synapse) between nerve cells. The first process is that of a propagated electrochemical change in the state of the nerve cells (nerve impulse), and the second is a chemical process. The role of physostigmine in demonstrating the chemical nature of transmission, and in the identification of acetylcholine as a transmitter substance, has already been discussed.

Consider a simplified synapse, as shown in Fig. 11.2. The transmitter substance is formed in the pre-synaptic nerve cell, and transported into the terminal branches of that cell. There it is stored in minute sacs or vesicles. The arrival of a nerve impulse at the terminal branches causes the rupture of many vesicles and the release of a small amount of the transmitter substance into the synapse. There are two types of transmitter substance: excitatory and inhibitory (see Chapter 5). An excitatory substance, for example, acts in the following way. The transmitter crosses the gap by the simple process of diffusion,

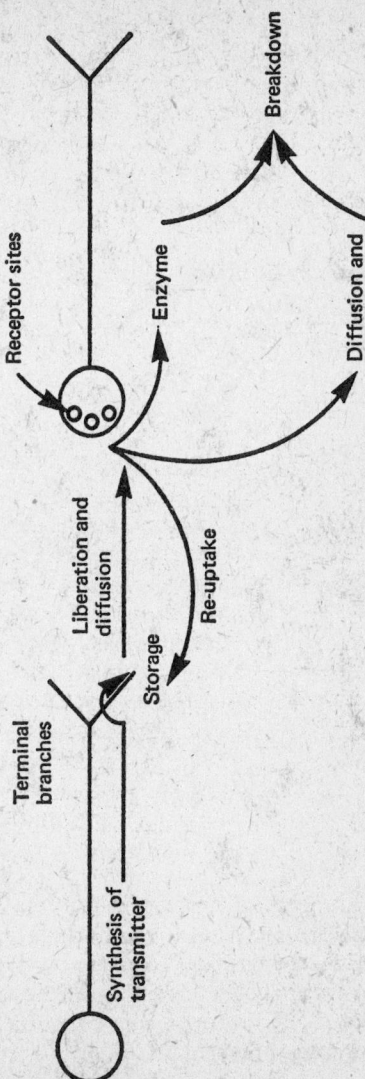

Fig. 11.2 A simplified model of synaptic transmission.

and some of it impinges on the post-synaptic cell. There are special areas on the surface of nerve cells, receptor sites, which respond to transmitter substances. If sufficient receptors are activated, a nerve impulse is produced in that cell. The liberated transmitter substance has to be removed from the synapse to prevent the continual activation of the post-synaptic cell. This is achieved by three different means. Enzymes may be present on either the pre- or the post-synaptic cells to break down the transmitter substance as it is released. Alternatively, continued diffusion may carry the transmitter substance away from the synapse, and it may then be broken down elsewhere by the enzyme. The third possibility is that it is taken up again by the pre-synaptic cell.

2 Transmitter substances

During the last two decades many substances have been shown to occur naturally in brain tissue, and any one of these could be critically involved in the function of the brain and in the control of behaviour. However, acetylcholine is the only chemical that has been shown conclusively to be a transmitter substance at central as well as peripheral synapses. Studies have shown that nerve cells sensitive to acetylcholine are widely distributed throughout the brain. They have been found in the brain stem, in the thalamus, hypothalamus and basal ganglia, in the cerebellum and in the cerebral cortex (see Crossland, 1967; Bradley, 1968). However, it cannot be assumed that all cells sensitive to acetylcholine are activated through cholinergic synapses. Despite this, Crossland (1970) has tentatively estimated that something in the order of 30% of central synapses may be activated by acetylcholine. It is therefore rational to assume and look for a relationship between brain acetylcholine metabolism and behaviour. For those studying cholinergic involvement in behaviour, drugs like atropine and the anticholinesterases offer useful ways of interfering with central cholinergic function. Several of the studies that have used these drugs to these ends have already been discussed.

Noradrenaline has been shown to be a transmitter substance at certain peripheral sites, and there is much evidence to suggest that it is also a transmitter in the central nervous system. One of the ways in which the role of brain noradrenaline in the control of behaviour has been studied is by bringing about a depletion of this transmitter substance, and by then observing the resultant changes in behaviour. A drug that has been popular in this respect is reserpine. Studies on its pharmacological properties in the late 1950s showed that it brought about a marked depletion of noradrenaline through an interference with the storage mechanisms in the pre-synaptic neural components. The most obvious effect of reserpine in both the clinical and the laboratory situation is that of sedation, and many studies have suggested that the drug-induced depletion of noradrenaline is responsible for this effect. However, it has been shown that reserpine also depletes another possible central transmitter substance, 5-hydroxytryptamine, and some researchers have linked this action with its sedative properties. This seems unlikely for several reasons. For example, parachlorophenylalanine, which selectively depletes 5-hydroxytryptamine, does not depress activity in rats, but alpha-methyl-paratyrosine, which selectively depletes noradrenaline, does.

Many other substances have been named as possible central transmitter substances. Perhaps the most likely are 5-hydroxytryptamine, gamma-aminobutyric acid and dopamine. Others include the polyamines, spermadine and spermatidine, the prostaglandins, glutamic acid, histamine, and adenosine triphosphate.

Classification of drugs

The drugs which are of interest to the psychologist and to the behavioural pharmacologist have been classified in many different ways: according to their chemical structure, mode of action, pharmacological properties and clinical application. Very few schemes agree, but there appear to be three generally recognised drug groups:

1 drugs which bring about inhibition (depression)—tranquillisers, sedatives;
2 drugs which bring about excitation—antidepressants, stimulants;
3 drugs which cause 'model' psychoses—hallucinogens, psychotomimetics.

A major difficulty is that a drug may inhibit central nervous system activity and as a result cause behavioural excitation, or vice-versa. However, a classification is offered by way of conclusion. This is loosely based on the above distinction between three drug groups, and is drawn from Clark and del Guidice (1970) and Crossland (1970).

1 *Depressants*

(a) Major tranquillisers or antipsychotics:

phenothiazines	chlorpromazine
reserpine and derivatives	reserpine
	tetrabenazine
butyrophenones	haloperidol
	trifluperidol

(b) Minor tranquillisers or antianxiety agents:

benzodiazepines	chlordiazepoxide
	nitrazepam
	diazepam
	oxepam
substituted diols	meprobamate
diphenylmethane derivatives	benactyzine

(c) Sedatives:

barbiturates	amylobarbitone
	pentobarbitone
	phenobarbitone
alcohol	ethanol

2 (i) *Antidepressants*

    (a) Monoamine oxidase inhibitors:

hydrazine derivatives	iproniazid
nonhydrazines	pargyline
	harmine

    (b) Tricyclics: imipramine
                                      amitriptyline

(ii) *Stimulants*
    (a) Agents related directly to neurohumoral substances:

                                      amphetamine
                                      atropine

    (b) Xanthines: caffeine

3 *Psychotomimetics and hallucinogens*

    (a) Agents containing an indole nucleus:

                                      LSD_{25}
                                      psilocybin
                                      bufotenine

    (b) Compounds related to noradrenaline:

                                      mescaline

    (c) Others: phencyclidine
                                      tetrahydrocannabinol

The value of any classification is largely one of economy, and not only should the properties of the drugs covered in that classification be investigated, but the scheme itself should be constantly evaluated and modified. For example, it is now apparent that the terms 'stimulant' and 'depressant', as applied to amphetamine-like and barbiturate-like drugs respectively, do not refer to intrinsic properties of those drugs but to an interaction between the drug and test environment. In certain situations and in certain doses, amphetamine can depress the activity of behaviour and barbiturates enhance it.

References

Bignami, G., & Gatti, G. L. (1966), 'Neurotoxicity of anticholinesterase agents: antagonistic action of various centrally acting drugs'. In *Proceedings of the European Society for the Study of Drug Toxicity.* Vol. III, *Neurotoxicity of Drugs.* Prague.

Bradley, P. H. (1968), 'The pharmacology of synapses in the central nervous system.' In Robson, J. M., & Stacey, R. S. (eds), *Recent Advances in Pharmacology.* London: Churchill.

Clark, W. G., & del Guidice, J. (1970), *Principles of Psychopharmacology.* London: Academic Press.

Crossland, J. (1967), 'Psychotropic drugs and neurohumoral substances in the central nervous system'. In Ellis, G. P., & West, G. B. (eds), *Progress in Medicinal Chemistry.* Vol. 5, London: Butterworths.

Cox, T., & Tye, N. (1973), 'Effects of physostigmine on the acquisition of a position discrimination in rats'. *Neuropharmacology, 12,* 477-84.

Cox, T., & Tye, N. (1974), 'Effects of physostigmine on the maintenance of discrimination behaviour in rats'. *Neuropharmacology, 13,* 205-10.

Fisher, S. (1970), 'Nonspecific factors as determinants of behavioural response to drugs'. In DiMascio, A., & Shader, R. I. (eds), *Clinical Handbook of Psychopharmacology.* New York: Science House.

Hines, G., Lee, A. E., & Miller, W. T. (1970), 'Effect of atropine dose level on the suppression of water-reinforced VI responding'. *Psychonomic Science, 20,* 37-8.

Kelleher, R. T., & Morse, W. H. (1968), 'Determinants of the specificity of behavioural effects of drugs'. *Ergeb. Physiol. Biol. Chem. Exp. Pharmak., 60,* 1-56.

Warburton, D. M. (1969), 'Behavioural effects of central and peripheral changes in acetylcholine systems'. *J. Comp. Physiol. Psychol., 68,* 56-64.

Recommended further reading

Claridge, G. (1970), *Drugs and Human Behaviour*. Harmondsworth: Penguin Books.

Crossland, J. (1970), *Lewis's Pharmacology*. London: E. & S. Livingstone.

Rech, R. H., & Moore, K. E. (1971), *An Introduction to Psychopharmacology*. New York: Raven Press.

Thompson, T., & Schuster, C. R. (1968), *Behavioural Pharmacology*. New Jersey: Prentice-Hall.

12

Parapsychology

A. Gauld

'Parapsychology' is a term for which it is very difficult to find a satisfactory definition. Dr John Beloff, a leading British parapsychologist, calls it 'the scientific study of the paranormal', but this merely raises the question of what is meant by 'the paranormal'. Professor J. B. Rhine, the pioneer American parapsychologist, defines parapsychology as 'a division of psychology dealing with behavioural or personal effects that are demonstrably nonphysical', while an older, roughly equivalent, term is 'psychical research'. The British Society for Psychical Research (the 'SPR') states that its purpose is 'to examine without prejudice or prepossession and in a scientific spirit those faculties of man, real or supposed, which appear to be inexplicable on any generally recognised hypothesis'. But since there are a good many 'faculties of man' on whose proper explanation psychologists are unable to agree, this definition, if interpreted too strictly, would be liable to bring a good part of 'psychology' into 'parapsychology'. However, it does have the merit of making clear, in retrospect, why certain phenomena have been classed together under the heading of 'parapsychology' or of 'psychical research'.

During the early and middle years of the nineteenth century the 'Mesmeric' movement spread rapidly across Europe and America, and in its wake came numerous, and often startling, reports of the novel faculties which certain persons might allegedly display whilst under the mesmeric or, as we should now say, hypnotic influence. These faculties included 'clairvoyance' (the 'seeing' of distant scenes or events), thought-transference (later called 'telepathy') and 'precognition' (clairvoyant or telepathic apprehension of future events). In the second half of the nineteenth century the Mesmeric movement was succeeded, and to a considerable extent absorbed, by the Spiritualist movement. 'Mesmeric clairvoyance' was extended to include ostensible perception of the spirits of deceased persons, and the 'mesmeric trance', in which subjects were obedient to the commands of the mesmerist, developed into the 'mediumistic trance', in which they seemed to fall under the influence of departed spirits. The spirits were also said to 'communicate' or make their presences known by raps and object-movement of a kind very similar to those alleged to occur in 'poltergeist' cases. The raps and so on were supposed to occur chiefly in the presence of persons ('physical mediums') whose organisms were somehow able to supply the energy requisite for the phenomena. In addition to taking over and enlarging upon the principal phenomena of Mesmerism, Spiritualism formed a natural soil for stories of poltergeists, portentous dreams, monitions, doubles, death-wraiths and so forth, stories of kinds which had always been noised abroad but which now gained a fresh currency.

The period in which reports of these various kinds of odd happenings were circulating widely was also a period in which physical science was advancing rapidly. By the 1870s many people had come to think that a full account of the behaviour of material objects could be given in terms of the masses, motions and interactions of minute, billiard-ball-like atoms, and that the phenomena of life and of mind would shortly yield to a similar analysis. Within the framework of this somewhat cocksure 'materialist synthesis' there could be no place for such alleged human faculties as clairvoyance, telepathy and precognition, and still less for the contacts with another world claimed by Spiritualist mediums. Thus in the 1880s, when the SPR and its American equivalent, the ASPR, were founded, there was, on the one hand, an established or almost established framework of scientific thinking and, on the other hand, a body of ostensible evidence for phenomena or 'human faculties' which that framework could not accommodate. It was the aim of the founders of these societies to sift the evidence for the outlawed phenomena (often no doubt in the hope of overthrowing the 'materialist synthesis'), and these phenomena have remained the central study of parapsychologists, even though the framework of thought which proscribed them has been much modified since the nineteenth century.

Parapsychology and testimony

In the field of parapsychology one inevitably and at every turn runs upon psychological problems relating to the trustworthiness of evidence. This is mainly because it is not often possible to repeat the alleged phenomena to order. Someone who wants to convince others that parapsychological phenomena really take place cannot simply set up some standard situation or experiment and say 'look and see'. He has to build his case upon the testimony of persons who claim to have met poltergeists, seen ghosts, had premonitions, experienced telepathy and so on, and upon the reports of the rather limited number of workers who have obtained positive results in laboratory experiments on telepathy and clairvoyance. Now there is some psychological evidence that witnesses of exciting events are liable in retrospect to forget, or confuse, vitally important details. The mistakes are commonly such as to distort the witnesses' accounts in the direction of their preconceived notions. How much greater may the distortions be when the event concerned is one so bizarre as, for example, the appearance of a ghost! Before one could unreservedly accept the testimony of the witnesses of such an event, one would need to be assured as to their intelligence and general integrity, to have their signed testimony (preferably written down immediately after the occurrence described), to have separate concordant statements from a number of witnesses, and so on and so forth. These conditions are sometimes, but not frequently, fulfilled. Even reports of apparently successful laboratory demonstrations of telepathy and clairvoyance require careful scrutiny. One needs to be sure that an overenthusiastic experimenter has not misrecorded the results in such a way as to exaggerate their significance, that the experimental subjects did not achieve their successes by picking up small sensory clues or by the practice of deceit, and so on. These dangers can be guarded against in various ways, for instance by the use of electronic machinery in the running of the experiment and the recording of results.

It will be possible to discuss only a few of the kinds of parapsychological phenomena for which it is alleged that we have satisfactory evidence.

Apparitions

Stories of apparitions have been widespread in most cultures and in most periods of history, and our own are no exception. However, a distinction must be made between the dramatic and terrifying ghosts of folk lore and legend, and the ghosts of which, mainly through the efforts of the SPR and kindred societies, we have first-hand accounts from seemingly trustworthy witnesses. 'Real' ghosts tend (with some exceptions) to look and behave much like ordinary persons, except that they vanish inexplicably, sometimes through walls in the traditional manner. It has been remarked that a collection of 'real' ghost stories is more likely to provoke sleep in the reading than to banish it afterwards.

The popular idea of ghosts is that they are the spirits of deceased persons. However, this supposition faces obvious difficulties, not the least of which is that the 'deceased persons' commonly appear clad in the very same clothes which they wore in life, and the spirit of a pair of trousers is an impossible conception. Psychologists who have subjected first-hand accounts of ghosts to detailed study usually assert that figures and clothes are alike hallucinatory, that they exist only in the minds of the people who see them. This is borne out by the fact that they leave no physical traces behind them. Sometimes an apparition is seen to wreak physical effects on its surroundings—it may, for instance, open a locked door—but such effects are generally found to have been part of the hallucinatory drama—the door has remained closed and locked all the while.

Ghosts—visible apparitions—thus emerge as hallucinations of the sense of sight. And, of course, there are comparable hallucinations of the sense of hearing. Voices, cries, even music, may be heard for which no external physical cause can be discovered. Sometimes the senses of sight and of hearing may be conjointly hallucinated, and a visible phantasm may speak or its footsteps be heard. In rare cases the senses of sight, hearing and touch may all be affected.

To say that ghosts are hallucinations is, however, to oversimplify. For sometimes the hallucinations may correspond to external events in a way for which it is hard to find an ordinary explanation. There are, for instance, many first-hand accounts of 'crisis' apparitions—recognised hallucinations which closely correspond in time to a crisis (usually death) in the affairs of the person whom the hallucinatory figure represents. Again, there are on record a number of cases in which an apparition has been simultaneously perceived in the same place by several different witnesses. The experiences of the witnesses correspond, and the hallucination is, as it were, shared. Somewhat similar are cases of 'haunting' apparitions, in which the same figure is seen in the same locality on a number of different occasions.

It is impossible here to go into the problems raised by all these classes of apparently 'veridical' hallucinations. A few remarks concerning the largest class, that of 'crisis' apparitions, will have to suffice. An intensive study of crisis apparitions was undertaken in the later part of the nineteenth century by an exceptionally able British psychologist, Edmund Gurney (Gurney, Myers and Podmore, 1886). Gurney attempted, first, to disprove a certain obvious explanation of crisis apparitions and, secondly, to provide an alternative explanation of his own.

The explanation which Gurney attempted to disprove is as follows. Let us suppose that hallucinations of recognised persons or of recognised voices are commoner among sane persons than has hitherto been supposed. Then we can expect that from time to time one of these hallucinations will just by chance more or less coincide with the death of the person recognised. Now people will tend to remember and talk about the hallucinations which coincide with deaths or other external circumstances; but they will tend to forget and to keep silent about hallucinations which do not. Hence stories of 'crisis' apparitions will gain currency.

In order to assess this explanation Gurney instigated a 'Census of Hallucinations' which was carried further by a group of his colleagues after his premature death (Sidgwick *et al.*, 1894). Seventeen thousand persons were asked whether they had ever experienced a visual or auditory hallucination. Just under 1700 replied that they had. These 1700 persons had between them had roughly 350 recognised visual hallucinations of persons known to them. Some 80 of these coincided within twelve hours either way with the deaths of the persons recognised. However, when cases which were evidentially unsatisfactory or in which the percipient might have had good reason to anticipate the death were removed, this number was reduced to 32. The Census Committee made certain allowances for the fact that people were obviously more prone to forget non-coincidental hallucinations than to forget ones which coincided with deaths, and concluded that overall 1 recognised visual hallucination in every 43 was a death-coincidence. A calculation based upon the death-rate for that period suggested that only 1 such hallucination in 19 000 should be a death-coincidence. The actual figures exceeded the predicted ones by a factor of 440.

Although the methods by which the Census was conducted and its returns evaluated would today be regarded as antiquated and unsatisfactory, it is hard to explain the results away, and they pose a considerable puzzle. Gurney had his own answer to the puzzle, namely that 'crisis' apparitions are to be regarded as telepathically induced hallucinations. The percipient becomes at some, probably subconscious, level of his personality telepathically aware of the dying person's situation, and this information, for reasons which we do not wholly understand, finds its way into the percipient's ordinary consciousness in the form of an hallucination, the details of which he has himself constructed. Gurney endeavoured to support this view (a) by showing that there is adequate experimental and anecdotal evidence that telepathy does occur, and (b) by demonstrating that 'crisis' apparitions fall at the end of an unbroken series of instances of 'spontaneous' telepathy, a series in which vivid mental images, sudden inexplicable emotions or impulses to action, or dreams, may be the vehicles of the information received.

Extra-sensory perception

Is the evidence for telepathy satisfactory? Many people would say that it is not. Certainly the early experiments left a great deal to be desired. To begin with, even if the results are accepted as indicating the operation of some paranormal factor, it does not follow that the factor involved must have been telepathy. If, for instance (as in so many of the early experiments on telepathy), a 'percipient' successfully reproduces a drawing upon which an 'agent' (the person 'transmitting') is concentrating, it by no means follows that the percipient's mind has been in extra-sensory contact with the agent's. The percipient may have had some kind of direct extra-sensory awareness of the target drawing ('clairvoyance'). The early experimenters, however, for the most part found telepathy a more philosophically acceptable notion than clairvoyance:

> Star to star vibrates light; may soul to soul
> Strike thro' some finer element of her own?

and were inclined to disregard the possibility of clairvoyance. It is, in fact, far from easy to devise experimental set-ups which will in principle demonstrate 'pure' telepathy or 'pure' clairvoyance, especially if, as seems inescapable, the possibility of 'precognition' is also admitted. For this reason it is nowadays customary to use the neutral term 'extra-sensory perception' (ESP) to cover all apparent instances of the extra-sensory acquisition of factual information.

Another defect of the early experiments on telepathy was the widespread tendency of the experimenters to choose the 'targets' (the objects, pictures, etc. on which the agents concentrate) in a more or less haphazard manner. A drawing would be made, or an object selected, simply on the spur of the moment. When such conditions obtain it is extremely difficult to be sure that a successful 'guess' by the percipient is not due simply to his sharing certain habits of mind with the experimenters. Again, many of the early experiments were carried out with percipient and agent/experimenters directly confronting one another, a circumstance which might lead to the percipient picking up all kinds of small sensory clues unintentionally given by the agents.

A pioneer in the attempt to apply modern techniques of experimental design and statistical assessment in the conduct of experiments on ESP has been J. B. Rhine, for many years associate professor of psychology at Duke University, North Carolina. Rhine's experiments (Rhine, 1935) set a pattern which has been followed by many other experimenters in the field. As 'targets' in his experiments Rhine used cards—the so-called 'Zener' cards—on which were printed one of five kinds of geometrical symbols: circle, cross, square, wavy lines and star. These cards were made up into packs of twenty-five, containing five of each kind of card. When the order of presentation of the cards is randomised, the 'percipient' has obviously a 1 in 5 chance of correctly guessing each 'target' card. It is very easy to calculate the odds against any given score or sequence of scores being due to chance. In the early 1930s Rhine and his colleagues discovered a number of high-scoring subjects. One of them, a theological student named Hubert Pearce, averaged nine right in each of 30 runs of 25 guesses (odds against chance

100 000 000 000 to 1). During the experiments Pearce was 100 yards away from the experimenter/agent, Rhine's associate J. G. Pratt, who was in a separate building. In England in the late 1930s and early 1940s, Dr S. G. Soal worked with two subjects, Basil Shackleton and Mrs Gloria Stewart, whose scores exceeded chance expectation by even greater amounts.

A recent development has been the use of sophisticated electronic apparatus to present targets in a random sequence and to record subjects' guesses. In 1969 Dr Helmut Schmidt, an American physicist, published the results of some experiments on precognition which were carried out utilising such a machine (Schmidt, 1969). Schmidt's machine had four electric lamps of different colours, with corresponding buttons for each one. The subject's task was to guess which lamp would light next. Subjects made their guesses by pressing the appropriate button. This caused one of the lamps to light. Which lamp lit was determined by an electronic switch which 'changed position' a million times every second. No one could possibly stop such a switch so as to select a desired lamp. But as an additional safeguard Schmidt introduced a brief delay between the pressing of the button and the closing of the switch. The precise length of the delay was determined by the rate of decay of a piece of radioactive strontium-90—a randomly variable process. If the subject guessed correctly a 'hit' was registered.

Schmidt selected as subjects a number of persons who believed themselves to possess 'psychic gifts'. In an experiment with three subjects who each made rather over 20 000 guesses, the odds against chance exceeded 500 000 000 to 1. In a second experiment, in which four subjects were required to pick not which lamp would light but a lamp which would *not* light, the odds against chance exceeded 10 000 000 000 to 1. Schmidt and others have done further experiments utilising electronic machinery, and in the last few years a number of apparently successful experiments have been done on ESP in animals in which the experimental procedure has been entirely carried out by machine (Randall, 1972).

It will be observed that the case for ESP rests heavily on the outstanding performances of a relatively small number of gifted subjects. Many attempts have been made to hit upon some repeatable method of inducing above-chance scoring in ordinary people. Hypnosis, drugs, meditational techniques and methods of training persons to control their own brain rhythms have all been tried out. Promising results have occasionally been obtained, but so far the elusive 'breakthrough' has not taken place. It is noteworthy that the extraordinary successes reported by the mesmerists and early hypnotists have not been repeated in more recent times.

Seers, shamans and spirit mediums

Who are the 'gifted subjects' just referred to? Standard personality tests have been used in attempts to build up a 'personality profile' of the gifted subjects; but these attempts have not led to any very consistent or impressive results. The best way to find a high-scoring subject is still to seek people who fancy that they have 'the gift'. Of course, in many, perhaps most, societies, including our own, there are persons who are in effect professional 'psychics' or 'sensitives'. Their ranks include the 'oracles' of the ancient world, the shamans or medicine men of North America and Siberia, the witchdoctors of Africa, and our own 'cunning men', fortune tellers and spirit mediums. Such persons frequently enter a state of dissociation, trance or emotional uplift before exhibiting their gifts, and while in this state may assume the personality, or come under the influence, of a god, ancestral spirit, deceased person or extra-terrestrial being. Unfortunately, anthropologists have by and large shown little interest in the question of whether or not shamans have in fact the gifts which their admiring followers attribute to them. In the 1950s R. and L. Rose administered some standard ESP tests to Australian Aboriginal witchdoctors with statistically significant results (Rose, 1956). In our society such tests have sometimes been applied to spirit mediums. The results have for the most part not been exciting. A number of quite intensive investigations have, however, been conducted into spirit mediums in the exercise of their craft. The American trance medium Mrs Leonora E. Piper (1857–1950) and the British Mrs Gladys Osborne Leonard (1882–1968) were studied exhaustively over lengthy periods of years by prominent members of the SPR and the ASPR. The conclusion was reached that, while speaking or writing in the characters of deceased friends and relations of people present, both these ladies exhibited far more knowledge of the concerns of those deceased persons than they could have acquired by ordinary means. It must be borne in mind that the sitters were brought to the mediums at the discretion of the investigators, that they were introduced under pseudonyms, and so on and so forth. In Mrs Leonard's case, many seemingly successful 'proxy' sittings were held; that is to say, sittings in which the sitter acted on behalf of an absent third party of whose concerns he knew little or nothing.

Another class of 'gifted subject' is that of the person in whose presence inexplicable physical occurrences (especially rappings and the disturbance of small objects) are alleged to take place. This has been said to happen with certain shamans and mediums, but the best-known instances are perhaps those associated with 'poltergeist children'. Some remarkable poltergeist cases have recently been studied in Scotland by Dr A. R. G. Owen, in Germany by Dr H. Bender and in the United States by Mr W. G. Roll (Owen, 1964; Roll, 1972).

Parapsychology and psychology

Suppose that, for the sake of argument, one accepts that there is at least *prima facie* evidence for the genuineness of some of the sorts of phenomena studied by parapsychologists. Then the question naturally arises whether the findings of parapsychology can be accommodated within, or at least illuminated by, any theoretical framework so far developed by psychologists.

It is difficult to give a firm answer. Attempts have been made to treat some of the phenomena, and especially telepathy, in terms of 'communications theory', and to develop 'wireless' theories of thought-transference. It cannot be said that any of these attempts have been very successful. The most widely adopted general framework for thinking and talking about the phenomena of parapsychology is one derived from psychopathology. It is held that such 'faculties' as ESP characterise some unconscious or 'subliminal' level of the personality, a level which is thought by some to manifest itself in the production of hysterical and neurotic symptoms and other behavioural abnormalities. The reasons why this view has so often been found plausible seem to be these. First, many spontaneous examples of ostensible ESP—for instance, ESP occurring in the form of 'crisis' hallucinations, dreams and speaking or writing in trance—characteristically 'intrude' upon the subject's ordinary stream of consciousness and are outside his control. This seems also to be true of the peculiar physical phenomena which take place in the vicinity of so-called 'poltergeist' children. Similarly, successful subjects in ESP experiments commonly report that their guesses are made 'automatically' and without any conscious endeavour to summon up appropriate images, etc. Secondly, spontaneous cases of ostensible ESP frequently exhibit what might be described as a 'symbolic' quality. For example (to take some actual cases), in crisis apparitions the phantasmal figure may be seen as accompanied by a hearse or by Jesus Christ, or it may float off heavenwards like Mary Poppins. Now it has frequently been claimed by psychopathologists of certain schools that material in the unconscious mind can percolate into the conscious mind only by assuming some kind of symbolic disguise. Accordingly, when we find material whose form is obviously symbolic breaking into consciousness, we may infer that it has welled up from the unconscious.

In the light of speculations such as these, the 'gifted' ESP subject emerges as someone in whom the border between the conscious and the unconscious is more permeable or more shifting than it is with most of us. Whether explanations of parapsychological, or psychopathological, phenomena in terms of the working of an 'unconscious mind' or 'subliminal self' have value, or indeed logical coherence, is too considerable an issue to be tackled here; but there do seem to be some reasons for linking cases of 'spontaneous' parapsychological phenomena to phenomena often regarded as falling within the provenance of the psychopathologist.

References

Gurney, E., Myers, F. W. H., & Podmore, F. (1886), *Phantasms of the Living*. (2 vols) London: Trübner.
Owen, A. R. G. (1964), *Can We Explain the Poltergeist?* New York: Helix Press.
Randall, J. L. (1972), 'Recent experiments in animal parapsychology'. *J. Soc. Psychical Res.*, *46*, 124-34.
Rhine, J. B. (1935), *Extra-sensory Perception*. London: Faber & Faber.
Roll, W. G. (1972), *The Poltergeist*. Garden City, New York: Nelson Doubleday.
Rose, R. (1956), *Living Magic*. New York: Rand McNally.
Schmidt, H. (1969), 'Precognition of a quantum process'. *J. Parapsych.*, *33*, 99-109.
Sidgwick, H., *et al.* (1894), 'Report on the census of hallucinations'. *Proc. Soc. Psychical Res.*, *10*, 25-422.

Recommended further reading

Heywood, R. (1971), *The Sixth Sense*. London: Pan Books.
Thouless, R. H. (1972), *From Anecdote to Experiment in Psychical Research*. London: Routledge & Kegan Paul.
West, D. J. (1962), *Psychical Research Today*. Harmondsworth: Penguin Books.

13
Educational Psychology
W. E. C. Gillham

The *Journal of Child Study* for February 1913 included the following item in its Editorial Notes: 'After the school doctor comes the school psychologist, and both have come very much too late and very inadequately. The London County Council have appointed Mr Cyril Burt, MA, as school psychologist. This is excellent; other education authorities will please copy. Unfortunately Mr Burt is only to be a half-timer. There is work enough for several full-timers.'

It was, in fact, not until 1931 that the next psychologist was appointed by a local education authority—the City of Leicester. In 1932 the first LEA Child Guidance Clinic—consisting of psychologist, psychiatrist and psychiatric social worker—was established in Birmingham, and by the time war broke out in 1939 there were twenty-two such clinics; by the end of the war the number had risen to seventy-nine. At that time the typical organisation was that of the Child Guidance Clinic team headed by a medical director (a psychiatrist), who had case responsibility and took the major diagnostic role; the educational psychologist, whose main work was with children in schools or administering tests supplementary to the clinical 'diagnosis' of the psychiatrist; and the psychiatric social worker, whose responsibility it was to obtain a background case-history from the parents and sometimes to do 'case-work'—verbal therapy aimed at increasing insight into problem relationships. This pattern, American in origin, was introduced into this country in the late 1920s under the auspices of the New Commonwealth Fund of America. Although abandoned in its country of origin, this organisation is still the formal reality in England and Wales, although informally there are wide variations—a function of individual personalities and attitudes as much as local traditions. During the past twenty years, however, there have been major changes in the status and role of psychologists, in part due to their great increase in numbers not paralleled by a comparable increase in the number of psychiatrists and social workers.

Up to the beginning of the 1950s educational psychology was predominantly a woman's profession, but starting with the increased number of male entrants to the profession after the war this has now changed. At the time of writing (1973) approximately three-quarters of the 600 or so educational psychologists in England and Wales are men.

The typical, but by no means universal, organisation of services is as follows. Educational psychologists are appointed by the LEA and are expected to divide their services between the Child Guidance Unit, where they are a member of the 'team', and the School Psychological Service, which is headed by the Senior Educational Psychologist. Both services are primarily concerned with children of school age, but there has always been some work with pre-school children and this is increasing. The psychiatrist is appointed by the Regional Hospital Board (soon to become the Area Health Board) and the psychiatric social worker—now known just as a 'social worker'—by the Social Services Department. An unusual and, unfortunately, little-known feature of both services is that referral is 'open', i.e. parents can refer their children directly without going through a doctor, headteacher or other professional worker. As a general rule, medical referrals go to the Child Guidance Unit and referrals from educational agencies to the School Psychological Service, but this is not always the case and, since the CGU and the SPS are usually housed together and share common secretarial and administrative facilities, which service deals with which referral is often decided after it has been received and appraised. The range of problems referred is as wide as the concerns of the adults making the referrals—in other words, referral depends upon the recognition of a problem and the feeling of a need for help. Typical problems referred might be, for example: a ten-year-old boy who seems very intelligent but has great difficulty in reading; a seven-year-old girl who stammers and wets the bed; a three-year-old who does not seem deaf but has not begun to talk; an adolescent girl, doing well at school, who suddenly refuses to attend and panics when her parents try to force her to do so; and so on.

Attempting to help with problems which can cause so much unhappiness is obviously an important professional service, and the significance of the work being done by psychologists employed by LEAs was marked by the publication in 1968 of the report of a working party which had been set up by the Secretary of State for Education and Science to consider the nature and development of their service. This report, entitled *Psychologists in Education Services* but generally known as the Summerfield Report after the Chairman of the Working Party, Professor Arthur Summerfield, has been a major policy document in determining the growth of LEA services.

The independent development of psychological services is largely due to the fact that educational psychologists have felt constricted in a role just as a member of a child guidance team. The compartmentalisation of the 'team's' roles in dealing with children's problems has often meant that action is slow and cumbersome—a common complaint about child guidance services. In addition, working with a colleague who, being medically qualified, has been assigned the direction of the team has necessarily meant the psychologist having dependent status. This liaison with a profession noted for its hierarchical structure and its autocratic traditions and practice has only rarely been a happy one and more usually an uneasy compromise on both sides. In Scotland, in marked contrast, the Child Guidance Service consists entirely of educational psychologists who have little contact with psychiatrists. Scottish educational psychologists are, in effect, specially trained teachers and their identification is very much with teachers and the education service.

A definition of educational psychology—as an area of study and as a clinical occupation—presents difficulties because any generalisation is easily controverted. Certainly educational psychology as practised in Scotland is different, as a general rule, from educational psychology in England and Wales, although some psychologists working south of the border see themselves—and are seen—in an identical role to their Scottish counterparts. But it is also common for educational psychologists in England and Wales to be engaged in the investigation and treatment of psychologically disturbed behaviour, whether at home or at school.

In the United States school psychologists work independently of psychiatrists and exclusively in the field of education, and this is reflected in their conception of educational psychology as a subject of study. A recent American text on the subject (Travers, 1973) is subtitled 'A scientific foundation for educational practice'. Another American author (Ausubel, 1968) defines educational psychology as being 'primarily concerned with the nature, conditions, outcomes, and evaluation of class-room learning'. Lovell (1973), in a standard English text on the subject, defines educational psychology as 'the laws and principles learned in general psychology ... applied to all manner of problems in the education and upbringing of children'—a much wider definition.

The current content of any professional practice or academic discipline is obviously an outcome of an evolutionary, historical process. As might be inferred from the quotation in the opening paragraph of this chapter, the need for specialist help to deal with children's problems followed on from the establishment of compulsory elementary education. Compulsory school attendance was of more than educational significance: it meant that children of all social classes were subjected to the detailed and regular scrutiny of members of the socially conscious middle class, and the defects of health and development which became apparent led society into a wider consideration of the welfare of children.

In Paris, at the beginning of this century, the education authorities became concerned about the special needs of those children who were, or appeared, intellectually retarded; they engaged the services of a scientist, Alfrède Binet, who was interested in the more systematic appraisal of human abilities, particularly in relation to the clinical assessment of what was then called 'mental deficiency'. In conjunction with a colleague, Théophile Simon, and over a period of some years before the First World War, he developed an individual test of general ability, or 'intelligence', and was able to demonstrate that the typical clinical assessment of mental deficiency was extremely unreliable. The Binet–Simon test was being developed at a time when social and educational concern about individual differences was increasing and when technical and theoretical developments in psychology and related disciplines were geared for a rapid advance in the scientific measurement of mental abilities. An American version of Binet's test, with norms for the American population, was published in 1916 and entitled the Stanford–Binet, having been developed at the University of Stanford by Lewis Terman. An English translation was produced by Burt in this country and included in his comprehensive book *Mental and Scholastic Tests* published in 1921. The twenties and thirties were the heyday of the mental testing movement and its diminution has been slow because many psychologists concerned with individual differences, particularly educational psychologists, came to see themselves—and to be seen—as applied scientists whose reputation for this claim rested upon the use of standardised tests. Having made their bed in this fashion, it is hardly surprising that others expected them to lie on it.

Although the establishment of psychological services is not a statutory obligation for local authorities, the provisions for the ascertainment of children in need of special education included in the 1944 Education Act served to perpetuate the role of educational psychologist as tester (recall that Binet's tests were originally designed for such a purpose). And professional colleagues in other roles and disciplines saw security in their own tenure by the encouragement of the psychologist in the performance of this function.

Doubts about the value of the concept of intelligence—and mounting evidence about the very modest predictive power of intelligence tests (e.g. Nisbet and Buchan, 1959)—combined with the uncertain value of special schools (Presland, 1971), have served to make educational psychologists increasingly intolerant of such restriction. Yet if 'mental testing' has not kept pace with professional needs and theoretical and experimental advances in the study of learning, understanding and problem-solving behaviour, in its time the systematic assessment of abilities was an exciting, even momentous advance. Consider, for example, this quotation from a paper published by Binet and Simon in 1908: 'During the past year one of us examined twenty-five children who for various reasons had been admitted to Sainte-Anne and later confined at the Bicêtre, at Salpetrière, or at other places. We applied the procedure of our measuring scale to all these children, and thus proved that three of them were at-age in intelligence, and two others were a year advanced beyond the average.' Such discoveries have the quality of a revelation, and since intelligence was regarded at that time as innate mental ability—a relatively unchanging commodity which determined the capacity for attainment in other areas, particularly the subjects taught in schools—this was seen as a discovery of the first importance. But if tests 'saved' those who achieved high enough scores, correspondingly it condemned those who failed to do so. Such a view of intelligence and intelligence tests was widely taught in this country by educational psychologists of great influence—for example, Burt, Schonell and Alexander—and remains influential, although discredited for many years (Crane, 1959). We now recognise that inferences about a hypothetical general ability derived from a given set of performances can be a very doubtful procedure because of the *variety* of factors influencing that performance; and in so far as it is reasonable to talk about a general intellectual ability, we have also come to recognise that it is essentially an attainment (Vernon, 1970)—influenced by all the factors (including *teaching*) that influence other attainments. We are also aware of what Mittler (1973) has called 'the failure of the intelligence test to provide information which can be positively harnessed to the design of a programme of education and habilitation'. Mittler is particularly referring to that group of children who are sometimes known as 'severely subnormal'. This group, which has only recently (1971) become the responsibility of LEAs, has highlighted the need for techniques of assessment which are specific in their guidance as to remediation needs. This very practical trend is allied to the increasing concern in developmental psychology to place the description and evaluation of children's behaviour in the context of a natural environmental setting—the ethological approach. Some teachers and parents have, for a long time, complained that the educational psychologist, seeing the child in an alien setting (e.g. a clinic or an interview room in a school) and giving him tests of unfamiliar materials according to a 'standardised' and inflexible procedure, was not seeing the child they knew. Talking about the psychologist's contribution to education, Ausubel (1968) comments on 'the serious decline in knowledge and theorising about school learning that has taken place over the past half-century, accompanied by the steady retreat of educational psychologists from the classroom'. This failure to work (and theorise) alongside teachers is surpassed by the failure to work with parents; when it *is* considered, which is rarely, it tends to be dismissed because they are not 'professionals' or because they are too 'emotionally involved'; these may be valid reasons sometimes but not as often as they are invoked. Furthermore, parents' motivation and availability may be greater than a professional worker's could be—and in particular situations, and with specific guidance, of comparable technical competence.

The traditional pattern of training and experience for a career in educational psychology is a long and somewhat arduous one.

The Summerfield Report says: 'An educational psychologist who is taking up a first appointment at the present time is commonly expected to have the following qualifications: (a) an honours degree in psychology (or an equivalent qualification in psychology); (b) postgraduate training in educational psychology; (c) experience of teaching in schools extending over three years (in which a year spent in teacher training may be included).' These are, in fact, the minimum requirements for membership of the Association of Educational Psychologists—the professional body representing psychologists employed by LEAs. Apart from the fact that a significant minority of practising educational psychologists has little or no teaching experience (20% having one year or less in 1965, according to the Summerfield Report), the usefulness of teaching experience is by no means generally accepted and was, in fact, challenged by the authors of the Summerfield Report. The real value of the psychologist's contribution may be that he sees things differently and so is able to add something, in terms of understanding or practice. Seth (1972) goes so far as to say that 'long-continued "ordinary" teaching is for the psychologist counter-productive, likely to be harmful rather than beneficial . . . the most "child-centred", activity-biased school has a pedagogic job to do, and the teacher very rapidly acquires the attributes of his special role . . . and these are likely to be constricting in his relationships with children and parents in a different setting.' Whitmore (1972) comments: 'The argument that the psychologist in the education service needs to be a qualified teacher to be accepted by teachers in school is no more than a confession that teachers do not yet appreciate the relevance of psychology to children in school. Doctors don't have to be teachers for medical advice to be accepted!' Whitmore goes on to say, 'In fact, what is really needed is a child psychology service that is competent to provide psychological help to children (including handicapped children) of all ages, *in all situations*' (my italics).

The expansion of services, and the development of specialist competences amongst individual educational psychologists, is clearly going to be the pattern during the next decade. There are several reasons why this is likely to be the case. First, there has been a considerable increase in the number of educational psychologists, and this rate of increase is accelerating as new training courses are established in universities and elsewhere and as existing courses take on more students. At the time the Summerfield Report collected its data in 1965 there were 326 educational psychologists in England and Wales (or the equivalent in full-time terms); by January 1971 this had risen to 500, and at the time of writing (1973) the number is probably in the region of 650, with approximately 90 to 100 intending entrants to the profession in postgraduate training (mostly on one-year courses). Secondly, the reorganisation of local authorities in April 1974 means that services will be fewer in number but increased in staff establishment as part of the 'redesigning' and development that the new LEAs will have to implement. Thirdly, there are the new and sometimes rather different demands which are being, and will be, made on psychological services: for example, the needs of Social Service Departments (in themselves, developing services); the expansion of nursery education; the greater responsibility for the mentally handicapped; and the reorganisation of health services—with the School Health Service moving from the Education Department to the new Area Health Boards. (At the present moment School Medical Officers do a great deal of the work involved in the ascertainment of children in need of special educational treatment.)

To move from looking towards the future to looking into the past: it is clear that the heavy workload and the small size of many services have impeded development and have appeared to limit the work of psychologists to an often cursory examination of those children who are in manifest difficulties. As Westland (1970) says, 'the picture (is) of an educational psychologist as a specialised clinical psychologist, whose function is to treat problem cases—that is, he is concerned with the educationally abnormal, with the things that go wrong, rather than with the optimal functioning of the normal processes of educational learning.' Since the psychologist's workload is determined by the referrals he receives, and since it is tempting for teachers and others to regard problem children as the psychologist's responsibility, the situation can easily arise where he is continually battling with a waiting list of individual 'cases' when the main solution, if there is one, may be in influencing educational policy, school organisation, the attitudes and practice of teachers, or the patterns of child-rearing in the home. For example, it is possible to see children's failure to learn to read as the child's learning failure or learning disability—a 'case' which has to be 'diagnosed' and 'remediated'; but many of the problems thus thrown up are likely to be due to the priority given to reading in the curriculum or the competence of the teaching the children have received. Tackling this sort of general problem at the individual level can be futile. Todd (1973) demonstrates a more general approach to the problem which has been effective. As psychologist in charge of the Leicestershire SPS he was concerned about the large number of reading failures referred, and in 1969 initiated a survey of reading attainment in the County at 11+, sampling one-third of the age group.* Having demonstrated the extent of the problem, with the support of his colleagues he developed courses for teachers and a remedial advisory service with the following discernible effect on reading attainment (Table 13.1):

Year	% below reading age 7 yrs	% below reading age 9 yrs	% below reading age 11 yrs
1969	4.7	18.6	39.0
1971	3.5	15.4	36.7
1973	3.2	14.4	36.5

Table 13.1 Percentages of children below the reading age levels indicated at 11+. Total number of children: approximately 2500 for each year. Reading test: Burt (Rearranged) Word Reading Test (1938 norms).

* I am indebted to the Director of Education for Leicestershire, Mr A. N. Fairbairn, for permission to quote these results.

This sort of general influence helps many more children than an educational psychologist could hope to help individually. Indeed, one of the merits of the examination of individual children can be, as in the instance quoted here, to indicate a general situation which needs modifying: action taken along these lines can prevent problems arising—or at least reduce their number or severity. Whitmore (1972) observes, 'the child guidance service is often thought of as a preventive service and it was the dream of the pioneer clinics that they would reduce the incidence of mental disorder in children. This dream has not really come true, for children only make contact with the service when a problem has arisen that their parents and/or teachers cannot manage.' Increasing the number of educational psychologists alone is not going to solve the problem of a queue of children waiting to be seen; waiting for difficulties to occur, and then get out of control before referral, can only perpetuate the situation. There will, of course, always be children who will need specialist, individual help; at the moment this group receives inadequate attention because it has to compete with those groups where problems are symptomatic of wider social or situational factors, or problems that could be dealt with by others. Helping parents and teachers to be their own 'experts'—which they certainly can be—and preparing them so that problems are avoided are roles which the psychologist needs to develop if he is not to continue as a harassed, and relatively impotent, first-aid man, as in many cases he is at the moment. The extent to which parents, teachers and other adults professionally concerned with children can act as therapists or remediators in ways different from their 'normal' role is still largely unexplored territory. In part, of course, this rests upon the philosophy that children's problems are not somebody else's business but the business of every adult in a responsible relationship with children. This is not an anti-expert view but a view which expects the expert to share his knowledge and understanding—and his ignorance and bafflement—and to encourage other adults to contribute accordingly.

Changing those situations which create problems demands a

kind of activity which educational psychologists have engaged in to a negligible extent, namely investigation or *research*. Research is usually seen as a university activity of high status but, in the social sciences particularly, of uncertain value—or at least uncertain relevance to real-life problems. But the massive significance of educational and social services (and their equally massive budgets), the cost of children's problems—in human and economic terms—all point to the need for research into the most effective use of resources, research designed to obtain information as a basis for making rational decisions, and research designed to evaluate the outcome of what has been implemented. Without such data, decisions can only be made on the basis of personal conviction, or information of uncertain interpretation. As a case in point, we have no proof that psychological services actually do any good to the children they see; conversely, we have no proof that they do not. The same applies to many aspects of the developing educational and welfare services; it may be, of course, that many of those engaged in such services are more concerned with their beliefs than with evidence.

Educational psychology is, in various forms, studied, taught and researched in universities. But those engaged in such activities are not usually qualified and experienced as practitioners (unless they are tutors to courses training educational psychologists) and their activities may bear little relationship to the concerns of those who are. It is, perhaps, for this reason that working educational psychologists tend to feel rather cut off from universities and inadequately considered in the latter's scheme of things. However, the increasing interest in applied psychology in university departments and the professed desire on the part of the Research Councils to sponsor socially relevant research may bring about a *rapprochement* which could be mutually beneficial.

In this respect university fears about a reversal of traditional academic priorities are almost certainly unfounded. There is no reason why 'applied' research in educational psychology (or any other branch of applied psychology) should just be of the 'bread-

and-butter' variety. Remedial action taken by psychologists dealing with children in difficulties, the organisation and provision of educational and other services for children—all of these things make assumptions about how children feel, think, react and so on. These assumptions presuppose explanations or *theories* about what determines behaviour; and the validity, or otherwise, of these assumptions is related to the validity, or otherwise, of remedial provision or action. Talking about learning failure, Ausubel (1968) says, 'There is ... a very close relationship between knowing how a pupil learns and the manipulable variables influencing learning, on the one hand, and knowing what to do to help him learn better, on the other.' In other words, to be practical one must understand, and to understand one must theorise—and test out one's theories; such a continuity could be seen as the link between universities and local authorities.

If the need for complementary research seems to be much emphasised, it is because it has been much neglected by university teachers as well as by practising educational psychologists; yet it must be the basis for developing valid psychological services. A very distinguished British psychologist once wrote (Bartlett, 1950), 'I know of no practical problem of human behaviour whatever to which any genuine solution can be found without fundamental research ...' Bartlett was not talking about 'laboratory' research, but about research concerned with practical problems of living. An awareness of these problems, and a strong desire to help, is a notable characteristic of our times. An effective response to this prompting can only come if we keep in mind, and put into action, the need for the evaluation, or revaluation, of basic assumptions and existing practice.

References

Ausubel, D. P. (1968), *Educational Psychology: A Cognitive View*. New York: Macmillan.
Bartlett, F. C. (1950), 'Challenge to experimental psychology'. In

Proceedings and Papers of the Twelfth International Congress of Psychology, pp. 23-30. Edinburgh: Oliver & Boyd.

Binet, A., & Simon, T. (1908), 'The development of intelligence in the child'. Reprinted in Jenkins, J. J., & Paterson, D. G. (eds) (1961), *Studies in Individual Differences*. New York: Appleton-Century-Crofts.

Burt, C. (1947), *Mental and Scholastic Tests*. (3rd edition) London: Staples Press.

Crane, A. R. (1959), 'An historical and critical account of the accomplishment quotient idea'. *Br. J. Educ. Psychol.*, 29, 1, 252-9.

HMSO (1968), *Psychologists in Education Services* (The Summerfield Report). London.

Lovell, K. (1973), *Educational Psychology and Children*. (11th edition) London: Univ. of London Press.

Mittler, P. (1973), 'Purposes and principles of assessment'. In Mittler, P. (ed.), *Assessment for Learning in the Mentally Handicapped*. Edinburgh & London: Churchill Livingstone.

Nisbet, J., & Buchan, J. (1959), 'The long-term follow-up of assessments at age eleven'. *Brit. J. Educ. Psychol.*, 29, 1, 1-8.

Presland, J. (1970), 'Who should go to ESN schools?' *Spec. Educ.*, 59, 1, 11-16.

Seth, G. (1972), 'Some basic principles of professional training'. *J. Assoc. Educ. Psychol.*, 3, 2, 4-18.

Todd, G. B. (1973), '11+ reading survey in the county of Leicestershire'. *Leicestershire Education Committee*. (Unpublished report.)

Travers, R. M. W. (1973), *Educational Psychology*. New York: Macmillan.

Vernon, P. E. (1970), 'Intelligence'. In Dockrell, W. B. (ed.), *On Intelligence*. London: Methuen.

Westland, G. (1970), 'What is educational psychology?' *J. Assoc. Educ. Psychol.*, 2, 7, 10-14.

Whitmore, T. K. (1972), 'Maladjusted children'. Suppl. to *J. Assoc. Educ. Psychol.*

Recommended further reading

HMSO (1968), *Psychologists in Education Services* (The Summerfield Report). London.

Lovell, K. (1973), *Educational Psychology and Children*. (11th edition) London: Univ. of London Press.

14
Clinical Psychology
D. J. Smail

Now one of the major branches of 'applied' psychology, clinical psychology emerged as a clearly identifiable discipline, and as a profession, shortly after the Second World War. Wartime psychologists had had the chance to bring their theories and, more particularly, their methods to bear on problems like the selection of officers and men, and had learned a good deal about the measurement of relevant mental characteristics such as intelligence, as well as about factors more directly concerned with mental health. Armed with this experience, in addition to that of pre-war British and American psychologists who had had an interest in similar fields, a small number of psychologists became established in the brand-new National Health Service.

At this early stage, the most reasonable slot into which to fit this handful of pioneers seemed to be among the 'paramedical' professions in the general area of psychiatry. These psychologists thus became concerned with clinical problems almost exclusively within the field of mental illness. If psychologists were expecting to play a significant role in the actual treatment of such illness (which they almost certainly were not) they were to be disappointed, since the medical profession had got there first and was well in control of all matters relating to the theoretical formulation of mental health problems, diagnosis and treatment. For those readers unaware of the distinctions involved, it may be as well at this juncture to point out that psychiatrists differ from psychologists quite sharply in terms of background and training: they are medical practitioners with particular experience of mental health problems and with special qualifications, usually in the form of a Diploma in Psychological Medicine. This latter is not to be confused with a degree in psychology, though it does involve a smattering of psychological knowledge.

Academic psychology had, and to an extent still has, tended to steer clear of the gross, practical problems of psychological disorder, and to scorn the activities of those who, like Freud, ventured to handle such phenomena in the name of psychology. In this way Freud's creation, psychoanalysis, has not been accepted as really 'belonging' to academic psychology, where the emphasis on experiment and the step-by-step advancement of scientific knowledge has tended to preclude the kind of sweeping conceptualisation of man offered by the psychoanalysts. One consequence of this was that psychological ideas concerning mental health and illness were for a long time limited to psychoanalysis and its offshoots, and found their home (which, indeed, they had never really left) in the medical profession.

Some broadly psychoanalytic, or 'psychodynamic', ideas (e.g. concerning 'unconscious mental processes') had, however, found their way into psychology via the study of personality. Especially in American psychology, it came to be felt by some research workers that men's attitudes and motivations could not always be understood solely by reference to their conscious verbalisations and overt behaviour, and that ways needed to be found of measuring the contribution of unconscious factors. This led, for instance, to the development of so-called 'projective' techniques in personality measurement. These were psychological tests which aimed at providing a standard stimulus situation (e.g. a picture of people engaged in some kind of activity) to which a subject could respond without being aware that his response might reveal aspects of his own personality and personal problems (e.g. by telling a story about the figures in the picture, the details of which, by the very nature of the situation, he could only provide from 'within' himself). This, then, was one area in which a marriage was possible between Freudian ideas about unconscious influences and experimental psychology's concern with stimulus, response and measurement. How successful the marriage was is another question, and one which will not be developed here.

Thus the early clinical psychologists brought with them a tradition of scientific rigour and scrupulous measurement, a limited tolerance of some concepts on the periphery of psychoanalysis, and some expertise in the field of measurement of cognitive abilities, intelligence and some aspects of personality. As already suggested, had they had any crusading wish to apply their concepts therapeutically, they would no doubt have collided head-on with the medical profession, but as it was they were happy enough to adopt the role of precise scientists, providing, by means of psychological testing, exact and quantifiable data which could be used by their medical colleagues as the latter saw fit.

However, in applying the methodology of experimental psychology in clinical situations, these psychologists really lacked any fundamental conceptual system for their chosen field; they had at their disposal a variety of techniques, but they had to cast around for a framework in which to fit them. In the British National Health Service the most readily available framework was that of medicine, and, not unnaturally, this was the one which clinical psychologists were quick to adopt.

Clinical medicine tends to progress empirically, and certainly this seems to be the case in psychiatry: the methods of diagnosis and treatment which are used are those which, in the experience of the practitioners, appear to *work* and upon which they are as a result generally agreed (this does not, of course, mean that the theories on which they are based, if any, are *true*). The psychologist here sensed a good opportunity to apply his methods of experimental design and sampling, survey and questionnaire techniques, projective and cognitive psychological tests, in order to add a little precision and rigour to the somewhat loose clinical empiricism of psychiatry. Clinical psychology thus concerned itself with developing measures of psychiatric diagnosis and brain functioning, attempting by means of psychological tests to differentiate between patients of various types and to evaluate the success or otherwise of contrasting methods of treatment and therapy. In all this, very little thought was given, until relatively recently, to the question of whether the basic psychiatric concepts in use were themselves appropriate ones. For example, while a lot of time and effort was expended on attempting by means of objective tests to differentiate schizophrenic from non-schizophrenic patients, few psychologists raised the question of whether schizophrenia was a useful concept in the first place. It is only the present generation of clinical psychologists who are beginning to face seriously the possibility that this wholesale acceptance of a medical-psychiatric framework may have been unfortunate.

The first decade or so of clinical psychology in Britain was characterised by preoccupation with one or two quite well defined issues (still by no means resolved today), and the practice of clinical psychology involved reasonably uniform and clearly specifiable activities. First and foremost, the psychologist came to be recognised as a mental tester. By means of intelligence and memory tests, objective and projective personality tests, and specially developed diagnostic inventories, he would provide psychiatrists, at their request, with information which might aid them in reaching a diagnosis or in planning a course of treatment for patients about whom, for one reason or another, they felt uncertain. The psychiatrist's uncertainty might be occasioned by the confusing or mixed nature of the patient's symptoms, or by difficulties in communication, or he might for a variety of reasons wish for a check on, or corroboration of, his opinion. The psychologist would not see patients about whom the psychiatrist felt no such uncertainty nor required any such check. In cases where estimates of intellectual ability were required, the psychologist's role would be a little more positive, as an IQ score tends to give an air of precision to what would otherwise be a rather global judgement of intelligence, and hence psychologists would probably be referred a high percentage of those patients in whose diagnosis, treatment or management intellectual factors seemed to the psychiatrist to play an important role. In this way psychologists found themselves spending a large part of the day, if not all of it, administering a variety of psychological tests to a steady stream of patients referred by medical colleagues. Not surprisingly, the concerns of clinical psychologists at this time were heavily bound up with this testing role, and were reflected in a major controversy which split the clinical camp into two and, indeed, had reverberations in most other branches of the discipline. This was the issue of clinical versus statistical prediction.

Among clinical psychologists there were those who felt that one could not do justice to the individual patient on the grounds of objective psychological tests alone, and that one must take into account also his particular circumstances, the uniqueness of his personality and the clinician's intuitive 'feel' about him. For example, this kind of psychologist would feel unhappy about assigning a patient to the category 'schizophrenia' simply on the grounds of his having achieved a certain pattern of scores on a questionnaire test which had been shown to classify schizophrenics correctly at a level much better than chance. It may be, he might argue, that this questionnaire test correctly identifies 85% (say) of schizophrenic patients, but there may also be special circumstances in the case which the clinician can take account of and the test cannot; the clinician has the added advantage of being able to question the individual, to give him other psychological tests, to enquire into his history and to consider him in the context of long years of clinical experience. Clinical expertise would thus be seen as being more likely to be correct than the blind, probabilistic diagnosis arrived at by the questionnaire. There was probably also a tendency for clinicians such as these to prefer those psychological measuring instruments, such as projective tests, which were based on more 'liberal', or at least humanistic, theories like psychoanalysis rather than the coldly mathematical, actuarial questionnaires which categorised individuals simply on their achieving numerical scores of a kind demonstrably similar to a particular diagnostic group. The opposing camp consisted of the more 'tough-minded' psychologists who had little time for vague notions of clinical skills and intuitions or for loosely formulated and not easily testable conceptualisations derived from psychoanalysis. If clinical psychology was to be scientific, it had to stick to the accepted, disciplined approach from which it developed, and would stand or fall on the ability of objective, statistically based and standardised measures to make accurate and verifiable predictions about patients; the only way this could be done scientifically was to excise as far as possible the subjective influence of the clinician and to compare individuals' test scores with appropriate normative data. Accuracy of prediction must in this case inevitably be a question of probability—nobody could expect *every* patient to be correctly categorised, and any procedure which does better than chance is probably worth considering.

The principal arguments in this dispute can be found in Meehl (1954), whose book *Clinical versus Statistical Prediction* is a classic in clinical psychology. Meehl's findings, and they have not since been rebutted, point quite clearly to the superiority of the statistical approach. On the whole, 'clinically relevant' judgements about patients tend to be more accurate when they are made automatically on the basis of objective actuarial data than when professional experience is allowed free play. Although this controversy is by no means dead, clinical psychology has perhaps moved on to some extent, and the question has become one not so much of which method is better as of whether there is much point in the first place in trying to make 'predictions' of this kind. What is the significance, the modern clinician might ask, of assigning patients to diagnostic categories anyway? It has been argued also that probabilistic judgements are of doubtful usefulness in the clinical situation. Again, new sophistication in the development of psychological measurement, in which mathematical rigour has become associated with devices more subtle than the somewhat stark questionnaire, has perhaps blunted the formerly sharp distinction between what is statistical and what is clinical.

Before we move on to consider further the activities of the present-day clinical psychologist, and to speculate how these may develop in the future, it would be as well to mention one or two other aspects of the early clinician's role.

There is probably little doubt that most clinical psychologists were never entirely happy about getting landed with the job of mental tester. In the first place, once the appropriate tests had been developed, routine administration of them to patients became a somewhat humdrum chore which rarely required the degree of training and skill possessed by even inexperienced clinical psychologists. In the second place, psychologists became aware that they were finding themselves in a rather low status role within the Health Service, and were being used by psychiatrists much as laboratory technicians might be used: a psychological assessment would be requested in the same way and for similar reasons as a urine analysis. And in the third place, it began to dawn on many psychologists that the scientific philosophy of standardised psychological testing was not being supported by results; in other words, the application of rigorous methods to the clinical formulations of psychiatry did not seem to be paying off in terms of ultimate benefit to patients, or even increased scientific understanding of their condition. This last problem we shall return to shortly. The problems of boredom and low status were compensated for partly by an enduring tradition in clinical psychology of research. Since the very beginning it has been widely recognised that clinical psychologists have, by virtue of their training, a special expertise in research methodology, and that a significant proportion of their time may be devoted to the conduct of research into problems either of their own choosing or as part of a co-operative venture with psychiatrists or other interested professionals. In this way clinical psychologists have made research contributions in such areas as mental measurement, diagnostic formulation, treatment effectiveness, symptom formation, character structure, and so on, out of all proportion to their numbers as professionals in the mental health field. They have also provided their fair share of theoretical contributions. It is probably this role more than any other which helped preserve the dignity as well as the fundamental usefulness of clinical psychology during its formative years.

As time progressed it became the ambition of a gradually increasing number of clinical psychologists to become involved in treatment, and in cases where the psychologist had particularly good relations with medical colleagues (who are ultimately responsible for patients' treatment) the latter were often happy enough to refer one or two of their patients to the psychologist for individual or group psychotherapy. Most British psychiatrists have a marked bias towards organic, i.e. medical-physical, explanations and treatment of mental illness, but a small minority were ready enough to recognise that an interested and experienced psychologist might have a contribution to make in the strictly psychological problems which occasionally seemed to crop up. However, for psychologists to be involved in treatment was rare, and it was certainly not recognised as an accepted part of their role. A little over a decade ago, marked changes began to take place in this role, and it is probable that more than anything else these were due to the advent of behaviour therapy.

As already indicated, traditional forms of psychotherapy had on the whole a medical background, and there was little reason for the psychologist to feel that his training gave him any kind of licence to carry out such treatment. Behaviour therapy, however, represented a form of treatment having its roots very clearly in the psychological tradition. Students of the psychology of learning, one of the major branches of academic experimental psychology, had over the years developed an interest in so-called 'experimental neurosis'. This concept arose from observations that under certain circumstances animals could be made to show signs of disturbed or maladaptive behaviour. The kinds of circumstances involved were where laboratory animals were faced with conflicting stimuli which called for incompatible responses (e.g. 'pleasure' and 'pain' stimuli presented simultaneously), or where some kind of unpleasant stimulus was inescapable. In some cases it was also possible to demonstrate that maladaptive behaviour of this kind could be 'treated' by conditioning new, more adaptive responses to the anxiety-provoking stimuli. Here, then, was a new model for the understanding of 'neurotic' behaviour and symptomatology, and one that offered a reasonable alternative to the Freudian theories which psychologists had always found so distastefully unscientific. Coincidental with the crystallisation of this new approach, research reports began to appear, notably under the authorship of H. J. Eysenck (1960), which threw doubt on the efficacy of traditional forms of psychodynamic psychotherapy (i.e. treatment methods having their roots in Freudian psychoanalysis): treatment of neurosis by these methods could not be shown statistically to be any improvement on no treatment at all. Behaviour therapy thus offered a simple explanation of neurotic symptoms, i.e. that they are no more than maladaptive conditioned responses, which was eagerly taken up by experimental as well as clinical psychologists, and the evidence in favour of this view was popularised and augmented by writers such as Eysenck (1959) and Wolpe (1958).

Suddenly, therefore, clinical psychologists found themselves in possession of a 'respectable' and well-supported scientific theory of neurosis and its treatment, just as confidence in psychoanalytic techniques was at a low ebb. As a result, treatment of a wide variety of patients by a wide variety of methods (see, for example, Meyer and Chesser, 1970) is now a well-recognised part of the clinical psychologist's role, even though the *responsibility* for patients is still in the hands of the psychiatrist. Furthermore, the explanation of many kinds of mental disorder in terms of learning and conditioning now competes on at least equal terms with more traditional medical and psychoanalytic approaches.

In conjunction with the explosion in research into behavioural methods of treatment of the kind mentioned, new interest was also stimulated in examining more closely the more psychodynamic methods of therapy. Eysenck's criticisms of psychotherapeutic effectiveness provoked a quick reaction from psychologists whose sympathies lay with the more humanistic psychological theories, and in the flood of research which followed it soon became clear that one could not talk simply of the efficacy of 'psychotherapy', since the psychotherapeutic situation was an enormously complicated one. To understand what goes on in the therapist–patient relationship, one must examine the situation very minutely indeed—one cannot simply generalise about all therapists and all patients as if they did the same things in the same ways. Particularly interesting research was carried out by American psychologists who subscribed to the therapeutic approach developed by Carl Rogers (1961). What emerged from this was an emphasis on the importance of the therapist's personality characteristics, quite apart from his theoretical views or technical procedures. Indeed, some therapists may, because of anti-therapeutic personal characteristics, do their patients more harm than good. The important factors here seem to be the degree to which the therapist is able to communicate warm acceptance to his patients, to understand them empathetically (from their own vantage point) and to be genuinely himself in the therapeutic situation. Much of this work is summarised in Truax and Carkhuff (1968).

It is, however, not yet possible to draw very general conclusions from the research which surrounds the controversies in the field of psychological treatment methods. The tough-minded 'scientists' of the behavioural persuasion are still to an extent opposed to the tender-minded humanists who have succeeded to the psychodynamic tradition, but the research sophistication and the strength of the scientific foundation of both camps is much more equal than was once the case, and the issues are not therefore quite as crudely obvious as they once were (see, for example, Bergin and Garfield, 1971).

One very clear result of these developments, then, is that, no matter where his sympathies lie, the clinical psychologist can justify his involvement in therapeutic activities by reference to an extensive research literature and a body of well-founded theory which have grown up almost entirely within the discipline of psychology, and he need no longer feel that a medical qualification, or a period of initiation under the supervision of psychoanalytic authorities, is a necessary prerequisite for the practice of psychotherapy. Of course, medical safeguards are necessary in cases where patients may well have organic factors involved in their condition, and clinical psychology at the present time is still very much in the shadow of the medical profession; nevertheless, psychologists' confidence and self-respect have been greatly enhanced by the developments outlined.

The clinical psychologist's concern with psychological testing has also undergone changes. The somewhat crude comparison of an individual with group norms on an objective test, in order to arrive at a statement of the probability of his belonging to a certain diagnostic or behavioural category, seems to be giving way to a more sophisticated approach in which scientific methodology is applied directly to the individual case. Thus methods have been developed in which controlled and quantitative measures can be applied to individuals in a kind of miniature experimental situation, and by means of which their behaviour or mental state can be monitored from one occasion to another, or the structure of their conceptual system analysed.

A cool appraisal of the aims and methods of traditional psychological testing has revealed a number of difficulties, inaccuracies and logical inconsistencies. For example, a 'test' of schizophrenia would be held to be valid if it correctly identified patients who had been labelled schizophrenic by an experienced psychiatrist. In the first place, one may ask, what is the point of constructing a test to do something which has already been done (i.e. diagnose a patient who has already been diagnosed by psychiatrists); and in the second place, what is the point of a psychiatrist referring a patient to a psychologist for a test result which simply 'predicts' what the psychiatrist's opinion would have been at the outset? Doubts such as these about the *relevance* of testing in clinical psychology, as well as a number of more technical difficulties with tests, have been voiced with increasing frequency in recent years, and for a detailed appraisal of the current status of assessment in this field the interested reader could not do better than consult Mittler (1970).

Psychological theories such as those of George Kelly in psychology (see Bannister and Fransella, 1971) and R. D. Laing in psychiatry (Laing, 1967) have had a heavy impact on clinical psychology, and have tended to switch attention away from the degree to which the individual conforms to social norms towards an understanding of the person as the centre of his world. In other words, if you want to understand somebody, you have to discover and appreciate from his own point of view the way he organises and deals with the people and things around him, and not simply compare him with the statistical average to see how he deviates.

In this way many clinical psychologists nowadays see themselves in the role of experimental scientists, bringing a well-established body of theory and technique to bear on behavioural and experiential problems, whether of individuals or groups, which arise in the setting of the hospital service. There is no obvious reason why these problems should arise only in the psychiatric field, and clinical psychology is beginning to extend its influence into the provinces of other medical specialities. Psychological expertise is relevant to any area in which problems of communication, learning or interpersonal relations arise, and there is certainly no shortage of such problems in the Health Service.

Another major aspect of the clinical psychologist's role is teaching. Twenty years ago, perhaps, he had little to offer his professional colleagues in this direction. Since then, the rapid accumulation of psychological knowledge of practical relevance to the kinds of activity in which Health Service professionals are involved means that a good deal of his time should be spent in passing on knowledge and skills which can be put into practice by them.

Medical influence is, of course, extremely strong in the Health Service, and is likely to remain so. Not only is it taken for granted that a patient in hospital, even a psychiatric one, must be suffering from a medical illness, it is also assumed that the ultimate expert in all questions of treatment and management of patients—and also to a large extent of hospital organisation, staff relations, etc.—is the medical practitioner. There seems little doubt that the extent of this claim to authority and expertise is coming to be challenged at several points, largely through the activities of social scientists and clinical psychologists, who find themselves at the present time in a novel, if politically somewhat uncomfortable, position. In some respects, they feel, they have conceptual tools at least as powerful as those of medicine (in the field of psychiatry), and these should give them a right to take greater responsibility for some aspects of treatment and for some managerial functions at present seen as solely medical. It is apparent that it is no more than an assumption that much of 'mental illness' is illness at all (Szasz, 1962), and many psychologists feel that it is high time that the 'medical model' was, more publicly than has yet been the case, given the searching, critical scrutiny it deserves. It might, for example, prove more useful to view psychological disorder in terms of social factors, 'problems in living', etc., rather than as some kind of medical condition.

At the present time, the professional position of the clinical psychologist is in a state of rapid change. Not the least responsible for this state of affairs is the current total management reorganisation of the National Health Service. As a result of this, it seems likely that clinical psychologists will be less closely linked to individual psychiatric hospitals, as they tend to be at present, and will be able to offer their services on a wider basis to any medical speciality which requires them, and possibly also to local authority departments of social services. It seems likely also that the image of the 'mental tester' is now defunct, and that the functions of assessment, treatment, research and teaching will develop in the directions already indicated, but with an emphasis on the clinical psychologist as a behavioural scientist in the hospital service rather than as a kind of second-class paramedical technician. There is no doubt that relations between clinical psychology and psychiatry are to an extent problematic, but one hopes they are not insoluble, and it is probable that British clinicians will follow their American counterparts in becoming gradually more able to carry on their profession without hindrance in those areas where it is appropriate for them to do so.

The training of clinical psychologists, not long ago a somewhat haphazard affair, is now becoming more standardised and rational. Eventually, it is probable that all clinical psychologists will be trained on two-year postgraduate courses based on a university, but until sufficient places on such courses (of which there are several) become available there will still be a necessity for the three-year, apprenticeship-type scheme, which was once the main method of training. In this the trainee clinician is supervised in the hospital setting by a senior colleague. The award of a British Psychological Society Diploma in Clinical Psychology to successful examinees at the end of such a training period ensures that they have reached a standard comparable with that of their university-trained fellows, at the same time encouraging supervisors to provide an adequate syllabus.

Whatever happens to clinical psychologists in terms of their professional role, it seems certain that clinical psychology will continue to be one of the 'applied' branches of the discipline, in which the theories and methods of psychology come up against real people in real situations, and hence will continue to attract students who wish to get to grips with truly human problems. To many clinical psychologists, the concerns of their academic colleagues have frequently seemed minute, trivial and irrelevant, just as the activities of the former may seem impressionistic and uncontrolled to the latter. There is no doubt, however, that the two mutually enrich each other: the clinician's basic training in academic psychology provides him with a core of scientific discipline which helps him keep his feet on the ground, while his concern with the stark phenomena of human existence serves to remind psychology that it is ultimately about people.

References

Bannister, D., & Fransella, F. (1971), *Inquiring Man*. Harmondsworth: Penguin Books.

Bergin, A. E., & Garfield, S. L. (1971), *Handbook of Psychotherapy and Behaviour Change*. New York & London: John Wiley.

Eysenck, H. J. (1959), *Behaviour Therapy and the Neuroses*. London: Pergamon.

Eysenck, H. J. (1960), *Handbook of Abnormal Psychology*. London: Pitman.

Laing, R. D. (1967), *The Politics of Experience and the Bird of Paradise*. Harmondsworth: Penguin Books.

Meehl, P. E. (1954), *Clinical versus Statistical Prediction*. Minneapolis: Univ. Minnesota Press.

Meyer, V., & Chesser, E. S. (1970), *Behaviour Therapy in Clinical Psychiatry*. Harmondsworth: Penguin Books.

Mittler, P. (1970), *The Psychological Assessment of Mental and Physical Handicap*. London: Methuen.

Rogers, C. R. (1961), *On Becoming a Person*. London: Constable.

Szasz, T. (1962), *The Myth of Mental Illness*. London: Secker & Warburg.

Truax, C. B., & Carkhuff, R. R. (1968), *Toward Effective Counselling and Psychotherapy*. Chicago: Aldine.

Wolpe, J. (1958), *Psychotherapy by Reciprocal Inhibition*. Stanford: Stanford Univ. Press.

Recommended further reading

Bannister, D., & Fransella, F. (1971), *Inquiring Man*. Harmondsworth: Penguin Books.

Bergin, A. E., & Garfield, S. L. (1971), *Handbook of Psychotherapy and Behaviour Change*. New York & London: John Wiley.

Meyer, V., & Chesser, E. S. (1970), *Behaviour Therapy in Clinical Psychiatry*. Harmondsworth: Penguin Books.

Mittler, P. (1970), *The Psychological Assessment of Mental and Physical Handicap*. London: Methuen.

15
Occupational Psychology
G. C. Simpson

Occupational psychology is the study and application of the psychological principles which affect the relationship between man and his working environment.

The area of interest is extremely wide, including the whole range of occupations from social work and the Health Service to the military, from bakeries to steel works, from finance and insurance to chemical and petroleum plants. It is because of this wide scope that the title 'Occupational Psychology' is preferred to the alternative 'Industrial Psychology', which has somewhat restrictive connotations.

Historical background

In Britain the growth of interest in the psychology of work began during the First World War with the establishment of the Health of Munitions' Workers Committee. The need to meet the high level of demand for war materials involved corresponding demands on the efficiency of workers in the armaments' factories. The Committee was established, therefore, to investigate methods of increasing output while decreasing lost time and fatigue. Some of the early studies investigated the relationship between production and hours of work, and the effects of changes in lighting and noise level on performance. After the War the

Committee was re-formed as the Industrial Fatigue Research Board and given the task of promoting the understanding of the relationship between the conditions of employment and the functions and capabilities of the human operator, with emphasis on both efficiency and preservation of health.

In 1921 the National Institute of Industrial Psychology was established to investigate similar problems with direct reference to individual firms. Gradually this became the centre for the investigation of the use of psychology in personnel selection.

The next major development also came about as a consequence of the outbreak of war. The Second World War brought with it much more sophisticated equipment, which demanded high concentration, technical skills and rapid decisions. An effective relationship between man and his equipment became a matter of great importance. Man and machine had to operate as an integrated system in order to ensure optimum performance. Shortly after the War this interest in man–machine systems was formalised as the new technology of Ergonomics (Greek *ergos*, work, and *nomos*, laws). The War also brought with it a greatly increased demand for men of officer calibre and hence the need to improve, very rapidly, the ability to select and train the potential officer; this provided the impetus for more careful and more extensive consideration of the psychological aspects of selection and training.

Scope of occupational psychology

Basically, occupational psychology falls into two divisions, which were described by Rodger and Cavanagh (1962) as:

1 Fitting the man to the job (FMJ).
2 Fitting the job to the man (FJM).

1 Fitting the man to the job
The aim of this area of occupational psychology is to investigate and implement methods of achieving an optimum allocation of individuals to jobs. There are, of course, two sides to this—the

individual's and the organisation's. In other words, the function could be restated as: achieving the optimum matching of the individual's and the organisation's aims and requirements. A schematic representation of this matching process is shown in Fig. 15.1.

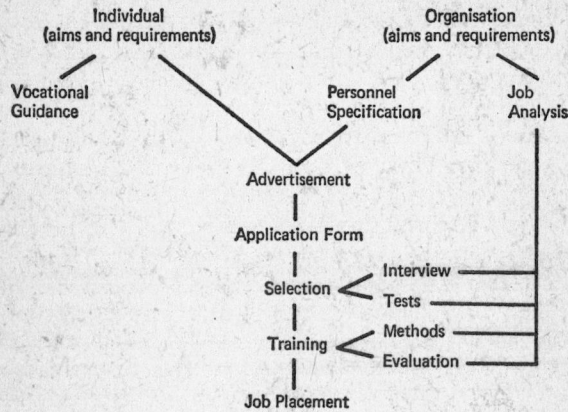

Fig. 15.1 Fitting the man to the job: a schematic representation.

As the diagram shows, the process begins with the aims and requirements of the two parties, and it is here that occupational psychology makes its first contribution through the use of *vocational guidance* and *job analysis* techniques. When this has been done the matching process begins with the advertisement and application forms. The next stage, short-list selection, is the principal area of psychological study. From selection the chosen individuals move on to training. Once again, occupational psychology has a significant contribution to make in the design and evaluation of optimal training schemes. At the end of training the new employee is finally placed in his job, where, after a time lapse, the whole process will begin again when he decides to change his job or becomes a candidate for promotion.

2 Fitting the job to the man (ergonomics)

This area is concerned basically with the direct relationship between man and the tasks which make up his job. It involves the study of all the aspects of man at his workplace, the equipment he uses, the information he needs and the environment he works in. All these aspects are combined in the concept of the man–machine system (see Fig. 15.2).

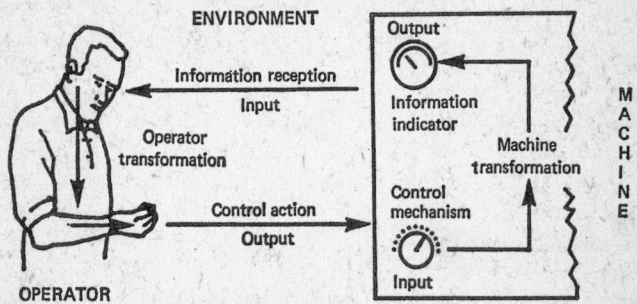

Fig. 15.2 The man–machine system.

Almost all forms of work constitute a man–machine system from the weekend gardener in his allotment to the fighter pilot in his supersonic aircraft. Just as the gardener works with a 'machine' (his spade), so the pilot works with his plane; just as the gardener uses information about how widely spaced he wants his potatoes, so the pilot needs information on windspeed, altitude, target definition and so on. Similarly, both work in particular environments which may necessitate specialised clothing, whether it be wellingtons or complete life-support systems. It is the aim of *ergonomics* to study, integrate and enhance the function of the man–machine system.

Whilst both occupational and experimental psychology are vital aspects of ergonomics, they are not always sufficient on their own. Often correct solutions to a number of man–machine system problems require the combination of knowledge from a number of sciences, as shown in Fig. 15.3.

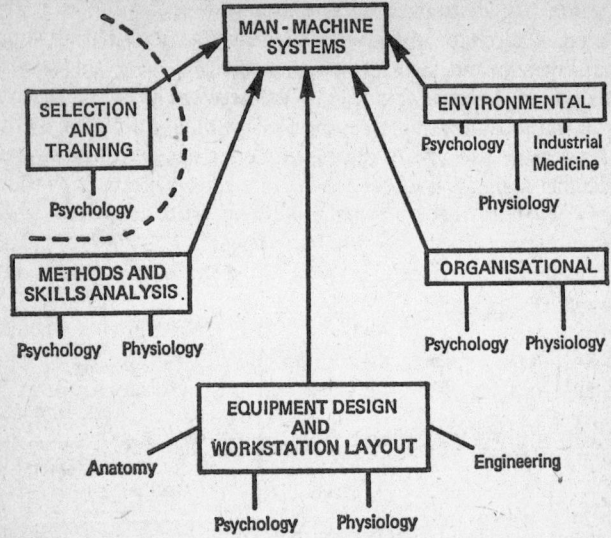

Fig. 15.3 The interdisciplinary nature of ergonomics.

Fitting the man to the job—1 Selection

As is shown in Fig. 15.1, selection is a matching process, a process of finding the most suitable individuals for particular jobs. In order to do this efficiently an applicant must have a clear and realistic picture of his aims, requirements and capabilities. Similarly, the organisation must have a precise conception of their aims and requirements for the particular job in question. Occupational psychology has developed techniques to aid both the individual (vocational guidance) and the organisation (job analysis).

Vocational guidance is a technique which utilises personal interviews, psychological tests, scholastic records and the individual's occupational interests, in conjunction with the counsellor's experience, in order to guide the individual into the most appropriate type of job. Whilst this has obvious value to school, college and university leavers, it is wrong to think of its being restricted to those groups. The average working life is in the region of forty to fifty years, and clearly an individual's aims, requirements and abilities will change and develop throughout this period. Vocational guidance can therefore be of great assistance at almost any stage in a person's working life. It is also of considerable use to the organisation; for example, the overall selection procedure will be much more efficient if the individual knows exactly what he wants and exactly what he is capable of. When this is the case, the number of people who apply for a job without much chance of getting it will be considerably reduced.

Job analysis is a methodology of data collection which allows us to identify aspects of the job which are relevant to what Rodger (1965) calls the 'difficulties and distastes' of a job. On the basis of the job analysis it is possible to devise a job specification which gives detailed requirements of the most appropriate person for that job, thus aiding the organisation in its selection procedures.

The process and methods used vary considerably but essentially consist of a systematic job study to define the duties, responsibilities, activities and special skills required to carry out a particular job. The type of factors covered by job analysis are as follows:

(a) educational or other qualifications and experience required;
(b) physical expenditure, physical workload and stress;
(c) mental workload and psychological stress factors;
(d) social factors, work groups;
(e) medical considerations;
(f) special aptitudes;
(g) responsibilities, leadership potential, etc.;
(h) contractual and legal details;
(i) management and union policies;
(j) promotion prospects, salaries, etc.

While most of these factors will be important for the great

majority of jobs, the emphasis will change from one to another and a close definition of where the emphasis lies will be of extreme value in selection.

In ergonomics, job analysis can be used to isolate problem areas in work procedure, information 'bottlenecks' and so on; while in training, a detailed job analysis is invaluable in designing training schemes and manuals.

These two processes, therefore, provide the ideal situation in which to carry out the selection procedures themselves.

Selection procedures

Various surveys conducted to isolate what types of procedures are used in selection suggest that almost all firms employ some kind of interview technique, and a small but increasing number of firms use psychological tests (mainly intelligence and aptitude tests).

The interview is the most commonly used technique and also the one surrounded with the greatest mystique. No one likes to admit he is a bad interviewer, especially if interviewing is an integral part of his job, yet one of the most consistent findings of psychological research on interviewing is that most people are not as good as they think they are!

The general theme of research results was established as long ago as 1915 in a paper by Scott. This experiment involved six personnel managers who each interviewed the same thirty-six candidates for a sales position. Each manager ranked each candidate on his suitability for the post. The results showed that there was very little relationship at all between the rankings of the six interviewers. In a later study by Scott (1916) the experiment compared the performance of interviewers rating the same candidates on two separate occasions. Again very little relationship was found. These early studies, therefore, suggested that there is a considerable difference not only in the various individuals' assessment of the same candidate but also in the assessment of interviewers on different occasions. This type of finding has been confirmed by subsequent studies.

More recent research has suggested ways in which interview consistency can be improved. One of the more promising of these techniques is interview-structuring; this is an attempt to increase the relevance of the interview by ensuring that the most salient points are dealt with consistently and systematically in each interview. Structuring is therefore a type of *aide memoire* or interview guide, covering the most important areas to be discussed. A good example of structuring is the *Seven Point Plan* (Rodger, 1965), which is designed for general selection interviews, and covers physical make-up, attainments, general intelligence, special aptitudes, interests, disposition and circumstances.

A typical study in the area of structuring is that of Hovland and Wonderic (1939). They used interview-structuring to provide ratings on a number of points which were then built up into an interview score. In all they obtained 300 such scores. After some time they followed up the candidates and divided them into three groups:

(a) those who were still on the job;
(b) those who had resigned;
(c) those who had been dismissed.

The tendency was for a greater proportion of those who had obtained high interview scores (based on the structuring technique) to remain on the job, whereas the majority of those who had obtained low interview scores had been dismissed. Thus the type of structuring used to produce the interview scores proved to be an extremely useful technique for improving the predictive value of the interview.

Unfortunately, although it is now well established that interview-structuring is a valuable aid in improving the validity and reliability of interviews, it does have one disadvantage: by increasing structure you are, by definition, decreasing one of the greatest assets of the interview, its versatility.

This double-sidedness of research recommendations on interviewing is quite common; for example, a 1:1 interview situation (one interviewer to one candidate) is much less daunting and much more relaxing for a candidate than a panel interview. However, a panel interview will significantly reduce the possibility of a candidate being subject to the whims and bias of a single assessor.

Numerous other aspects of the interview situation have been investigated with similar and somewhat inconclusive results, and this apparent lack of directly applicable research findings is probably a function of the research orientation. In the past too much research has been oriented towards *whether* one technique is better than another and too little emphasis on *why* certain techniques are better. It is only by understanding the underlying mechanisms that we can generalise and develop more appropriate techniques. Some attempts have been made to develop this line of research, one example being the consideration of interviewing in terms of decision-making (e.g. Lowe-Holmes and Brocklesby, 1968; Holdsworth, 1971). However, this kind of approach is relatively new, and while it shows considerable promise it will be some time before a valid evaluation can be made.

A psychological test is essentially a standardised, objective measure of a sample of behaviour. There is a large variety of techniques included under the heading of psychological tests, but the two most common types used as selection instruments are intelligence and aptitude tests. Intelligence tests can be described in more detail by considering which aspects of 'intelligence' they take into account. There are three major divisions: numerical, verbal and spatial. A test may deal with any one of these exclusively or with a combination of them. Similarly, aptitude tests may be subdivided into cognitive ('mental') and psychomotor ('performance').

Perhaps the most important single aspect of the use of tests in selection is emphasised in the above definition, that is a test covers only a 'sample of behaviour'. It is vital, therefore, that the sample is genuinely relevant to the job in hand. This is well shown by an experiment to investigate the value of intelligence tests in selecting clerical workers for banks (Shore, 1958). The study used two intelligence tests, the Otis test and the Thurstone Test of Mental Alertness. The results of the Otis test showed correlations ·41, ·15 and ·53 with subsequent performance of individuals on three types of clerical job. It is clear therefore that, while all the jobs were clerical, this particular test is a better predictor for some types of clerical work than others. The Thurstone test is made up of two sections, a linguistic or verbal section and a quantitative or arithmetic section. The correlations between test score and subsequent performance were ·63 and ·53 respectively. Again the two sections were different in their value as predictors, even for the same job. Many other studies have shown similar results; it is therefore essential to be sure of the relevance of a test before it is used as a selection technique. The only sensible way to do this is to evaluate the test since, as the above experiment shows, without an evaluation, using an inappropriate test can be positively misleading.

Aptitude tests are concerned with specific abilities or potential ability, for example mechanical understanding, musical ability, etc. The performance tests are, as they imply, tests of actual ability; would-be musicians may be asked to play a particular piece or would-be carpenters may be asked to make a particular joint. The cognitive tests are oriented more towards the appreciation of particular abilities; for example, mechanical appreciation can be assessed by presenting the candidates with drawings of various lever or cogwheel systems and asking them to describe the expected output for a given input.

As with intelligence tests, relevance or *validity* is essential. Cambell (1963) compared three tests (two intelligence, one mechanical aptitude) as possible techniques in the selection of gas fitters. As might be expected, the mechanical aptitude test proved to be much more valuable as a predictive technique. Similarly, Durrett (1961) compared the value of three tests in selecting face workers for mines. One test was a general intelligence test, the second a mechanical comprehension test (cognitive aptitude) and the third a two-handed co-ordination test (performance aptitude). The correlations were 0, ·12 and ·57 respectively.

Spencer and Reynolds (1961) report an evaluation of the use of an aptitude test in the selection of graduate engineers for a calculating machine company. The interesting aspect of this study was that the experimenters correlated test score with performance rating, as is the normal procedure, but correlated on three different occasions; the results are shown below:

Training programme performance rating—6 months after joining—·40 correlation

Job performance rating—12 months after joining—·58 correlation

Job performance rating—18 months after joining—·64 correlation

The correlation, and hence the test's value as a predictor, increased with time. If the only correlation taken had been the initial, post-training measure (which it often is), this test could easily have been abandoned, whereas the later results show it to be quite a useful predictor.

In conclusion, therefore, it has been shown many times that psychological tests can be of great value in personnel selection, but extreme care must be taken in the choice of tests and there is no real alternative to serious evaluation before use.

Fitting the man to the job—2 Training

At the present time there is more training in industry than ever before, largely because of the accelerating rate of technological change, which makes it almost impossible for industry to rely on the skills of the old-time craftsman, who, having served his apprenticeship, could survive all his working life on the abilities developed during his youth. It is becoming increasingly true that what one learns at twenty-one will be, at best, outdated and often irrelevant by the age of thirty-one. This has meant, in conjunction with a number of other factors, that training, which was once restricted to the early part of an individual's career, is now a continuous process, often occurring several times during a person's working life.

Tilley (1968) has said of occupational training: 'The aim of a technology of training is to expedite the process of learning by arranging conditions so that the students learn more rapidly and more efficiently.' Although initially this may appear a rather obvious statement, it contains three important points:

(a) By talking of a 'technology of training', Tilley implies that training is itself a skill and should be subject to all the usual rigours of a technology. This will include a highly systematic and functional approach to research and implementation combined with extensive testing and evaluation.
(b) In using the phrase 'by arranging conditions' the author is emphasising that the onus for success of a training scheme should lie directly on the shoulders of the trainer. For far too long educationalists, trainers and teachers have been able to overlook their own shortcomings by resorting to such defences as 'How can I train someone who isn't interested?', whereas in fact it is clearly their responsibility to develop the interest.
(c) The final point is the emphasis placed on *learning* as a control point in training. No training can occur without learning.

From this last point in particular it might appear that psychology has a major contribution to make, for one of the traditional areas of psychological research has been the learning process. Unfortunately, much of this previous research is of limited application in the occupational setting. As McGehee (1958) comments: 'An experiment which demonstrates conclusively that white rats tend to repeat rewarded responses on an elevated maze does not lead easily to the generalisation that "Rosie the Riveter" responds in a similar manner as that of a lower order mammal.'

One technique developed from the traditional psychology of learning, however, has proved to be of considerable utility in occupational training. This is Skinner's development of programmed instruction (PI).

PI is, in fact, a very broad area, ranging from programmed books through 'teaching machines' to large multi-terminal computer systems. Essentially, it is a process which 'routes' the individual through the material to be learnt dependent upon his success at each stage. The system has a number of advantages over more traditional training schemes, for example:

(a) It requires an active response from the student at each stage.
(b) The process uses small steps, the careful control of which produces a gradual increase in mastery.
(c) It provides immediate feedback for each response.
(d) By using small steps it ensures a low error rate.
(f) It frees the instructor to provide individual attention where necessary.

Over the past twenty years there has been a large number of research projects to evaluate the use of programmed instruction in occupational training, typical of which is the study reported by Hickey (1961). This research was carried out in conjunction with a mail-order company. The project studied training workers for the job of package billing, the last clerical job before the article goes to the customer. The experiment compared two training schemes: the 'normal' one, which had been in use for some time, consisted of 40 hours of lecture, demonstration and practical work; the second method was a specially designed programmed book. The study investigated 120 trainees in all, 60 on each of the procedures. The trainees using the programmed book system reached the required level of competence in 26 as opposed to 40 hours, constituting a saving in training time of 34%. To the worker it meant a reduction of about a third in the total time she spent on trainees' wages. For the company, who hired approximately 500 girls per annum for this job, a 34%

reduction in training time meant an overall saving in the region of $20 000 per year.

Another example is given by Annett (1971), reporting a series of investigations to evaluate the use of PI in the training of gas fitters on natural gas conversions. His results were similar to those of Hickey, in that the PI group took considerably less time to reach the criterion level. For one particular job the reduction in training time was as much as 50%.

Whilst there are examples, such as these, of a direct transfer from traditional psychological research to operator training, a much broader impact has been made by the direct employment of psychologists on general occupational training problems.

The work of Belbin and her colleagues (e.g. Belbin *et al.*, 1957) typifies this. The researchers were asked to investigate the training problems associated with invisible mending in the textile industry. Invisible mending is an extremely important, skilful and demanding task, especially in terms of visual acuity and manual dexterity. Because of the nature of the work, the firm believed that it was unsuitable for older women and therefore always employed young girls on this particular job. This created difficulties, for a lengthy training period was involved and as the staff were exclusively young girls they often left to marry shortly after reaching a skilled level.

The real importance of this study, though not part of the original objectives, was that it showed conclusively that older women could do the work very well if the training scheme was designed to suit their specific needs. (For further details of the special training requirements of older workers, see Belbin, 1958.)

Another, more recent, example of the general importance of choosing the correct training procedure was reported by Smith and Pearn (1972). Their study was concerned with the apparent lack of success of immigrants training to be bus conductors (10% compared with about 50% success rate for non-immigrants). The experiment compared conventional lecture with discovery training methods for teaching 'road sense'. The conventional training was a normal classroom situation; the discovery technique was a method of concrete examples using a table-top road plan with model buses, cars, road signs, etc. The significant, and perhaps surprising, result was that the conventional method of classroom lectures was more efficient for the immigrant trainees.

Both these studies, while contrasting in their results, show that great care must be taken in the choice and design of a training scheme, and that all possible alternatives must be given serious consideration. The correct training scheme will not be found fortuitously or by guesswork, but only by the application of scientific methods of development and evaluation.

Fitting the job to the man—ergonomics

We stated earlier that the real impetus for the development of ergonomics began during the Second World War with the necessity to ensure the optimal relationship between man and his equipment, a particular problem being aircraft cockpit design. In consequence, one of the early major areas of research was in the design of controls and displays. During the last twenty-five years detailed research has been carried out to define the most appropriate type of 'display' (e.g. the altimeter) for particular usage. This research is summarised in Table 15.1.

A considerable amount of research has also been invested in display design *per se*, the first important question relating to the general characteristics of a good display. Rolfe and Allnutt (1967) summarise the requirements as follows:

Displays should be:

1. *Unambiguous*—they should not be open to misinterpretation.
2. *Readable*—they should not demand undue time to obtain a reading.
3. *Precise*—they should not present information to an accuracy which exceeds the sensitivity of the sensing equipment (i.e. it should not exceed the accuracy of the 'information' it obtains).

Information type	Display technique		
	Analogue		Digital
	Moving index	Moving scale	
Quantitative	Fair	Fair	GOOD
Check reading	GOOD	Poor	Poor
Setting	Fair/Good	Fair	GOOD
Correction of continuous process	GOOD	Poor	Poor
Comparison			
(a) Quick	GOOD	Poor	Poor
(b) Highly accurate	Fair	Poor	GOOD

Table 15.1 Summary of information type and associated recommended display type.

4. *Concise*—a display should not exceed the accuracy which the operator needs.
5. *Capable of indicating failure*—it should be possible to note any malfunction of the instrument.
6. *Readily distinguishable*—it should be possible to recognise a given display in the company of other instruments.

In other words, the essence of good display is simplicity and clarity. A prime example of the importance of these factors is shown in the design of aircraft altimeters. The problem here is that the range of readings required is extensive, involving a wide range of numbers. Many displays include three scales and three pointers (one each for 100's of feet, 1000's of feet and 10 000's of feet). A typical example is shown in Fig. 15.4. This creates a number of problems. First, the display is cluttered and therefore difficult to read. Secondly, the exact order of reading must be remembered at all times, for reading the scales in the wrong order can lead to catastrophic errors. Thirdly, there is a possibility on some altimeter designs of relating the wrong pointer to

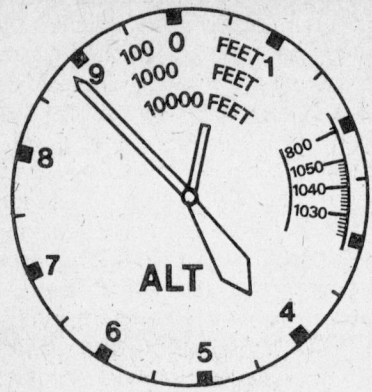

Fig. 15.4 A typical multi-pointer altimeter.

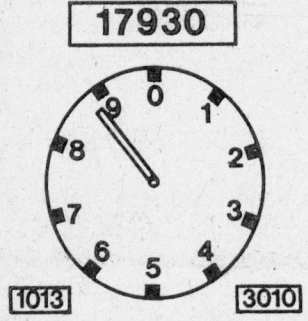

Fig. 15.5 A typical counter-pointer altimeter.

the wrong scale. The simple alternative to overcome the problem of a vast range of possible readings is to use a digital (direct reading in numerical form) display. However, this also has major shortcomings, for not only does the pilot take straight height readings from the altimeter but he also relies on it for information on rate of change of height and this is difficult to assess from a digital display. A viable alternative—the counter-pointer display (see Fig. 15.5)—has been suggested, where the major height component is given in digital form and the scale and pointer part of the display gives the information on rate of change. An experiment discussed in Rolfe (1969) compared the traditional altimeter with a counter-pointer altimeter. The results showed that the counter-pointer altimeter had a mean time to obtain a reading of 1·34 seconds compared with 3·90 seconds for the traditional altimeter, and the reading errors were 0 and 20% respectively. Clearly, therefore, considerable improvements can be made in the design of displays on the basis of the experimental investigation of the relationship between the displays and the operator who is going to use them.

Another interesting example of the ergonomic approach to the study of displays was the discovery of population stereotypes. Loveless (1962) reviewed a long series of experiments in which subjects had been asked 'Which way would you expect the display to move to indicate an increase in value?' It became obvious that the majority of the population had very definite expectations of what represented an increase. This became known as the *population stereotype*. The experiments were continued and developed to include controls and the question reframed to ask which way the subject would expect the display to move if he moved the control to the right (left, up, down, etc.). A summary of the display and control movements which conform to population stereotypes is shown in Fig. 15.6.

Controls and display movements which conform to population stereotypes are said to be *compatible*. The importance of compatibility is shown by the following points paraphrased from a paper by Taylor and Garvey (1959):

(a) Learning time will be shorter with compatible displays and controls.
(b) There is a much greater risk of error and accident with incompatible display–control relationships.

(c) Performance with incompatible displays and controls will decrease under any form of stress.
(d) All the above effects will become even more marked with increasing age of the operator.
(e) A mixture of compatible and incompatible display–control relationships is potentially so dangerous that it would be better to have them all incompatible if it is not possible to have them all compatible.

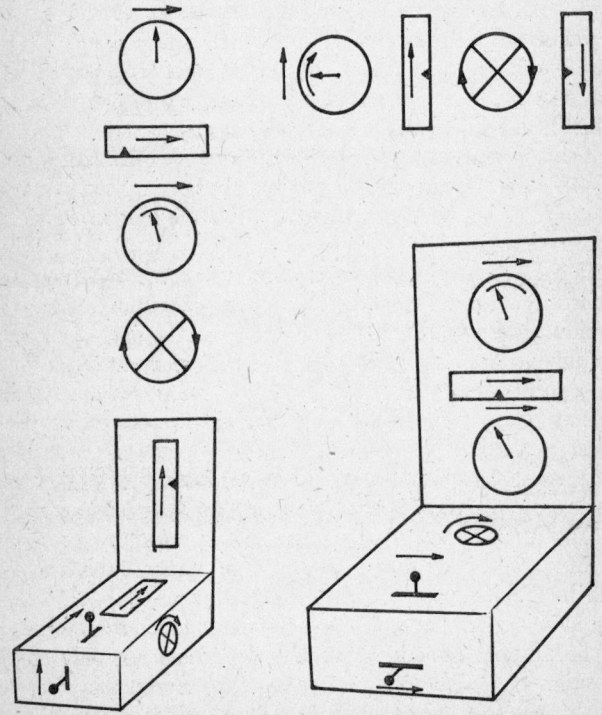

Fig. 15.6 Established compatible control display relationships. (After Murrell, 1965.)

Considerable work has also been done on the layout of displays and control panels, for it is the control station which provides the basis for operator–system interaction and communication, and it is possible that lack of forethought in the design stage will lead to a reduction in overall system efficiency. With the introduction of more sophisticated systems and a growing tendency to 'centralise' control, the importance of this communication link is steadily increasing.

Concomitant with this rise in system sophistication is a growth in the amount of information that has to be dealt with in the operator–system link, making it necessary for far greater amounts of information to be displayed on each panel. To ensure optimum use of the information it must be presented in a way which will enable ease of identification and operation and which will also reduce the possibility of error.

To achieve good design standards there are three major areas of consideration: the information requirements of the task; the physical aspects of the work station; and the interaction of the two previous factors.

It is vitally important to define exactly those aspects of the information which are necessary to the operation as this will avoid *unnecessary* information appearing on the operator's panel —(unnecessary information is at best redundant, at worst it can be positively confusing). Next the relative importance of the various types of information and their relative frequency of use must be specified as these provide a structure for the layout of displays and controls so that appropriate decisions can be made.

Physical aspects of the control station layout include such factors as reach, viewing angle, working position and so on. While these may seem minor points, the effect of ignoring them can be complex and dangerous. For example, approximations based on how far an operator can reach to touch something are of little value. Functional reach is dependent not only on the position of the control but also on type, speed and required accuracy of the control action, as well as frequency and duration of control use. Similarly, a bad working position may seem a minor inconvenience, but it can affect reaction time, fatigue absenteeism and even labour turnover. The human's ability to adapt may seem a valuable asset, but by relying on it the designer runs certain risks, for example:

(a) long- and short-term injury and strain due to bad working posture;
(b) less spare capacity to deal with emergency conditions;
(c) greater probability of accidents;
(d) greater probability of error.

The skill of good design, in ergonomic terms, is matching the information and control requirements of the task to the physical aspects of the operator and the workspace available, the basic building block of which is job analysis. This serves to emphasise again just how important consideration of job analysis is to the whole of occupational psychology.

Another large area of study in ergonomics is that of environmental stress and its effect on the operator in terms of both health and performance. Numerous stresses have been investigated, including high-level noise, extremes of temperature and humidity, localised and general vibration, sleep loss, speed stress, boredom, etc. Some of these stresses, for example noise, temperature and vibration, have been considered in terms of defining both physiological tolerance limits and psychological, or *performance*, limits. Research results in this area suggest that performance starts to deteriorate well below the limits of strictly physiological tolerance. For example, numerous researchers have showed physiological tolerance at temperatures well above normal deep body temperatures, whereas most studies of performance suggest a decline around 80% of deep body temperature. Definition of the relationship between extremes of environmental stress, in particular temperature and noise, has led to considerable research effort to develop and evaluate protective clothing, and important steps have been made towards establishing legal limits to exposure to stresses (especially noise) which may cause long-term health impairment.

Recent research on the short-term performance effects of stress (e.g. Cox *et al.*, 1973) is also suggesting possible preventive measures in terms of dietary intake. These studies have suggested that performance decrements (or 'loss') caused by exposure to high-intensity noise can be reduced by the prior administration of glucose. Considerably more research is needed in the study of stress effects, however, especially as most laboratory studies are restricted to single stress factors whereas very few work situations, if they are stressful, contain only single stresses.

The study of ergonomics embraces many other occupational problems such as inspection, fatigue, the organisation of work/rest schedules, shift work, design considerations for the handicapped and also the design of products from the consumer's viewpoint as well as that of the manufacturer. It does in fact cover, as was emphasised earlier, all aspects of man–machine systems whether at work or at home, in the factory or office, and even in sport and leisure.

Occupational psychology is a rapidly growing specialism within the parent discipline in terms of research and practice. More and more organisations, especially the larger ones, are finding it useful to employ occupational psychologists at both the research and practitioner level. The major problem is to ensure that in a subject so closely allied to application, the research stays firmly embedded in its original aim of providing results that are not only meaningful but useful.

References

Annett, J. (1971), 'Learning in practice'. In Warr, P. B. (ed.), *Psychology at Work*. Harmondsworth: Penguin Books.
Belbin, E. (1958), 'Methods of training older workers'. *Ergonomics*, *1*, 3.
Belbin, E., Belbin, R. M., & Hill, F. (1957), 'A comparison between the results of three methods of operator training'. *Ergonomics*, *1*, 1, 39–50.

Cambell, J. T. (1963), 'Validity information exchange'. *Personnel Psychology*, *16*, 4, 181–3.

Cox, T. R., Simpson, G. C., & Rotheschild, D. (1973), 'Blood glucose levels and skilled performance under stress'. *Journ. of International Research Communications*, *1*, 9, 30.

Durrett, H. L. (1961), 'Validity information exchange'. *Personal Psychology.*, *14*, 3, 453–5.

Hickey, A. E. (1961), 'Programmed instruction in business and industry'. In Margulies, S., & Eigen, L. D. (eds) *Applied Programmed Instruction*. New York: John Wiley.

Holdsworth, R. F. (1971), 'Mathematical models and selection decisions'. *Occ. Psychol.*, *45*, 99–109.

Hovland, C. I., & Wonderic, E. F. (1939), 'Prediction and success of a standardised interview'. *J. App. Psychol.*, *23*, 537–46.

Lowe-Holmes, A. R., & Brocklesby, I. (1968), 'A factor analytical study of selection decision-making'. *Occ. Psychol.*, *42*, 85–8.

Loveless, N. E. (1962), 'Direction of motion stereotypes: a review'. *Ergonomics*, *5*, 2, 357–83.

McGehee, W. (1958), 'Are we using what we know about training?—learning theory and training'. *Personnel Psychol.*, *11*, 1–12.

Rodger, A. (1965a), 'The seven point plan'. *National Institute of Industrial Psychology Paper* No. 1.

Rodger, A. (1965b), 'The criterion problem in selection and guidance'. *Occ. Psychol.*, *39*, 2, 77–82.

Rodger, A., & Cavanagh, P. (1962), 'Training of occupational psychologists'. *Occ. Psychol.*, *1 & 2*, 82–8.

Rolfe, J. M. (1969), 'Human factors and the display of height information'. *Applied Ergonomics*, *1*, 1, 16–24.

Scott, W. D. (1915), 'The scientific selection of salesmen'. *Advertising and Selling*, *25*, 94–6.

Scott, W. D. (1916), 'Selection of employees by means of quantitative determinations'. *Annals American Academy Political & Soc. Sci.*, *65*.

Shore, R. P. (1958), 'Validity information exchange'. *Personnel Psychol.*, *11*, 22, 435–9.

Smith, M. C., & Pearn, M. A. (1972), 'Conventional lecture versus discovery training methods in the preparation of immigrant bus conductors'. *Jour. Cross-Cultural Psychology*, *3*, 4.

Spencer, G. M., & Reynolds, H. J. (1961), 'Validity information exchange'. *Personnel Psychol.*, *14*, 4, 456–8.

Taylor, F. V., & Garvey, W. D. (1959), 'The limitations of the Procrustean approach to the optimisation of man-machine systems'. *Ergonomics*. 2, 2, 187–94.

Tilley, K. (1968), 'A technology of training'. In Pym, D. (ed.) *Industrial Society*. Harmondsworth: Penguin Books.

Recommended further reading

Holding, D. (1969), *Experimental Psychology in Industry*. Harmondsworth: Penguin Books.

Murrell, K. F. H. (1965), *Ergonomics*. London: Chapman & Hall.

Pym, D. (1968), *Industrial Society*. Harmondsworth: Penguin Books.

Schultz, D. P. (1970), *Psychology and Industry*. London: Macmillan.

Tiffin, J., & McCormick, E. J. (1970), *Industrial Psychology*. London: George Allen & Unwin.

Warr, P. B. (ed.) (1971), *Psychology at Work*. Harmondsworth: Penguin Books.

16
The Uses of Psychology

C. I. Howarth

In this chapter I shall attempt to answer two related questions. What use is psychology, and what use is it likely to be in the future? These questions must be taken together since the second can only be answered by a modest extension of the answer given to the first.

The arguments which follow will be used to justify three conclusions:

1 that psychology as a branch of pure science is flourishing and that it is fairly easy to predict how it will develop;
2 that inappropriate assumptions about the nature of applied psychology have made it much less effective than it should be;
3 that the applications of psychological knowledge are hampered by the assumption that it should, like medical knowledge, be administered only by professional experts.

Psychology as a pure science

In themselves the scientific achievements of psychology are impressive. Chapters 2 to 12 have described the nature of some of these. Here I shall merely comment on them.

Methods of enquiry are well developed. Old controversies about whether psychology should be concerned with 'mental life' as revealed by introspection or with 'behaviour' as revealed to an outside observer are now happily of little interest, since so many studies have shown the usefulness of both introspection and the observation of behaviour, particularly in checking conclusions based on the other. It should always have been obvious that, after asking a man what he is doing, we should observe him to see if he is telling the truth. Similarly, after observing a piece of behaviour, it is foolish not to ask the person why he is doing it. Philosophical debates, in the past, prevented psychologists adopting this commonsense approach, but experience has prepared us to use a wide range of both behavioural and observational techniques, in the laboratory or in 'real life'. Experience has also taught us to mistrust results based on only one method of investigation.

Technical advances have increased the sophistication of our laboratory experiments. The most notable advance is the use of computers to control the apparatus. They make it possible to do experiments which would be beyond the capacity of simpler devices or of an unaided human investigator. For example, in studying the learning of a complex artificial language, the computer can check, instantly, the correctness of the subjects' use of the language. A human experimenter might require three months to learn the language well enough to achieve the same confidence and accuracy.

A special form of laboratory experiment is the simulator. With the aid of a computer and elaborate display and recording apparatus, simulators reproduce in most essential details the characteristics of a real-life situation. They make it possible to predict how people will react in a new environment, such as a space capsule or the cab of a revolutionary new train, before subjecting them to the possible dangers of the real thing. When applied to more mundane problems, such as driving a car, a simulator will enable the psychologist to control the situation and to measure it, in a way which would not be possible in 'real life'. Simulation is, in a sense, halfway between the laboratory and the real-life situation.

In addition to these technical advances, psychologists have learned to make more effective use of naturalistic observation (Willems and Rausch, 1968). The traditional methods of the interview, the participant observer and the concealed observer have been strengthened by the use of film and videotape. These make it possible to observe the same piece of behaviour over and over again. Such is the complexity of even the simplest forms of behaviour that new insights may arise every time one looks at a recording of it. The more often one looks, the greater the degree of understanding which develops. Such recordings also allow accurate measurements to be made on spontaneous behaviour in natural surroundings.

Statistical, mathematical and descriptive techniques have been developed to deal with the increasing complexity of the material which psychologists handle. But the greatest aid to understanding comes from an adequate theory. Theories in psychology can be as precise, testable and elegant as those of any other science. In some branches of the subject, such as psychophysics, the physiological psychology of the sense organs, memory, thinking and intelligence, there has been a pleasing continuity of development over a hundred years or more. In others, such as psycholinguistics, there have been dramatic developments within the last ten years.

A major difficulty for theorists in psychology has been the difficulty of expressing their theories in mathematical terms. This is due, not to any shortcoming in the theories, but to the paucity of mathematical techniques for describing the behaviour of complex interacting systems. Economists, meteorologists and others have the same difficulty. The digital computer now goes a long way towards overcoming this problem. It can work out predictions from theories which cannot be handled by conventional mathematics. In this mode the computer is used to simulate, symbolically, the behaviour of the theoretical system. This use of the computer is perhaps even more useful than its use to control experiments. It has added a new dimension to the development of psychological theories.

There have been some dramatic theoretical failures in the past. One of these is learning theory, where experiments yielded no clear-cut verdict between alternative views, so that theories have come and gone at the dictates of fashion rather than by the exercise of scientific judgement. But such failures occur in all sciences and, in a healthily developing subject, need not be taken too seriously.

Another type of failure, which is of greater significance, is the lack of any all-embracing theory comparable to relativity in physics or to evolution in biology. Psychoanalysis, gestalt psychology and some branches of learning theory have all aspired to this elevated status, but are now discredited, or seem to have only limited scope. It is interesting to speculate why there are no large-scale theories in psychology. Perhaps it is because the complexity of the subject makes it difficult to set it all within a single framework. Perhaps it is because the domain of psychology is less well defined than that of physics or chemistry or biology. If the latter is the case, then large-scale theories will only be successful when the subject-matter of psychology has been reorganised. How this could happen is beyond the scope of this chapter, but it seems likely that the developments in applied psychology discussed later will have considerable influence on psychological theory.

A comprehensive and successful theory confers a type of understanding which is very useful, but not essential. People trained to use such a theory have the status of experts and can sometimes use the theory to solve practical problems. In psychology, at the present time, our intuitive understanding of ourselves and of others must substitute for a global theoretical understanding. Fortunately, our psychological intuitions are based on a lifetime of experience. One important consequence of this is that the professional psychologist shares many of his insights with the 'man in the street', so that his status as an expert is rather different from that of experts in other fields such as nuclear engineering or medicine.

An exciting characteristic of psychology as a science is the degree to which it shares ideas with other sciences. Workers in control theory, computer theory and artificial intelligence, whose main aim is to design ever more intelligent machines, make use of ideas about human intelligence and about how people solve problems, which are derived from psychology. In turn, psychologists have borrowed ideas from workers in artificial intelligence as, for example, the theories of memory and problem-solving discussed or referred to in Chapter 4. Medicine and psychiatry deal with disorders of behaviour, while the description of the relevant normal behaviour is often done by psychologists. An example of this is the use of personality and intelligence tests, developed by psychologists, to compare the behaviour of a mentally ill person with that of normal people. Social anthropology and sociology deal with the behaviour of social groups and make use of ideas about the behaviour and motivation of individuals which are drawn from psychology. In turn, social psychologists are greatly indebted to social anthropologists and sociologists (see Chapter 6). Economics and business studies use theories of choice and rational decision-making, which are of equal interest to psychologists and which are perhaps most effectively tested by psychological experiments. Physiologists and biochemists study the physical functions of man within a framework that depends heavily upon psychology, particularly when they are studying the brain, the sense organs or other parts of the nervous system. Education depends on psychology for ideas about what is appropriate teaching material for children of different ages, and in this respect has probably been too much influenced by the ideas of Piaget. Recent work by Bruner and others (see Chapter 2) will probably be as influential in the future. Education also takes from psychology various ideas about the nature of learning on which new teaching technologies can be based. A recent example of the latter is the development of teaching machines and programmed instruction. Philosophy and political science deal with concepts of free will and freedom which are greatly influenced by psychological studies of conditioning, learning, choice and problem-solving.

In future, psychology as a pure science will build on its present strengths. Within the laboratory, more and more complex forms of behaviour will become accessible to experimental treatment. The computer is likely to play an increasing role in experimental work. Perhaps the most interesting development here is the possibility of using the computer in an adaptive mode. It can adjust the experiment to the responses of the subject. A well-known example of this is a chess competition between a chess player and a computer. This has been used to test the effectiveness of ways of programming the computer, but it could also be used to investigate how the man plays chess. Methods such as these, coupled with the computer modelling of theories of pattern recognition, decision-making, problem-solving and language, make it seem likely that the present rapid developments in these areas will continue.

There is a longer term prospect of major advances in the understanding of behaviour by reference to the working of the brain. These advances are likely to be rather slow because physiologists still lack techniques appropriate to investigating an organ as complex as the brain. The techniques which uncovered so much of the working of the spinal cord, and which enabled us to understand so much about the nature of simple reflex behaviour, were successful only because of the simple structure of the spinal cord and the small number of nerve cells involved in reflex activity. The study of the biochemistry of the brain and the investigation of the effects of drugs on behaviour face a similar difficulty, and here also progress is likely to be slow.

In recent years there has been a pleasing convergence of interest on the part of social psychologists and experimental psychologists. The social psychologists are now more adventurous in devising ways of studying social situations experimentally (see Chapter 6), while experimental psychologists have been made very uncomfortably aware of the fact that the laboratory experiment is itself a social situation subject to subtle social pressures (see, for example, Rosenthal, 1966, on the 'experimenter effect').

The study of human behaviour and of man's mental life is clearly central to all the human sciences. It is no surprise that psychology contributes to so many of them, but the extent and importance of the contributions is perhaps the best measure of the success of psychology as a science. But, despite this, and despite its success within its own defined area of study, psychology is not usually seen as the most important of the sciences of man. Since no other subject has contributed ideas on such a scale to such a wide range of other disciplines, this is perhaps surprising and needs explaining. It is sometimes suggested that this is because psychology has failed as a science, either because it has produced no comprehensive theory of human behaviour or because the knowledge gained is somehow unreal or trivial (see, for example, Joynson, 1970). Both types of argument are unconvincing. Many sciences, for example geology and meteorology, have done important work despite the lack of a comprehensive theory, and the knowledge described in the preceding chapters is real and important whether derived from the laboratory or from 'real life'. I should like to argue that the surprising lack of respect for psychology is not, in fact, due to its status as a pure science but is due to a lack of understanding of how psychological knowledge should be applied within society, and to a lack of understanding of the effective skills of applied psychologists.

Psychology as an applied science

While psychology as a pure science has been comparatively successful, attempts to apply psychological knowledge have often been unimpressive and, because of this, non-psychologists do not take the subject as seriously as they otherwise might. Psychologists hope to understand all human behaviour and all human experience. But what success they have had has been limited to behaviour which can be studied in the laboratory or which is comparatively easily accessible to superficial observation outside the laboratory. Attempts to achieve deeper insights by the techniques of psychoanalysis or by other forms of depth psychology have been disappointing, but it is significant that these fallible insights are the ones which have been most thoroughly absorbed by popular culture and which have had the greatest influence on related professions such as medicine or social work. When knowledge derived from laboratory studies or from superficial observation is applied to practical problems, it often seems to offer little that is not already available to common sense. For example, the study of learning in the laboratory, despite the absence of a large-scale theory of learning, has produced a considerable number of very precise studies, which have influenced teaching technology (e.g. programmed learning) and psychotherapy (e.g. behaviour modification) and which have stimulated a great deal of interesting work on brain mechanisms (see Chapters 5 and 11). But when we are making use of these studies in order to tell an aspiring student how to study his subject most effectively, the advice we give is almost totally unsurprising, although it is firmly based on experimental evidence. We would tell him to try to understand rather than learn by rote; to study small manageable amounts but not ones which are too small to be interesting or meaningful; to study in relatively short bursts with deliberate rest periods; to try to relate what he is studying to other things and experiences with which he is familiar and which are vivid for him; to motivate himself so that his attention may be given wholeheartedly to his studies; to avoid distractions; to work in quiet conditions when he is fresh but to use a discrete amount of noise or music to keep himself alert when he is tired; to learn anything likely to be particularly difficult to remember just before he goes to sleep because in that way he has a better chance of remembering it. Of this list of recommendations only the last may seem at all surprising and, unfortunately, it is probably the least reliable of them because it may conflict with another well-documented but unsurprising fact, that attention is more variable when you are tired. (Some of the experiments on which this advice is based can be found in the recommended further reading to Chapter 4 and others are described by Hunter, 1964).

If psychology told us nothing which we did not know already, there would be little point in studying it. If psychology could add nothing to common sense when dealing with practical problems, then there would be no need of applied psychology. Fortunately for the self-esteem of psychologists, there is more to it than that. Common sense is better at providing explanations *after* the event than in providing good advice *before* it. Proverbs come in contradictory pairs such as 'he who hesitates is lost' and 'look before you leap' so that one of them can always be applied after the event. Most statements made by psychologists can be related to common sense but, very often, so can their opposites. Hence the commonsense nature of the advice to the student given above does not in any way detract from its value. What is important is whether it will work.

A more serious shortcoming occurs when psychologists themselves make contradictory recommendations. Unfortunately, this is rather common in just those areas in which the general public expects psychology to have the most to offer. One example of this is the competing schools of psychotherapy. Psychoanalysis and behaviour therapy are totally different in conception and in practice, yet both may be recommended for the same condition by different psychologists. What is worse, the psychoanalyst does not regard the results of behaviour therapy as a cure, while the behaviour therapist can usually quote good statistical evidence to prove that psychoanalysis does no good at all.

Another example is the different views about how children should be treated in school and by their parents. Some psychologists insist that they be given the maximum possible freedom, so that their development may be entirely natural and unforced. Others favour greater discipline for the sake of an orderly curriculum or in order to produce a tolerably well-behaved child. It is characteristic of these debates that in the absence of adequate evidence they resemble religious controversies, depending more on faith than on science. It is not surprising that many people decide to ignore the recommendations of psychologists and to rely on common sense or instinct, or on whatever is currently fashionable.

The simplest explanation of the contrariness of common sense and of these unresolved controversies in psychology is provided by the sheer complexity of human behaviour. Behaviour varies from one situation to another so that apparently contradictory types of advice may both be appropriate, but on different occasions. It seems likely that children need both discipline and freedom. The problem is to find out when either is more appropriate and what is the best way to combine them. The psychological study of child-rearing can only be held back by a doctrinaire controversy between opposing views. It is often relatively easy to find out, by a small-scale study, just what is the best thing to do in a specific situation. It is much more difficult to make recommendations which can be followed in *any* circumstances. This is, of course, the same difficulty that we meet in trying to formulate large-scale theories. We have the techniques and the skills to answer specific questions by doing tailor-made pieces of research, but we cannot give confident answers based on existing theories. This characteristic of psychology seems likely to persist. It is therefore very important that professional psychologists should adjust their behaviour accordingly.

Psychology as a profession

Most professional people assume that their expertise will, in appropriate circumstances, enable them to make better judgements and to give better advice than a layman can. Thus the doctor can diagnose and prescribe for a limited range of diseases. The engineer can calculate the strength of a bridge provided that its design is not too revolutionary. The lawyer can predict the judgement which a court will give, and so on. It is interesting that the history of some professions shows that their expectations preceded their performance. Before about 1912 it is doubtful whether the attentions of a doctor were, on average, of any benefit to a sick person. In some periods, and in some places, notably when bleeding was used excessively and when disease was spread in insanitary hospitals, the attentions of doctors were positively harmful. Psychologists, along with many other aspiring professionals, also show signs of aspiring to a role they cannot honestly or effectively play. Perhaps our image of a profession is more primitive than we realise, being modelled on the priest or the wizard rather than being realistically related to the abilities of the people in the profession.

Whatever the explanation of the unrealistic aspirations of professional people, it is particularly important that psychologists should be realistic about their capacities, since these are far from negligible.

Not all applied psychology is unimpressive. We can learn a great deal from the successes and failures of the three main branches of professional psychology. These correspond to the three professional divisions of the British Psychological Society, and their activities have already been described in Chapters 13, 14 and 15. Educational and clinical psychology are relatively well established, with about 600 practitioners employed in each. Occupational psychology is much smaller and is not yet fully established as a professional body.

Educational psychologists are employed to help children who get into various kinds of difficulty at school or at home. They assess children by observation and by tests. In some cases they will treat them. Too rarely do their tests reveal things which were unknown to the child's teachers or parents, so that the educational psychologist's report may be treated with contempt. This is not because the tests are bad ones but simply because the tests have been developed to discover in twenty minutes what the teachers and the parents learn about the child over a much longer period. So it is inevitable that the results of the tests will rarely surprise anyone who already knows the child well. If the tests were used to check the teacher's report as a preliminary to *treatment*, there would be little objection to their use. But educational psychologists can rarely treat more than a small proportion of the children who are referred to them. Even those they do treat, they are unable to treat as they would wish, because of shortage of time. Either there is a very great shortage of educational psychologists or there is something wrong with the way they do their job. The Summerfield Report (1968) recommended that the number of educational psychologists be doubled, but even if that target were reached, one can be fairly certain that educational psychologists would still be treating only a small proportion of their clients and spending less time with each than they, the psychologists, would wish.

There is no doubt that when a good educational psychologist can spend a great deal of time with a child, the child can be very effectively helped. But most of the successes have involved an expenditure of time which would require an enormous increase in staff if all problem children were to receive comparable treatment. There is a mismatch between the role the psychologist is expected to play and the methods he wishes to use. We expect psychologists to deliver snap diagnoses and instant advice, while the psychologists want to spend long periods of time with their clients since they know that emotional difficulties and learning difficulties can only be overcome by slow and patient methods.

In clinical psychology the situation is rather similar, involving a great deal of not very informative testing and continual complaints about lack of time to give adequate treatment. The situation here is complicated by the fact that most clinical psychologists work with and under a psychiatrist. Psychiatrists are medically qualified and for that reason take ultimate responsibility for the treatment of the patient. Although there are more psychiatrists than psychologists, they also face the dilemma of being unable to spend enough time with individual patients, and in the recent past a large proportion of mental patients actually got worse as a result of the treatment, or lack of it, which they received in hospital. A particularly clear account of the history of psychiatry is given by Ullman and Krasner (1968). Various methods have been used to overcome this difficulty. In the past twenty years there has been an enormous increase in the use of drugs which enable mental patients to return to their homes and often to their jobs. Many would claim that the drugs do not 'cure' the disorder, but provided that the home or work environment is reasonably satisfactory, the patient may be 'cured' by the very fact of being able to leave hospital. However, many patients do not respond to drugs, and those who do may have to return to the hospital many times. While they are in hospital, group therapy may be tried in which, in effect, large groups of patients 'treat' each other with a little unobtrusive assistance from a therapist who may be a psychiatrist or a psychologist. Behaviour therapy may also be tried and, like group therapy, is more time-consuming than drug treatment but less so than individual psychotherapy.

Since most mental patients are adults, their treatment raises issues of freedom and responsibility which do not arise in relation to children, whose parents are expected to be responsible for them. To a greater extent than other sicknesses, mental illness affects people's ability to make sensible decisions about themselves. For that reason many are treated without their consent, and there is considerable debate about the justification for doing so. This makes it all the more distressing that treatment should be such an uncertain affair and that non-drug treatments should be too time-consuming to be available to any but a minority of patients.

Occupational psychology has not yet had time to discover all its professional dilemmas, but there are signs that it may be able to avoid the characteristic difficulties of the other two. Occupational psychologists give tests to people in order to predict what sort of job will suit them. They also design training schemes and may be involved in the design of working situations.

When the occupational psychologist gives a test it is more informative than those administered by the educational psychologist or the clinical psychologist. This is not because they have more powerful tests but because they start with less relevant information about the person being tested. Their tests are designed to find out quickly what the man and his employer will discover when the man has been working at his new job for some time. To that extent the tests can tell us something we do not yet know and can be genuinely informative and predictive.

The occupational psychologist has no ambitions to treat people or to spend long periods of time with his clients for any other reason. Instead he expects his expertise to be used in counselling, and in designing training schemes or working environments. In doing this he will be involved intensively at first, but thereafter need make only periodic checks to see how things are going. Other people will be expected to run the training schemes and to supervise the work environment. In this way he avoids the heavy demands on his time which are characteristic of educational and clinical psychology.

Recent developments in educational and clinical psychology suggest that these professions may become more like occupational psychology. In both cases there are people available who must spend far more time with the clients than the psychologist can. Children must spend a great deal of time with parents and teachers, while hospital patients spend most of their time with nurses. Working through them need not involve them in additional work, any more than changing the layout of a factory need create more work for foremen.

Techniques of behaviour modification have been developed which would enable both educational and clinical psychologists to delegate to others the long-term treatment of children or patients. Considerable changes have been produced in the behaviour of whole wards of mental patients by psychologists who observed that the nurses and other attendants were rewarding deviant behaviour with attention and ignoring the patients when they behaved normally. Various techniques have been used to reverse this situation. Just making the attendants aware of it can have an appreciable effect, although it may be difficult to persuade people to ignore disturbed behaviour, which is often seen as a cry for help. 'Token economies' have been used to help change the pattern of informal rewards and punishments. In this system tokens are handed out for 'good' behaviour while 'bad' behaviour is ignored. The change in the patient's demeanour can make the job of nursing them less arduous. Very similar techniques can be taught to parents who are overwhelmed by a difficult child and, in favourable cases, can produce dramatic changes in the child's behaviour, thus making the parents' life much easier. 'Token economies' have also been used in the classroom with difficult children, to make them more amenable to discipline and to ordinary methods of teaching. These methods have usually been used on very disturbed people and the main effect has been to make life easier for those looking after them. Whether the same methods can produce any appreciable return to 'normality' among less disturbed people is still an open question, although there are indications that this may be possible, particularly with children.

If educational and clinical psychologists were to make greater use of behaviour-modification techniques, their activities would resemble those of occupational psychologists, and calculations of the number of professionals required could drop dramatically because of the reduction in the amount of time-consuming individual treatment. There is, at the present time, some opposition to the use of behaviour-modification and other behaviourist techniques, on moral grounds. These will be considered later.

These developments may also be endangered by restrictive practices among psychologists. The British Psychological Society, like the equivalent professional organisations in other countries, has taken responsibility for setting standards in its applied divisions. It does so in the usual way by insisting that people employed in these fields should have passed certain prescribed examinations and done some 'in service' practical training. This may make it more difficult, in the future, for psychologists to treat people by proxy. They may, as the medical profession has to some extent, be able to make use of auxiliary workers. But it seems equally likely that, like teachers, they will try to protect their professional status by preventing untrained people from dealing with their clients.

In still other ways psychologists are in the process of changing their ideas of what is proper professional practice. There is a danger that they may follow, inappropriately, the model of some other professions. Perhaps the most dangerous is the medical model. Many psychologists would like to treat people with psychological difficulties in the same way that doctors diagnose and treat physical illness, in well-equipped professional premises and institutions. There are two things wrong with this model. First, it is probably a mistake to attempt to understand someone's psychological difficulties by seeing them in an artificial environment; it is almost certainly better to see them in an everyday setting at home, at work or in school. In this way the difficulties can be seen in the context in which they usually occur, and so can the reaction of other people to them. Secondly, it is almost certainly impossible to treat people with purely psychological difficulties simply as individuals. These difficulties result from and cause other problems with the family, with workmates or with friends. It is usually as important to deal with these as it is to treat the individual.

But all these ideas are very far from being established and accepted. Until such basic issues are settled, it is probably unwise to be too dogmatic about how professional psychologists should behave and how they should be trained.

Research in applied psychology

It is often assumed that it is the function of pure research to make new discoveries and of applied research to find ways of making use of the new knowledge. In fact, and as many authors have pointed out, the relationship is more complex than that. In psychology, for example, intelligence testing was developed by Binet and Simon to help solve a particular problem, but their work revolutionised more academic studies of intelligence. The relationship between pure research, applied research and practical affairs involves a rich exchange of ideas and problems. It seems likely that the growing importance of occupational psychology and the development of new methods in clinical and educational psychology will influence both applied and pure research. The most obvious influence will be in applied research, and already it seems possible to give a 'prescription' which covers some of the most successful examples of applied research. The following prescription has been much influenced by Chapanis (1959) and Leonard (1972).

The first step is to check whether the problem has been adequately formulated. In some cases this may be quite straightforward, as when the Post Office asked for research on the sorting of mail (Conrad, 1960). Here the main problem was obviously to improve the efficiency and speed with which the men sort the letters. In other cases there may be related problems which must be considered at the same time. An example of this is the development of new mobility aids for blind people (Leonard, 1972). The aids must not only be effective in the hands of a competent operator, they must also be easy to learn to use; they must inspire confidence; they must not interfere with existing techniques, such as hearing, which the blind person has already learned to use; and, finally, they must not be conspicuous because blind people have a strong desire to appear as normal as they can and will be reluctant to use a conspicuous or bizarre aid. This sort of information can be obtained by observation, by talking to other professionals, such as social workers, who are involved with the clients and, above all, by talking to the clients themselves.

The second step is to improve one's understanding of the nature of the problem. Again, the most powerful techniques are observation and consultation. In the case of blind mobility, one might ask whether the blind persons' chief problem was getting lost or bumping into things, and what were the common circumstances in which they got lost or what were the kinds of obstacle they bumped into.

The third step is to look for methods to solve the problems as they have been formulated. Again, consultation is very useful since the clients often have very good ideas of their own. Ideas can often be found by looking at the way related problems have been solved by other applied scientists. One would consult the relevant work of pure scientists, who may be psychologists, physiologists, doctors, engineers or whatever seems appropriate. Finally, it may be necessary to do some contrived experimental work, perhaps by simulation, to develop and test ideas from any of these sources.

The fourth stage is the implementation of suggested new devices or systems. Here again, success depends on the co-operation of clients and other professionals. The new system must be acceptable to all concerned, at least for a trial period, and it must be introduced in ways which produce a minimum of disruption in their lives.

The fifth and last stage is the assessment of the new device or system. Its efficiency may be measured in various ways, usually dependent upon observation. For example, one could measure the speed with which a blind person walks along the street using his new aid. The acceptability of the new system is just as important as its efficiency, and this can only be assessed by again consulting the clients.

The most striking feature of this 'prescription' is the amount of consultation at all stages. Indeed, the clients may be said to participate in the research at all stages. When this does not occur, then quite disastrous mistakes can be made. Similar disasters occur in other professions such as architecture, town planning, engineering and social work, and these professions could make much greater use of psychologists, or of methods developed by psychologists, to avoid mistakes such as the building of blocks of flats in which people hate to live or the design of cars which are excessively dangerous or unpleasant to drive. The psychologist may be the expert whose chief function is to prevent other experts 'going it alone'.

Moral implications of applied psychology

The debate about the proper function of the applied psychologist is related to the philosophical debate about free will. This old philosophical problem now has practical significance for psychologists. It is a deeply held belief that man has some freedom of choice and that he has therefore some responsibility for his own actions. For this reason, some are afraid to think of psychology as a science, since science has been associated with determinism and the explanation of events in a mechanistic way. Since machines are not thought to exercise choice, they should not be considered responsible for their actions. If man's behaviour could be explained in mechanistic terms, then that would detract from his free will and reduce his responsibility. That this is a real possibility is shown by the concept of diminished responsibility in law and by our greater tenderness towards wrongdoers of all kinds when an explanation of their behaviour can be found.

Behaviourists, who tend to think in positivist or mechanistic terms, are sometimes accused of degrading man by doing so. But the problem of free will is just as difficult for those who have traditionally opposed the behaviourists. What is now called humanistic psychology attempts to deal with man as a whole rather than in mechanistic parts. But paradoxically, if such a psychology were successful, it would, to the extent that it could influence the whole man, pose an even greater challenge to free will than does behaviourism. After all, the behaviourist only claims to be able to cure symptoms or to teach skills. This leaves to the client the responsibility for taking the treatment or the training.

This dilemma of responsibility is at the core of the debate about the role of the applied psychologist. How can we give advice without taking from people some of their responsibility for their own actions and their own integrity? Should psychologists even attempt to define a healthy state of mind? Despite these worries about free will, the branch of psychology that has had the greatest impact on popular culture has been psychoanalysis, which has also been one of the most bold in prescribing ideal states of mind and the most dogmatic about how people should achieve them. Clearly there is as great a demand for guidance as there is fear that it may be successful.

The 'prescription' given, in the last section, of the characteristics of effective applied psychology is attractive because it leaves so much responsibility with the clients. If psychologists can only be successful when they work in that way, then popular worries about psychologists controlling people against their will are without justification, because the psychologist is, in all his activities, dependent on the co-operation and goodwill of his clients.

Summary

Psychology has not failed as a pure science, but is seen to be relatively ineffective because its applications are so uncertain and unsatisfactory. In turn, this is not because we lack basic knowledge but because applied psychologists have not yet discovered the most effective way to do their work. This is partly due to the use of inappropriate models, drawn from medicine or from teaching, of how professional people should behave. It is also a reflection of society's own uncertainty about what it should expect from psychologists.

If this analysis is correct, then the most significant advances in psychology will be concerned with the development of effective and acceptable techniques in applied psychology. It seems likely that these techniques will depend on a process of consultation and interaction with clients which will leave the ultimate responsibility with them rather than with the psychologist. These techniques are also likely to require the co-operation of many non-psychologists who interact with clients in real-life situations.

References

Conrad, R. (1960), 'Letter sorting machines—paced, lagged or unpaced?' *Ergonomics*, 3, 2, 149–57.

HMSO (1968), *Psychologists in Education Services* (The Summerfield Report). London.

Hunter, I. L. (1964), *Memory*. (2nd edition) Harmondsworth: Penguin Books.

Joynson, R. B. (1970), 'The breakdown of modern psychology'. *Bull. Brit. Psychol. Soc.*, *23*, 81, 261–9.

Leonard, J. A. (1972), 'Studies in blind mobility'. *Applied Ergonomics*, *3*, 37–46.

Rosenthal, R. (1966), *Experimenter Effects in Behavioral Research*. New York: Appleton-Century-Crofts.

Ullman, L. P., & Krasner, L. (1969), *A Psychological Approach to Abnormal Behavior*. Englewood Cliffs, NJ: Prentice Hall.

Willems, E. P., & Rausch, H. L. (1968), *Naturalistic Viewpoints in Psychological Research*. New York: Holt, Rinehart & Winston.

Recommended further reading

Chapanis, A. (1959), *Research Techniques in Human Engineering*. Baltimore: John Hopkins.

Kay, H. (1972), 'Psychology today and tomorrow'. Presidential Address British Psychological Society 1972. *Bull. Brit. Psychol. Soc.*, *25*, 88, 177–88.

Warr, P. B. (ed.) (1971), *Psychology at Work*. Harmondsworth: Penguin Books.

Index

acetycholine, 172, 184
adaptive behaviour, 140
Adler, A., 152
adolescence, 159
Alexander, 208
Allnutt, 246
Allport, G. W., 23, 24, 25, 26, 29, 34
alternation, 143
amnesia, 76
Anastasi, A., 30, 31
animal behaviour, 133–47
   definition, 136
Annett, J., 245
anti-social behaviour, 158–61
anxiety, 153, 156
apparitions, 193–6
applied psychology, 262–5
approach behaviour, 145
aptitude testing, 241–2
Asch, S. E., 92
attention, 58
attitude change, 85
auditory system, 10
Ausubel, D. P., 206, 209, 215
autism, 156
autonomic nervous system, 59–60

babbling, 103
Bannister, D., 29, 34, 153, 228
Barnett, S. A., 133
Bartlett, F. C., 215
behaviour, adaptive, 140
   animal, 133–47
     definition, 136
   anti-social, 158–61
   approach, 145
   exploratory, 142–6
   obsessional, 156
behaviour therapy, 154, 161, 224–7, 269–70
behavioural pharmacology, 170–88
   definition, 171
behaviourism, 2, 4, 154, 174
Belbin, E., 245
Beloff, J., 190
Bender, H., 200
Bergin, A. E., 226
Bever, T. G., 110
Bignami, G., 179
Binet, A., 207, 208, 271
Blackham, G. J., 154
Blakemore, C., 69, 70
Bower, T. G. R., 12

Bowlby, J., 159
Bradley, P. H., 184
brain, 59–60
  and drug action, 178
  equipotentiality, 75
  lesions, 71, 73, 165
  stimulation, 72–3
Brocklesby, I., 240
Brotherton, C. J., 94
Broughton, J. M., 12
Brown, J. A. C., 153
Brown, R., 112
Bruner, J. S., 12, 16, 18, 19, 20, 21, 260
Buchan, J., 208
Buros, O. K., 30
Burt, C., 203, 207, 208

Cambell, J. T., 241
Carkhuff, R. R., 226
Carlsmith, J. M., 85
Cattell, R. B., 27, 32
Cavanagh, P., 233
central nervous system, 59
Chapanis, A., 272
chemotherapy, 152, 161, 171, 267–8
Chesser, E. S., 225
Child, D., 26
Child Guidance Clinics, 203–4, 213
child-rearing, 264–5
Chomsky, N., 105, 106, 107, 108, 109, 110, 111, 112
clairvoyance, 191
Claridge, G., 180
Clark, W. G., 186
Clarke, A. D. B., 165
Clarke, A. M., 165
client-centred therapy, 226

clinical psychology, 217–31, 267–70
  scope, 229–30
  training, 230
cognitive development, 9–21
cognitive remediation, 166, 209
cognitive psychology, 4
Collins, B. E., 85
communication, 114
comparative psychology, 136
computer simulation, 130, 257, 261
concrete operational intelligence, 17
conditioning, 141, 161
  operant, 137, 154
Conrad, R., 272
conservation, 15
constancy, 50
Cooper, C. F., 69
Cooper, F. S., 103
cortex, 60
  visual, 69–70
Cox, T. R., 144, 176, 253
Crane, A. O., 208
Crossland, J., 184, 186
cultural differences, 18, 20

Darchen, R., 143
Darwin, C., 134, 139
Davidson, H. H., 31
Davie, R., 36
decision-making, 45, 55, 127, 240
'deep' structure, 109
delinquency, 159–60
Dember, W. N., 144
dependent variables, 44, 118
depression, 156
'depth' psychology, 2, 6, 28, 35, 36

Descartes, 58
developmental psychology, 9–21, 28
   definition, 9
Diesenhaus, H. I., 149, 150, 152
display design, 246–51
'distinctive features' theory, 102
DNA molecule, 140, 146
Dodge, R., 51, 53
Doise, W., 95
drugs, 170–88
   administration, 177
   classification, 185
   dosage, 174
   effects, 176
Durrett, H. L., 241

education, 21, 206–9
educational psychology, 203–15, 266–7, 269–70
   definition, 206
   scope, 210–11
   training, 209–11
ego, 28
Eisenburg, R. B., 10
electro-convulsive shock, 77, 152
electroencephalograms, 163
Elkind, D., 16
enactive representation, 18
enzymes, 75, 182, 184
epidemiological surveys, 157
epilepsy, 161, 163–4
Erdmann, B., 51, 53
ergonomics, 233, 235, 246–53
Ervin, S. M., 112
ethology, 136, 209
experimental method, 44–5, 174
experimental psychology, 6, 42–56, 81
exploratory behaviour, 142–6

extra-sensory perception, 196–9
extraversion, 24, 27, 38
Eysenck, H. J., 26, 27, 31, 32, 38, 161, 162, 225, 226

factor analysis, 26–7, 32
Fantz, R. L., 9, 10
fear, 145
feature analysis theory, 47
feature extraction, 68
Fechner, G. T., 118
Fisher, S., 180
Flavell, J. H., 16
formal operational intelligence, 17
Fraisse, P., 5
Frank, L. K., 30
Fransella, F., 29, 34, 153, 228
Fraser, C., 112
Freedman, J. L., 86
Freud, S., 2, 6, 7, 28, 35, 36, 149, 152, 153, 218

Garfield, S. L., 226
Garvey, W. D., 249
Gatti, G. L., 179
Gautier, M., 165
genetic factors, 25, 146, 161, 181
Geoffrey-Saint-Hillaire, I., 136
Gerard, H. B., 85
Gibbs, E. L., 164
Gibbs, F. A., 164
Gillham, W. E. C., 166
Glanzer, M., 143
Gordon, 155
Greene, J., 110
Greenfield, P. M., 16, 18
group conflict, 92
group conformity, 94
del Guidice, J., 186

Guilford, J. P., 25
Gurney, E., 194, 195, 196

Hall, C. S., 24, 28, 35
Halle, M., 102
hallucinations, 194
Hargreaves, D. H., 86
Harris, K. S., 103
Hartshorne, H., 25
Helmreich, R. L., 85
Hetherington, R. R., 34
Hickey, A. E., 244, 245
Hinde, R. A., 144
Hines, G., 178
hippocampus, 79, 143
Hippocrates, 24
Hodgkin, A. C., 61
Holdsworth, R. F., 240
Holt, R. R., 25
Hovland, C. I., 239
Hubel, D. H., 68, 69
Hull, C., 154
humanistic psychology, 226
hunger, 59, 73
Hunter, I. L., 264
Huxley, A. L., 61
hypothalamus, 72
hysteria, 156

iconic representation, 18
id, 28
imitation, 112
independent variables, 44
information, 59, 251
Inhelder, B., 11, 15
innate abilities, 12, 112, 140, 208
instinct, 140
intellectual development, 14, 17, 19, 207
intelligence, 208–9, 240–1
concrete operational, 17
formal operational, 17
pre-operational, 14–15
sensory-motor, 14
intelligence tests, 166, 207
Stanford-Binet, 207
interviewing, 32, 34, 238–40
introspection, 1, 4, 257
introversion, 24, 27, 38

Jackobsen, R., 102, 103
Jacobson, L. F., 87
James, H., 1
James, W., 1, 2
Janis, I. L., 84
Jehu, D., 155
job analysis, 234, 237–8, 252
Joynson, R. B., 262
Jung, C., 24, 38, 140, 152

Kagan, J., 159
Kelleher, R. T., 177
Kelly, G. A., 29, 33, 34, 153, 154, 228
Kendell, R. E., 155
Kenney, 19
Kirby, R. J., 143
Kline, P., 36
Klopfer, B., 31
Kolb, L. C., 163
Kornreich, M., 162
Koslowski, B., 12
Kraepelin, E., 152
Krasner, L., 267

Laing, R. D., 4, 228
language, 10, 100–14, 165
acquisition, 111
Lashley, K., 75
Lazards, R. S., 24

learning, 45, 54, 141, 243–4, 259, 263
Lee, A. E., 178
Lejeune, J., 165
Lenneberg, E. H., 112, 113
Lennox, W. G., 163
Leonard, G. O., 200
Leonard, J. A., 272
Levelt, W. J. M., 110
Levitt, E. E., 162
Lewin, K., 82, 91
Ley, P., 91
Lieberman, A. M., 103
limbic system, 143
Lindzey, G., 24, 31
linguistic competence, 106, 110
  universals, 104, 113
lobectomy, 77
Loveless, N. E., 249
Lovell, K., 206
Lowe-Holmes, A. R., 240
Luria, A. R., 165
Lyons, J., 110

Mace, C. A., 7
maladjustment, 28, 156–9
manic-depressive psychosis, 156
Mann, L., 84
maternal deprivation, 159
mathematical psychology, 118–32, 258
  definition, 118–19
Mathewson, G. C., 85
Maudsley Personality Inventory, 32
May, M. A., 25
McGehee, W., 243
McNeilage, P. F., 103
McNeill, D., 112

Mechanic, D., 155, 161
mediums, 191, 200
Meehl, P. E., 222
Meltzoff, J., 162
memory, 9, 11, 14, 45, 50, 58, 59, 74
mental retardation, 154, 164–6, 207, 209
mental testing, 208, 219–20, 223, 240–2
mesmerism, 190–1
Meyer, V., 225
Mikulas, W. L., 154
Milgram, S., 93
Mill, J. S., 136
Miller, W. T., 178
Millon, T., 149, 150, 152
Milner, B., 77
Mitchell, S., 157
Mittler, P., 209
Mischel, W., 24
mongolism, 165
Moore, M. K., 12
Morse, W. H., 177
Moss, H. A., 159
motivation, 58, 153, 218
  unconscious, 153
motor skills, 10, 165
Mowrer, O. H., 155
Myers, F. W. H., 194

Nakazima, S., 103, 104, 113
National Institute of Industrial Psychology, 233
Neisser, U., 4, 46, 48, 49, 54
neonate, 9
nerve impulse, 61–5, 182–5
nervous system, autonomic, 59–60
  central, 59

neurones, 61–5
neurosis, 27, 33, 153, 155, 158, 161, 225
Newcomb, T. M., 91
Newson, E., 6, 36
Newson, J., 6, 36
Nisbet, J., 208
non-verbal cues, 89, 114
normal distribution, 120

object permanence, 11, 13
observation, 6, 43, 137, 258
obsessional behaviour, 156
occupational psychology, 232–53, 268–9
  definition, 232
  scope, 232
occupational training, 242–6
Odbert, H. S., 25
Olver, R. R., 16, 18
O'Neil, W. M., 1
operant conditioning, 137, 154
Oppenheim, B., 157
Opton, E. M., 24
Ordy, J. M., 10
organic psychoses, 156
Owen, A. R. G., 200

paranoia, 156
parapsychology, 190–202
  definition, 190
Pavlov, I. P., 38
Pearce, H., 197, 198
Pearn, M. A., 245
Penfield, W., 77
perception, 9, 45–7
Perchonock, E., 107
personal construct theory, 29, 33–4, 153, 228
personality, 23–39
  and body-build, 36
  assessment, 29–30
  idiographic approach, 26
  inventories, 31
  nomothetic approach, 26
  tests, 30, 218, 227
  traits, 24–5
  types, 24
person perception, 87, 157
phenomenology, 154
phonetics, 102
philosophical psychology, 4
physiological psychology, 58–79
  definition, 58
Piaget, J., 11, 12, 13, 14, 15, 16, 17, 18, 19, 103, 260
Piper, L. E., 200
placebo effects, 180–1
play therapy, 161
Plunkett, 155
Podmore, F., 194
poltergeists, 191, 200
population stereotype, 249
Pratt, J. G., 198
prediction, 117, 221–2, 239, 241–2
pre-operational intelligence, 14–15
Presland, J., 208
problem-solving, 9, 21, 45, 55
professional psychologists, 7, 203–7, 259, 265–71
programmed instruction, 244, 263
psychiatric social worker, 203
psychiatry, 149, 152, 203, 218, 267–8
psychical research, 190
psychoanalysis, 149, 153, 218
psycholinguistics, 100–14, 258

definition, 102
psychopathology, 149–66
  and social class, 161
  and sex, 161
  definition, 149
  in adults, 155–6
  in children, 157–8
  incidence, 155–8
  theories, 149–55
psychopathy, 156, 159
psychopharmacology, 170
psychophysics, 118
psychosis, 27, 156
psychotherapy, 5, 161–2, 224–7, 264

Rachlin, H., 141
Rachman, S., 162
Randall, J. L., 198
Rausch, H. L., 258
reading, 51
  failure, 212
reinforcement, 54, 141, 154
repertory grid technique, 33
research, 5, 42–5, 116–17
Restle, F., 55
Reynolds, H. J., 242
Rhine, J. B., 190, 197, 198
RNA molecule, 141
Robins, L. N., 156, 158, 159
Rodger, A., 233, 237, 239
Rogers, C. R., 153, 154, 162, 226
role-playing, 84
role relationships, 82
Rolfe, J. M., 246, 249
Roll, W. G., 200
Rommetviet, R., 109
Rorschach, H., 31
Rorschach test, 31
Rose, L., 199

Rose, R., 199
Rosenthal, D., 161
Rosenthal, R., 87, 261
Rutter, D. R., 89
Rutter, M., 156, 157, 158, 159
Ryle, G., 1, 2, 4, 6

Sargant, W., 152, 162
Savin, H. B., 107
Schachter, S., 90
Schaffer, H. R., 36
schemas, 11
schizophrenia, 34, 155–6, 160, 220
Schmidt, H., 198
Schmidt, R. P., 164
School Psychological Services, 204, 210–13
Scott, W. D., 238
Sears, R. R., 36
Seaver, W. B., 88
selection, 217, 233–4, 236–42
self-concept, 153, 160
Selfridge, O. G., 46
Seligman, M. E. P., 141
sensory discrimination, 118
  thresholds, 118
sensory-motor intelligence, 14
set, 56
Seth, G., 210
Shackleton, B., 198
'shaping', 155
Sheldon, W. H., 24, 37
Shepherd, M., 157, 158
Sherif, M., 95
Shore, R. P., 241
Shvachkin, N. K., 103
Sidgwick, H., 195
Silberman, A., 154
Simon, T., 208, 271

Sinclair, A., 95
Sixteen PF questionnaire, 32
skill, 13, 16, 45, 54
Skinner, B. F., 111, 154, 244
Slater, E., 152, 162
Smith, M. C., 245
Soal, S. G., 198
social anthropology, 81, 260
social competition, 94
social conformity, 90
social facilitation, 82
social psychology, 81–98, 261
 definition, 81
Spelman, M. S., 91
Spencer, G. M., 242
Sperling, G., 51, 52, 53, 54
spinal cord, 59
spiritualism, 191
S-R psychology, 3, 42
Stein, Z., 159
Stellar, E., 74
Stephenson, G. M., 89, 94, 96
Stewart, G., 198
stress, 162, 179, 252–3
Streufert, S., 96
Summerfield, A., 205
Sundberg, N. D., 29
super-ego, 28
superordinate goals, 95
'surface' structure, 109
Susser, M., 159
symbolic representation, 18
synapse, 64, 182
syntax, 105
Szasz, T., 150, 229

Tanner, W. P. (Jr.), 125
Taylor, F. V., 249
telepathy, 191, 196–9

template-matching theory, 47, 102
Terman, L., 207
therapy, behaviour, 154, 161, 224–7, 269–70
 chemo-, 152, 161, 171, 267–8
 client-centred, 226
 play, 161
 psycho-, 5, 161–2, 224–7, 264
thinking, 9, 13, 56
Thorpe, W. H., 141
Tilley, K., 243
Tizard, J., 157
Todd, G. B., 212
Tonkova-Yampol'skaya, R. V., 104
transformational rules, 106
transmitter substances, 184
Travers, R. M. W., 206
Truax, C. B., 226
Turner, E. A., 109
Turpin, R., 165
Tye, N., 176
Tyler, L. E., 29

Udelf, M. S., 10
Ullman, L. P., 267
unconscious motivation, 153

Vernon, P. E., 24, 30, 33, 35, 209
vision, 59, 66
 colour, 68
visual system, 10, 50, 67
vocational guidance, 234, 236–7

Warburton, D. M., 179
Warrington, E., 79
Watson, J. B., 2, 3
Weene, P., 46
Weiskrantz, L., 79

Westland, G., 211
Whitmore, T. K., 157, 210, 213
Whyte, W. H., 33
Wiesel, T. W., 68, 69
Wilder, B. J., 164
Willems, E. P., 258

Wing, J., 155
Wolpe, J., 225
Wonderic, E. F., 239
Wright, D. S., 3

Yarrow, M. R., 36

MATHEMATICS, SCIENCE AND TECHICAL TITLES IN TEACH YOURSELF BOOKS

05501 4	**Algebra** P. Abbott	50p
05364 X	**Arithmetic: Decimalized and Metricated** L. C. Pascoe	50p
05524 3	**Biochemistry** P. H. Jellinck	40p
18265 2	**Biology** J. R. Hall	75p
18253 9	**Biology, Human** D. Taverner	50p
05528 6	**Botany** J. H. Elliott	40p
05536 7	**Calculus** P. Abbott	50p
05590 1	**Calculus, Further** F. L. Westwater	50p
18050 1	**Concreting, Practical** A. E. Peatfield	60p
05565 0	**Dynamics** C. G. Lambe	40p
05569 3	**Electricity** C. W. Wilman	40p
19410 3	**Electronics** W. P. Jolly	60p
05916 8	**Electronics, Industrial** C. W. Eggleton	50p

05949 4	**Engineering Science** C. B. Day & V. A. Jones	50p
18323 3	**Farming** James Merridew	60p
09681 0	**Genetics** R. J. Berry	50p
05594 4	**Geology** A. Raistrick	60p
05595 2	**Geometry** P. Abbott	50p
15250 8	**Human Anatomy and Physiology** David Le Vay	95p
15378 4	**Inorganic Chemistry** R. E. Morcom	60p
16804 8	**Mathematics** J. Davidson	40p
05971 0	**Mathematics, New** L. C. Pascoe	50p
	Mechanical Engineering A. E. Peatfield	
05650 9	Vol 1 Hand Tools	40p
05651 7	Vol 2 Engineering Components	50p
05652 5	Vol 3 Workshop Practice	50p
05653 3	**Mechanics** P. Abbott	60p
12473 3	**Metrication** J. Peach	40p
05254 6	**Microbiology** G. D. Wasley & R. W. Warner	60p

05672 X	**Nutrition** M. Pyke	40p
05157 4	**Organic Chemistry** K. Rockett	60p
05680 0	**Perspective Drawing** H. F. Hollis	40p
15251 6	**Physics** D. Bryant	50p
05689 4	**Plumbing** J. H. Innes	50p
05701 7	**Radio Servicing** L. Butterworth	50p
12494 6	**Seamanship** T. F. Wickham & N. Hefford	50p
15368 7	**Slide Rule** B. Snodgrass	40p
05727 0	**Statistics** R. Goodman	50p
05738 6	**Trigonometry** P. Abbott	40p
19083 3	**The Weather** Sir Graham Sutton	60p
15247 8	**Welding** C. Bainbridge	50p
05748 3	**Zoology** T. M. Savory	50p

BUSINESS, PROFESSIONAL, COMPUTERS AND OFFICE PRACTICE TITLES IN TEACH YOURSELF BOOKS

15252 4	**Advertising** E. McGregor	50p
16957 5	**Banking** J. P. Parker & B. D. W. Cox	50p
05527 8	**Book-keeping** D. Cousins	50p
05541 3	**Catering and Hotel Operations** V. G. Winslet & S. Blundell	40p
05914 1	**Commerce** Ronald Warson	60p
16757 2	**Commercial Arithmetic** J. H. Harvey	40p
05549 9	**Commercial Correspondence** F. Addington-Symonds	50p
19495 2	**Computer Programming/Fortran** A. S. Radford	80p
05557 X	**Costing** D. Cousins	40p
05941 9	**Cybernetics** F. H. George	40p
05398 4	**Data Processing** K. N. Dodd	40p
05564 2	**Dutton Speedwords** R. G. J. Dutton	40p
05566 9	**Economics** S. E. Thomas	40p

09702 7	**Electronic Computers** F. L. Westwater & D. H. Joyce	40p
19086 8	**Exporting** D. F. Taylor & E. A. Rutland	50p
05629 0	**Insurance** H. A. L. Cockerell	50p
16756 4	**Investment** W. L. B. Fairweather	40p
12495 4	**Management Accounting** B. Murphy	50p
05967 2	**Marketing** John Stapleton	85p
19496 0	**Office Management** P. W. Betts	95p
12450 4	**Office Practice** J. Shaw	50p
05975 3	**Operational Research** M. S. Makower & E. Williamson	60p
11593 9	**O & M** R. G. Breadmore	50p
05698 3	**Public Relations** H. Lloyd	50p
05709 2	**Salesmanship** S. A. Williams	40p
05712 2	**Secretarial Practice** Pitmans College	50p
05687 8	**Shorthand** Pitmans College	40p
18263 6	**Typewriting** Pitmans College	60p